BUSINESS ETHICS

BUSINESS ETHICS

An Interactive Introduction

ANDREW KERNOHAN

broadview press

BROADVIEW PRESS — www.broadviewpress.com
Peterborough, Ontario, Canada

Founded in 1985, Broadview Press remains a wholly independent publishing house. Broadview's focus is on academic publishing; our titles are accessible to university and college students as well as scholars and general readers. With over 600 titles in print, Broadview has become a leading international publisher in the humanities, with world-wide distribution. Broadview is committed to environmentally responsible publishing and fair business practices.

The interior of this book is printed on 100% recycled paper.

© 2015 Andrew Kernohan

Library and Archives Canada Cataloguing in Publication

Kernohan, Andrew, author
    Business ethics : an interactive introduction / Andrew Kernohan.

Includes bibliographical references and index.
ISBN 978-1-55481-150-2 (paperback)

    1. Business ethics. I. Title.

HF5387.K47 2015   174'.4   C2015-905065-0

Broadview Press handles its own distribution in North America
PO Box 1243, Peterborough, Ontario K9J 7H5, Canada
555 Riverwalk Parkway, Tonawanda, NY 14150, USA
Tel: (705) 743-8990; Fax: (705) 743-8353
email: customerservice@broadviewpress.com

Distribution is handled by Eurospan Group in the UK, Europe, Central Asia, Middle East, Africa, India, Southeast Asia, Central America, South America, and the Caribbean. Distribution is handled by Footprint Books in Australia and New Zealand.

Broadview Press acknowledges the financial support of the Government of Canada through the Canada Book Fund for our publishing activities.

Edited by Robert M. Martin
Book design by Michel Vrana
Interior typesetting by Jennifer Blais

PRINTED IN CANADA

CONTENTS

ACKNOWLEDGEMENTS

Though no students were killed or injured during the writing of this book, many did suffer through earlier versions of the material. I would like to thank students in my business ethics courses at St. Mary's University and Dalhousie University for their patience with the book's development.

Aaron Panych, then an Online Instructional Designer at Dalhousie University's Centre for Learning and Teaching, gave me enormous help in online implementation of this material. I wish that I had taken more of his advice. However, our collaboration indirectly shaped the design of this textbook.

My friend Chris McKinnon of Trent University gave me valuable feedback on some of the book's content about which I did not feel confident.

Stephen Latta, Philosophy Editor at Broadview Press, closely read the whole manuscript, offered many valuable suggestions on the content, and forced me to make extensive revisions. Our work together may have slowed production of the book, but it was well worth it in terms of decreased mistakes and increased clarity.

Bob Martin did the final edit of the manuscript for Broadview Press, and helped make the book much easier to read. I take full responsibility for all remaining errors.

My partner, Anne MacLellan, gave me continuous support during the long process of creating the book. Our two cats, Otis and Minou, kept me company through many hours at the keyboard.

I would like to thank all these people for their help and to dedicate this book to my mother, Mollie Kernohan, and to my sister, Ann Kernohan, who, by taking on caring for my mother, gave me time for writing.

INTRODUCTION FOR THE READER

I imagine you, my reader, as an ethical person. You are kind to animals, you are honest with your employer, you give to charity, you try to reduce your consumption of fossil fuels, and you are horrified at human rights violations around the world. If you are not already such a person, then this book is not going to turn you into one. Given, however, that you are already morally competent, this book will help you become more so. This book will help you think about complicated ethical decisions. You learned many of your ethical principles as a child, and the rest you internalized, with some critical reflection, as you grew into an adult. These gut reactions and rules of thumb are adequate for quickly making most of life's decisions. Yet sometimes the situation is trickier, and you have to think carefully about what you should do. Then knowledge of ethical theory starts to be useful.

This book offers you a conceptual toolkit that will help you better integrate ethical considerations into your business decisions. It will increase your competence in recognizing ethically problematic situations and in thinking through difficult ethical decisions. It does not offer a decision-making algorithm. It offers neither a professional code of ethics for managers, nor a manual for implementing Corporate Social Responsibility in your business. It is not a comprehensive discussion of all the ethical issues that may arise in the world of business. Instead, the book offers a set of ethical approaches that philosophers have formulated over many centuries of reflection. Taken together, these approaches will give you insight into making difficult decisions.

Applying abstract ethical theory to specific, ethically problematic, cases is a high-level intellectual task. It is not a skill that can be acquired simply through reading about it. Becoming competent at applying ethical concepts to business decisions requires not just passively listening to a lecture and reading a textbook, but also active engagement with both theory and cases. You have to practice on relatively simple case studies before moving on to the complexities of real business life.

This book offers you a solid grounding in all the various ethical concepts and theories. I assume that you are in a business program, that you know some economics, and that you are not terrified by numerical examples. I find numerical models illuminating, so, wherever appropriate, I have constructed tables and charts to illustrate the ethical theory.

What is really important, though, is that you learn how to apply theory to ethically problematic situations. The book offers you a graduated course in applying ethical theory to practice cases. Each chapter ends with a case study involving the material in the chapter. Before you attack the case study, however, I recommend that you work through each chapter's multiple-choice questions, available either on the book's website or on your institution's learning management system. There are two types of questions.

One type asks you to recall and apply the concepts covered in the chapter. The other type primes you for the case study by helping you to identify the ethical issues that the case study raises. When you have finished these exercises, you will be ready for the case study.

Together, the twelve case studies cover many important issues such as insider trading, whistle-blowing, preferential hiring, executive compensation, environmental pollution, and so on, that are the standard content of a business ethics course. Here, however, you will yourself work out the ethical issues involved rather than merely reading someone else's analysis. Active engagement with both theory and practice will increase your competence at ethical reasoning and decision-making. This increased ethical competence, together with your skills at accounting, marketing, finance, human resource management, and so on, will help you become an excellent manager or administrator.

INTRODUCTION FOR THE INSTRUCTOR

The methodology of this book is pluralistic. I believe that applied ethics is best done by taking a variety of ethical approaches—rights, consequences, virtue, care, justice, and so on—and using them to reveal the ethically salient features of problematic situations. Having done their ethical due diligence, decision-makers will reach a better informed and better reasoned decision than they would have before they studied ethical theory.

I planned the book around the problem of teaching ethics either fully or partially online. Teaching theoretical ethics is perhaps best confined to in-person seminars, but teaching applied ethics, where the goal is to apply ethics to cases, is more amenable to online methods. The textbook supports a highly structured approach to applying ethical theory. The book allows for twelve modules. Each module contains a chapter of theory, supporting lectures, multiple-choice homework to consolidate understanding of the ethical theory, a case study that involves aspects of this theory, and multiple-choice homework that helps the student apply the theory to the case study.

You will, of course, use this book in class as you think best, but it may be helpful to you to hear how I use it. For a regular class, I offer a lecture and an in-class discussion of the case that is based on small groups and the Case Analysis Worksheet available on the book's website. For an online class, I offer recorded lectures and a discussion session using the university's online meeting software. For both types of class, I use the university learning management system to refer students to the book's student website for their homework, and then add weekly quizzes and tri-weekly review tests based on random selections of the homework questions. I find that all students, particularly online students, respond to incentives for engaging in the course material, so the course's computerized gradebook becomes quite extensive.

Every week, I require a post to the class discussion forum on the relevant case. I suggest that students approach their post as if they were doing the writing sample on the GRE or the GMAT. They are to do the case study homework, conceptualize the case, write for thirty minutes, take some time to edit their work, and then post. Students learn from each other's posts. I also require students to submit the posts as assignments, so that the posts can be checked for originality. A good rubric facilitates marking their work. Weekly assignments help keep students engaged with the material.

The instructor's website for this book contains material that you may find useful:

- PowerPoint slides of the tables and figures in the book that you can incorporate into lectures.

- All the multiple-choice questions in machine readable format so that you can incorporate them into online assessments or print them for paper assessments.
- The same multiple-choice questions as above, in an interactive format that students can use directly on the website; if you would like students to have access to the book's many interactive resources but do not wish to upload the questions into a Learning Management System, you can simply provide the instructor companion site URL and passcode to your students for them to utilize on their own time (please contact customerservice@broadviewpress.com if you require the URL and passcode).
- Links to YouTube videos of the author's lectures on the book, all divided into short chunks that you can link into online courses.

As you can see, I am enthusiastic about the use of online methods in both fully online and blended university courses. I suspect you share some of this enthusiasm, since otherwise you would not be using this textbook. I hope that you find this book a useful support to your teaching.

Chapter 1

ETHICAL DECISIONS IN BUSINESS

How do we analyze an ethically problematic situation?

What sorts of ethical considerations are relevant to the case?

Whose interests should we consider?

Ethics is unavoidable. Some people think that business is simply a game played according to the rules of property and contract law. They think only of how to acquire as much income and wealth for themselves as they can. Nevertheless, they are acting on an unspoken ethical claim. They are implicitly claiming that it is ethically permissible to think only of their own advantage when transacting business. This claim, whether they like it or not, is an ethical judgment. Their judgment that everything legally permissible is ethically permissible depends on a background ethical theory for which they owe us an explanation.

In previous generations, people often believed that business transactions were immoral. Up until the seventeenth century, Europeans generally viewed lending money for interest as usury and viewed making a profit on a business transaction as avaricious. The view of entrepreneurs as heroes has developed only in the last couple of centuries. Each of these views—that business is a game, that business is immoral, or that business is heroic—is an ethical judgment grounded in a particular ethical theory. This is the macro-ethics of business.

Ethics permeates all the details of our commercial lives. Businesspeople are continually faced with decisions about how to treat their employees and how to compensate them, whether to be loyal to their suppliers, how much information to give to their consumers, what details to put into financial reports to investors and creditors, how much pollution they should allow their operations to create, and what arrangements they should make with their international partners. This is the micro-ethics of business.

Ethical theories provide a framework for thinking about ethical decisions, but they do not provide an ethical code of conduct covering all decisions that might ever arise. In this matter, ethical theory is similar to economic theory. Economic theory does not tell a businessperson how best to make a profit in each individual transaction. It provides, instead, a useful theoretical framework for thinking about commercial problems. Knowing some economic theory helps a business decision-maker to pay attention to opportunity costs, to ignore sunk costs, to think about people's incentives, and so on. Similarly, knowing some ethical theory helps the decision-maker to attend to and weigh all the ethical considerations that are relevant to a decision.

There is no recipe for making good ethical decisions, but we can identify some components of the ethical decision-making process. These components include:

1. Recognizing that an ethical decision is required
2. Deciding who is morally accountable for the decision
3. Identifying whose interests must be considered
4. Identifying the relevant types of ethical reasoning
5. Categorizing this ethical reasoning according to the ethical theories being assumed
6. Reflecting critically on the strengths and weaknesses of these ethical reasons
7. Distinguishing the ethically relevant facts of the case
8. Considering the alternatives
9. Making the decision

As we shall see, ethical theory informs each of these components. Making a good ethical decision is not like solving an economics problem. It is part of analyzing a business case. In solving an economics problem, we move step by step from the information given to a determinate solution. In analyzing a business case, we bring together a variety of considerations from cost accounting, marketing, production management, and so on, to recommend a decision about how the firm should proceed. Likewise, in making an ethical business decision, we consider alternative courses of action in the context of various different ethical theories, and put these ethical considerations together with strategic management considerations to decide on the best course of action.

RECOGNIZING AN ETHICAL DECISION

Whenever we consider what we ought to do, what we should do, what it is our duty to do, whether we would be a bad person if we did something, whether something is right or wrong, or whether the results of a decision will be fair to all concerned, then we are making an ethical decision. Ethical decisions signal themselves by the presence of code words such as "ought," "should," "good," "duty," or "fair." These code words, however, can sometimes mislead. Suppose Amy asks herself, "Should I propose to the cost-cutting committee that our firm outsource the production of a popular clothing item to an offshore contractor operating in a lower wage environment?" Here Amy may be thinking strategically rather than morally. Amy's concern may be whether this is a good strategy for her company in terms of making higher profits, or her concern may be whether this is a good strategy for herself in terms of obtaining a year-end bonus. The use of code word, "should," in her question is not an ethical use in this context. In making an ethical decision, Amy should not confine herself to consideration only of her firm and herself. A fully ethical decision would consider the impact of outsourcing on the present employees of the firm, the fairness of paying lower wages in a developing country, the potential for human rights abuses in sweatshops, and so on.

Ethical judgments typically arise in situations that involve (1) a moral agent (which could be a person, organization, or corporation) (2) making and implementing a decision that (3) results in consequences for others. Figure 1.1 shows schematically a typical situation to which an ethical judgment applies.

Figure 1.1: Components of a Typical Ethical Judgment: A person or organization implements a decision that produces various consequences.

A **moral agent** is an entity to whom we are prepared to assign praise or blame, who can understand moral principles, who can respond to moral reasons, and whom we hold morally accountable. Adult human beings are typically moral agents. A large question in business ethics is whether an organization, a corporation, or a government department possesses moral agency, and whether we can hold them morally accountable.

DECIDING WHO IS MORALLY ACCOUNTABLE

Once we have decided whether a person or organization is generally capable of being morally accountable, a second question arises. We must determine which person or organization is morally accountable for the particular results of doing a particular action, and the degree to which he, she, or it is accountable. If the company proceeds on Amy's suggestion to hire an overseas contractor, and a worker injures herself because of the contractor's poor safety precautions, is Amy accountable, is her company accountable, or is it only the contractor who is morally accountable? An agent is **morally accountable** for an action and its consequences if we are prepared to praise or blame her for her freely made decision and for its results.

For example, let us add some details to Amy's situation. The company's stockholders are dissatisfied with the company's returns. The Board of Directors tells the CEO that profits must improve. The CEO tells the VP in charge of production to cut costs, but does not say how. The VP convenes a cost-cutting committee to make a recommendation. Amy proposes using an offshore contractor. The committee recommends this to the VP. The company signs a contract with an offshore firm. The offshore firm takes few safety precautions in its factories. A factory worker loses her fingers because the production line is moving too quickly. Who is morally accountable for the factory worker's injuries? Is it the supervisor overseas who raised the speed of the line? Is it the CEO who ordered the cost cutting?

3

Is it the committee that recommended moving production offshore? Alternatively, is it Amy who suggested employing an overseas contractor? Is everyone in this diffuse chain of control fully morally accountable? Is everyone partially accountable? Is the chain so diffuse that no one is morally accountable? We will return to these questions later.

IDENTIFYING WHOSE INTERESTS MUST BE CONSIDERED

It is a truism that our actions have consequences for others. It is, however, a difficult problem in ethics to determine which others we must consider when we are making an ethical decision. We will call this the issue of moral standing. A person, organization, or nonhuman entity has **moral standing** if we must consider his, her, or its interests in making an ethical decision. One view is that Amy has an obligation to consider only the interests of the owners of the firm. This is a version of the so-called **shareholder view of moral standing** in business ethics. (Friedman, 1970)

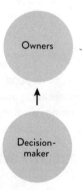

Figure 1.2: Shareholder View of Moral Standing:
The view that only company owners have moral standing in business
decisions, and that the only ethical obligations of managers
are to promote the interests of the owners.

Another view is that Amy also has an obligation to consider the interests of the firm's employees, suppliers, customers, and members of the community in which the firm is located. This is the so-called **stakeholder view of moral standing**, which is associated with the doctrine of corporate social responsibility. (Freeman and Evan, 1990) The stakeholder view gives a more complete picture of moral standing than the shareholder view, but it nonetheless fails to include some important groups that are affected by the actions of businesses. A still wider view is that Amy has an obligation to consider the interests of people in distant countries, of future generations, and of animals and the environment. This **comprehensive view of moral standing** brings up issues of globalization, sustainability, and the environment. (Goodpaster, 2010) Figure 1.4 represents this view schematically.

Figure 1.3: Stakeholder View of Moral Standing:
The view that various stakeholders have moral standing in ethical decisions
in business, and have interests that a manager must consider.

Figure 1.4: Comprehensive View of Moral Standing:
Schematic representation of all those who might be affected by a business
decision, and whose interests should be considered by managers.

This widest view requires that we carefully consider all those whose interests our business decisions will affect.

IDENTIFYING RELEVANT ETHICAL REASONING

We can use the components of an ethical situation to classify the different sorts of ethical theories that are possible. As shown schematically in Figure 1.5, a situation requiring an ethical judgment typically comprises a decision-maker with a certain character making a decision according to certain principles that leads to results that affect the interests of others. Ethical reasoning can focus either on the character of the agent, on the principles that the agent follows in making the decision, or on the net benefits of the results of the decision. When Amy is deciding whether to propose moving production offshore, she has to decide issues such as whether she wants to be the sort of person who will go to any length to make more money, or whether moving production offshore may violate principles of human rights, or whether new jobs in a developing country will benefit its workers. An **identity-based approach** to ethical reasoning focuses on what sort of person (organization) the agent (organization) is becoming, on whether she (it) is virtuous and has a good character. A **principle-based approach** to ethical reasoning looks at the decision-maker's motivations. It assesses the decision as right or wrong according to what ethical principles the agent follows, or does not follow, when she makes her decision. The agent might worry whether her decision stems from a desire for revenge or some other nasty motive, or if it is a principled decision that complies with her duties, shows respect for human rights, and is fair to all concerned. A **consequence-based approach** to ethical reasoning focuses on the results or outcomes of the action, and maximizes net benefits to all concerned.

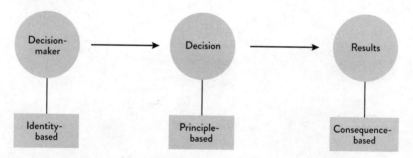

Figure 1.5: Schematic Diagram Showing Three Broad Approaches to Ethical Theory: Identity-based theories look at the sort of person the agent is. Principle-based approaches look at the principles that the agent follows in her decision. Consequentialist theories judge the decision according to the net benefits of its outcomes.

If Amy considers whether she wants to be the sort of person who will do anything to make more money, then she is wondering if she will become avaricious. Avarice is a vice of character, so her consideration is character or identity-based. She is wondering what sort of person she may become. If Amy considers whether her decision will lead to human rights abuses in the Special Economic Zone where offshore production will take place, then she is considering whether the principle of respecting human rights should motivate her decision. Similarly, if Amy worries whether it is fair to take jobs from members of the local community and give the jobs to people overseas, she is again wondering about the principles that should motivate her decision. When Amy weighs the cost and benefits of offshore production (lost jobs in the local community, new jobs in the developing country, poor pay and bad working conditions in the developing country, and so on), then she is taking a consequence-based ethical approach to her decision.

Ethical theory enables us to observe the different sorts of ethical considerations that go into a decision. When we pass a beam of white light through a prism, the prism breaks the white light down into its component colours: red, orange, yellow, green, blue, and purple. The optical prism is a useful metaphor for the role of ethical theory. (Crane and Matten, 2004:104)

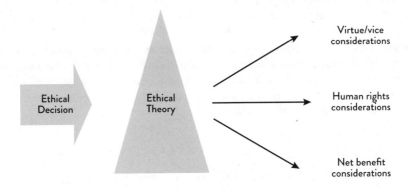

Figure 1.6: An ethical decision passes through the "prism" of ethical theory to reveal the different sorts of ethical considerations relevant to the decision.

Figure 1.6 illustrates the prism metaphor for Amy's decision whether to propose moving production offshore. Looking at her decision according to different approaches to ethical theory divides her decision into character-based considerations (for example, acquiring the vice of avarice), principle-based considerations (for example, respecting human rights), and consequence-based considerations (for example, the net benefits to people in both her local community and the developing country).

CATEGORIZING ETHICAL REASONING ACCORDING TO ETHICAL THEORY

We can make the metaphorical prism of ethical theory into a more precise observational tool by making exact distinctions between different types of ethical theory. We will begin here with a survey of the principal types of ethical theory. In later chapters we will discuss these types of ethical theory in much more detail, and further distinguish them into subtypes. To repeat, what follows is a brief, preliminary survey. Further chapters will cover the theories in more detail and make them more understandable.

1. Identity-Based Ethical Theories

The identity-based approach to ethical reasoning leads to ethical theories that assess the sort of person the moral agent has become. A virtue ethics holds that persons and organizations ought to cultivate a virtuous or morally excellent character. A virtue is a stable character trait with positive moral significance. Examples are courage, generosity, benevolence, and fairness. A vice is a stable character trait with negative moral significance. Examples are avarice, cowardice, dishonesty, and sleaziness. A virtue ethics holds that both persons and organizations ought to cultivate a morally excellent character.

If we understand the identity-based approach more widely so that it encompasses the nature of the agent, then we can think of a feminist ethics of care within this framework. Some feminist ethicists argue that the biological nature, upbringing, and education of women gives women a perspective on ethical decisions that is different from the dominant perspective of men. A feminist **care ethics** is concerned with establishing and preserving harmonious social relationships and with caring for others. This contrasts with traditional ethics, mostly developed by men, that tends to be concerned with following principles and calculating net benefits. A feminist care ethics, like a virtue ethics, emphasizes the role of discussion, wisdom, and judgment in ethical decisions and downplays the role of principles and calculations.

2. Principle-Based Ethical Theories

The principle-based approach to ethical reasoning says that each agent should be motivated by ethical principles when making a decision, and not be concerned with the consequences of the decision. There are several different types of principle-based ethical theories.

In **duty-based theories** of ethics, the agent should follow the principle of doing his or her duty, regardless of the consequences. An example is the set of duties imposed by the ten commandments in the Jewish and Christian Bibles. These are mostly negative duties, of the form, "Thou shalt not...."

In **rights-based theories**, the moral principles that agents should follow in their decisions involve respecting the moral rights of others. Respecting the moral rights of others may include respecting their freedom to do as they wish without coercing them into doing otherwise, respecting their autonomous choices without trying to manipulate them, or respecting their private property rights to use things that they own in ways that they choose.

In **justice-based theories**, the moral principles that agents should follow in their decisions involve treating others fairly. Treating others fairly requires treating everyone in the same way unless there are morally relevant reasons for treating them differently. Justice may require, for example, that businesses install access ramps for people with disabilities. Doing so treats some customers differently, but the different treatment is not morally arbitrary. Because some customers have disabilities that make using stairs impossible, there is a morally relevant reason for providing special ramps.

3. Consequence-Based Ethical Theories

In consequence-based approaches to ethical reasoning, what matters is that the outcome should be as good as possible. To use a cliché, the end justifies the means, when the end is the best end possible. The goodness of the end can be measured in several ways, each giving rise to a different type of consequentialist theory. If we value the outcome of the decision as a good state of the world, then we have an objective form of consequentialism. **Objective consequentialism** requires agents to make those decisions which lead to the best consequences from a point of view that is independent of the psychological states of individual people. For example, someone might claim that the international prestige of her nation is a good thing whether or not it makes citizens happier, and that maximizing her nation's international prestige should be a goal of ethical decision-making.

Objective consequentialism contrasts with forms of utilitarianism, which judge the goodness of outcomes purely in terms of the positive and negative psychological states that they bring about. **Utilitarianism** requires agents to make those decisions which maximize positive mental states in both themselves and others. The original developers of utilitarianism thought that ethical decisions should aim at producing the maximum amount of human happiness, which they equated with pleasure and the absence of pain. Modern versions often talk of ethical decisions aiming to bring about the greatest amount of satisfied preferences. Modern economics is a descendent of utilitarian thinking. Economists have shown that markets in perfect competition are optimal for satisfying people's preferences. We will later look at the efficient market justification for the capitalist system and consider issues of market failure, where the assumptions of perfect competition break down and markets do not deliver maximum preference satisfaction.

Another type of consequence-based ethical theory is ethical egoism. **Ethical egoism** is the ethical theory that agents ought always to maximize only their own self-interest. Ethical egoists believe that they should strive for results that maximize their own happiness, pleasure, or preference satisfaction. Ethical egoism is an ethical theory and not a psychological theory. It is not the empirical theory, sometimes accepted in economic theory, that rational agents always *do* make choices that maximize the satisfaction of their own preferences. It is the ethical theory that moral agents always *should* make choices that maximize satisfaction of their own preferences.

We have now developed a preliminary theoretical framework into which we can put many of the considerations that come up in making an ethical decision. This theoretical framework will help us to think about the ethical decisions that we must make. We can also use it as a sort of checklist that will help prevent us from neglecting any important ethical considerations. Table 1.1 displays this preliminary theoretical framework. The table has a column for each group whose interests the decision and its implementation will affect. The table has a row for each of the various types of ethical theory that we have

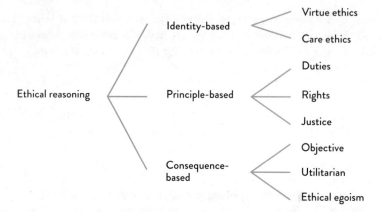

Figure 1.7: A preliminary taxonomy of ethical theories classified according to the different types of ethical reasoning involved.

just discussed. In succeeding chapters, we will look at distinctions between ethical theories that will make the framework more complicated. The table does not display issues of moral agency and moral accountability, which we will leave aside for the moment.

To see how this framework works, let us go back to Amy's decision whether to propose moving production offshore. Here are some of the considerations that we have discussed:

A. Amy realizes that if the company implements her proposal, then she will receive a handsome year-end bonus. From the point of view of ethical egoism, this is an ethical consideration because putting forward the proposal will maximize Amy's self-interest. We can classify this consideration as falling under the theory of ethical egoism and affecting the interests of Amy herself. Therefore, we can put an "A" in the cell where the row representing ethical egoism intersects with the column that acknowledges the moral standing of the self.

B. Amy worries whether in putting forward the proposal, and thinking only of her own gain, she is becoming greedy and avaricious. This virtue ethic consideration again affects her self. Therefore, we can put a "B" in the cell where the virtue ethics row intersects the column representing moral standing of the self.

C. Knowing that human rights abuses often occur in Special Economic Zones, Amy worries that implementation of her proposal will fail to respect the rights of overseas workers. These overseas workers will be working for contractors and not for her company. Therefore, we can put a "C" at the intersection of rights and a concern for members of the global community.

D. Amy knows that if her firm implements her proposal, then it will fire many of its present employees. This will have a very bad effect on the local community. This is a utilitarian consideration affecting the interests of employees and members of the local community. Therefore, we can put a "D" at both the intersection of utilitarianism and employees and the intersection of utilitarianism and community.

E. Amy also knows that the overseas contractor will pay the women sewing the clothing in a developing country much less than her company is paying its present employees for doing the same work. This is a justice consideration affecting her firm's present employees and the new workers overseas. Therefore, we can put an "E" where justice considerations intersect with employees and with people overseas.

	Self	Owners	Employees	Suppliers	Customers	Community	Globe	Posterity	Environ- ment
Identity									
Virtue Ethics	B			G					
Care Ethics									
Principle									
Duties		F							
Rights							C		
Justice			E				E		
Consequence									
Objective									
Utilitarian			D			D			
Ethical Egoism	A								

Table 1.1: A theoretical framework for thinking about ethical decisions showing whose interests we should consider and which ethical theories we should apply.

We can also see how to use this theoretical framework as a checklist to help us find other relevant ethical considerations. Here are some examples:

F. Amy should think of her duties to the owners of the firm. By taking on her role as a manager, Amy acquired a duty to benefit the interests of the owners. This role includes doing what she can to lower the firm's costs and maximize profits. We should put an "F" in the duties to the owner's cell of the table.

    G. Amy should think of the firm's suppliers. Moving production offshore will mean not renewing contracts with suppliers. Should the firm be loyal to its long-time suppliers? Loyalty is a virtue, and here it affects the interests of the suppliers, so we should put a "G" in that cell.

Using this theoretical framework as a checklist, we could discover other relevant considerations, but we will leave that as an exercise for the reader. The case of Amy's decision is becoming very complicated. Some ethical considerations point toward Amy making the proposal, and some count against it. What we need now is some way for looking at the strengths and weaknesses of these ethical reasons so that Amy may judge what she should do.

REFLECTING CRITICALLY ON ETHICAL REASONS

This taxonomy of ethical theories is a preliminary one that we will make more detailed in suceeding chapters. In applied ethics, which is what we are doing here, we use a knowledge of ethical theories in order to understand all the ethical reasons that are relevant to a decision. Academic ethics is different. Academic ethicists will typically make a career out of defending one particular ethical theory against all objections, and of pointing out the weaknesses of all competing theories. In applying ethics to business issues, we will, however, adopt a pluralist attitude to ethical reasoning, using many different theories in order not to miss any important ethical considerations relevant to a decision.

The arguments of academic ethics are still useful to us. Academic ethics has compiled a great deal of information about the strengths and weaknesses of each ethical theory. Often the motivation for one type of ethical theory is the discovery of weaknesses in another. We can often see the weaknesses of one type of ethical theory from the perspective of another type. For example, rights-based theories reveal a common weakness of utilitarian theories. Suppose, as a thought experiment, that the greatest happiness of humankind could be achieved if a few people became the slaves of all the others. The unhappiness of the slaves, we will suppose, is greatly offset by the increased happiness of the majority. Taking the perspective of human rights, however, we can see that there is something morally wrong with making some people into slaves, no matter how much happiness it produces. Business decisions do not typically turn on issues of slavery. Instead, the general point is that when we apply utilitarian considerations, we should always look for problems with rights abuses. A knowledge of the intellectual interactions between ethical theories will help us see the strengths and weaknesses of ethical considerations when they are applied to particular cases. Her college course in business ethics will remind Amy to investigate problems of human rights abuses in Special Economic Zones when she is doing a cost-benefit analysis of the decision to relocate production offshore.

When we finish analyzing a problematic decision from the perspectives of different ethical theories, we will frequently find that ethical considerations conflict with one another. For example Amy's duty to promote the interest of the shareholders by proposing going offshore will conflict with her obligation to promote the welfare of local empoleyees and suppliers. The best that anyone can do in situations where ethical considerations conflict is to clarify carefully what is at stake and then reflect critically on what is the best overall decision. We have no clear recipe for making such a decision. However, only if we have clearly understood all the relevant ethical considerations will we make the best possible decision.

DISTINGUISHING ETHICALLY RELEVANT FACTS

The facts are the facts. There are, however, a huge number of facts about the world, and knowing which ones are relevant to the case at hand can be tricky. This is analogous to the Frame Problem that computer scientists ran into when they tried to create artificial intelligence. A big problem with programming a computer to perform like a human being is that the computer faces too much information. Humans intuitively know which facts are relevant to decisions about the task at hand; computers do not. Without this intuitive knowledge, the computer is forced to investigate each and every fact in its memory to see if it is relevant to the task. Is the distance from the Earth to the Moon relevant? Is the mass of the electron a relevant factor? Without some guidance to what sort of facts are relevant, the computer will become bogged down in checking the relevance of everything. Tasks that are easy for humans become computationally impossible for an artificial intelligence.

In a similar way, the ethical decision-maker is confronted with too many facts, and must somehow decide what facts about the case are ethically salient. A knowledge of ethical theory is useful here. Different types of ethical theories require different types of information. Virtue ethics requires information about the character of the decision-maker. Rights-based theories require information about potential abuse, coercion, and manipulation. Metaphorically, we can reverse the earlier prism metaphor, and think of ethical theory as a sort of optical filter through which we can examine the case. The coating on the lens will filter out the facts of the case that are not morally relevant, and enable us to see more clearly the facts that are ethically salient.

Her knowledge of various ethical theories will enable Amy to see what facts she should examine. Virtue ethics will make her think about what sort of character traits she is displaying. Human rights considerations will make her think about problems of worker abuse overseas. Utilitarianism gets her to look at the various costs and benefits of the decision to all those concerned, present employees, the local community, customers, and new workers in a developing country. Justice considerations get her to look at how the benefits and burdens of the decision will be distributed among these different groups of people. In general, ethical theory helps us to see the sorts of facts which are relevant for ethical decisions.

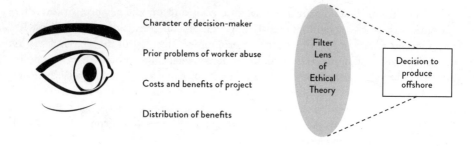

Character of decision-maker

Prior problems of worker abuse

Costs and benefits of project

Distribution of benefits

Filter Lens of Ethical Theory

Decision to produce offshore

Figure 1.8: The coated "lens" of ethical theory filters out the irrelevant facts and reveals the ethically salient facts.

CONSIDERING ALTERNATIVES

Knowledge of ethical theories also helps us to discover alternative decisions that we should consider. Just as there is a problem of finding the ethically relevant facts, so too there is a problem of finding a manageable number of ethically salient alternatives. The space of alternative decisions is always vast, but most choices are morally irrelevant and we should rule them out. Again, ethical theory provides a filter. The number of ethically permissible possible choices is much smaller than the total number of possible choices. For example, justice considerations rule out potential choices that are flagrantly unjust. At the same time, justice considerations should also lead us to search for alternatives that are fairer to all concerned. Amy and her company, for example, could look at ways of compensating the company's present employees when the company moves their jobs offshore. Perhaps the company could offer them retraining, or positions in a newly expanded warehousing and distribution centre.

It is important to remember that staying with the status quo, or business as usual, is also an ethical decision. We can usually make the status quo better, fairer, or more respectful of human rights. We cannot avoid making ethical decisions by just doing business as usual.

MAKING AN ETHICAL DECISION

Making an ethical decision would be easier for us if we were committed to just one ethical theory. If we were ethical egoists, for example, then we should consider only our own interests, and we would neglect the interests of others except as those interests impact our strategic game plan. If we were libertarians, people who believe only in moral rights of liberty, property, and contract, then we could rule out considerations of maximizing net benefits or distributing benefits fairly. Nevertheless, we cannot avoid ethical theory by announcing our commitment to what we regard as the one, correct theory. We must be able to justify our theory, say why it is better than competing theories, and show how it avoids the apparent weaknesses that other theories point out in it.

Those of us who are not committed to one favourite theory will have to weigh competing considerations pointed to by the whole plurality of ethical theories. This will not be easy, and few cases will have one obvious best answer. Knowledge of applied ethics will help us weed out ethically inferior alternative decisions. Knowledge of applied ethics will also help us to weigh the competing considerations in terms of their well-known strengths and weaknesses. This process may leave us with a range of options that, from an ethical point of view, are all equally good. Then we can use strategic business considerations to narrow the range of options down further. Sometimes we may face a range of options that are all bad ones, and we may be unable to decide between them. Then we face an ethical dilemma. Applied ethics will help us make better ethical decisions in business, but it will not tell us what to do in every case.

SUMMARY

1. Our first task is to recognize when an ethical decision is required regarding a business issue.
2. Our next task is to decide which person or organization is morally accountable for the decision.
3. Then we identify whose (or what's) interests must be considered. We must determine who or what has moral standing in the case.
4. We must think about which ethical considerations are relevant to the case. Ethical considerations are either character-based, principle-based, or consequence-based. Ethical theory is a sort of prism which refracts an ethical decision into its component considerations.
5. We classify these ethical considerations according to the ethical theories that they assume. Virtue ethics and care ethics use a character-based approach. The principle-based approach appeals to either duties, rights, or theories of justice. A consequence-based approach tries to maximize either objective values or the happiness of everyone. The latter variant is utilitarianism. Another variant is ethical egoism, where the agent considers only her own self-interest.
6. The strengths of one type of ethical theory complement the weaknesses of others. We can use our knowledge of ethical theory to critically reflect on the ethical considerations relevant to a decision.
7. Knowledge of ethical theory also functions as a filter that helps us to distinguish those facts that are ethically relevant to the case from the huge number of facts that are irrelevant.
8. As in all decision-making, we must brainstorm the alternatives, including business as usual. Again ethical theory helps us to look only at the ethically relevant alternatives.
9. Ultimately we must make an ethical decision. To do this we must weigh the alternatives, reject those that are ethically inferior, and leave a selection of options that are ethically acceptable.

ONLINE LEARNING RESOURCES

You will find a collection of learning resources associated with this chapter on the book's website: http://sites.broadviewpress.com/businessethics/. Working through this material will help you understand and remember important concepts that we have discussed, and will help you apply them to issues in business ethics.

STUDY QUESTIONS

Answering the following questions will help you to understand the ethical theory in this chapter and will help you to create a set of review notes on the textbook.

1. Illustrate the difference between moral standing and moral accountability.
2. Describe the difference between identity-based ethical reasoning and principle-based ethical reasoning.
3. Describe the difference between principle-based ethical reasoning and consequence-based ethical reasoning.
4. Describe the difference between utilitarian ethical reasoning and rights-based ethical reasoning.

DECISION QUESTIONS

The whole point of learning ethical theory is to understand and ask questions like the following when you are analyzing an ethically problematic situation or case.

- Whose interests will the decision affect?
- Should we consider the owners of the business?
- Should we consider employees, suppliers, customers, and the local community?
- Should we consider the global community, posterity, or the environment?
- Which facts are most relevant from an ethical point of view?
- Does our analysis of the ethical situation lead us to require more information about the case?
- After our analysis of the ethical situation, can we see alternative decisions that we should consider?
- Which of the alternative decisions is the best from a business point of view?

CASE STUDY

Analyze this case study using the ethical theory that you have learned so far. You will find a collection of learning materials applying to the case on the book's website: http://sites.broadviewpress.com/businessethics/. These materials will help you in your analysis.

Should Amy Go Offshore?

Amy Johnson graduated two years ago from the business program at a well-known local university. Immediately after her graduation, the Seinfeld Textile Corporation in Truro hired her as a junior manager in the production department. Her boss is the Vice President for production, Tom Harris. She is mostly happy in her new job, but feels that her pay should be higher. She and her partner have recently become engaged to be married, and they would like to be able to buy a house. Amy would like to do a good job helping ST become more profitable and she would like very much to get a good year-end bonus and a promotion as soon as possible.

Amy is from Truro and knows many of the people who work at Seinfeld Textiles. She has made friends at the company, both with some of the managers and with some of the workers. She does find the other managers to be rather competitive, particularly the older and more senior ones. She worries about the demands of her work, about the sort of person she must become to compete in the company, and the effect of her time commitment to the company on her relationship.

The stockholders of Seinfeld Textiles are dissatisfied with the company's returns. The Board of Directors has told the CEO that profits must improve. The CEO has told the VP in charge of production, Tom Harris, to cut costs, but has not said how. Tom has convened a cost-cutting committee to make a recommendation. Amy has thought about this problem and is wondering to herself, "Should I propose to the cost-cutting committee that our firm outsource the production of our most popular clothing item to an offshore contractor operating in a lower wage environment?"

From her research, she has identified a particular operator in Bangladesh, the Chittagong Clothing Company, which can do this sort of work well and cheaply. Amy also knows that this company, CCC, has had complaints against it for how it treats its workers, who are mostly young women. She knows that it pays its garment workers reasonably well by Bangladesh standards, but realizes that these wages are far less than they are in Truro. She has also found indications that CCC is rather lax about the safety standards in its factories. CCC's factories are often shoddily constructed, and its supervisors often pressure its employees to work faster than is safe. However, Bangladesh sorely needs the new jobs that this contract will bring.

Amy realizes that if the company implements her proposal, and the strategy works, then she will receive a handsome year-end bonus and possibly a promotion. Amy knows that if her firm implements her proposal, then it will fire many of its present employees. This will take jobs from members of the local community and give the jobs to people overseas. Amy also knows that CCC will pay the women sewing the clothing in a developing country much less than ST is paying its present employees for doing the same work. As well, moving production offshore will mean that ST will not renew contracts with its present suppliers.

Should Amy recommend that ST contract with CCC in Bangladesh to produce clothing?

Chapter 2

THE NATURE OF ETHICAL REASONING

How can we identify ethical reasons?

Are any of these ethical reasons relative to cultural membership?

How do we balance conflicting ethical reasons?

When we make decisions, we make judgments about what is the best thing to do, and we make these judgments for reasons. Here it is important that the word "reasons" be in the plural. If we think about almost any decision we have ever made, then we can find reasons pointing both one way and the other. Some reasons are stronger than others are, and sometimes one reason may have overriding importance. Nevertheless, we usually judge what is best and decide what to do, not for one reason, but according to the balance of many reasons.

For example, suppose that Ben is in a situation where he could easily steal $500 from the holiday-bonus fund at work. He may just act impulsively, but if he thinks before he acts, then he will find reasons both pointing toward taking his opportunity and pointing against doing so: He feels that he is underpaid. He needs the $500 to buy holiday gifts for his children. Someone might catch him, and then he will lose his job. His employer recently passed him over for a promotion, and he would like revenge. Someone will miss the money, and there will be an atmosphere of suspicion in his department for some months after people notice the loss. And so on. How these reasons balance out will affect his judgment about how to act. If he is a competent decision-maker, then he will consider all of them.

This list of reasons is far from complete, because so far Ben has not considered important ethical reasons that bear on his decision: He should not be the sort of person who is dishonest and disloyal to his fellow employees. He should not poison the work relationships in his department. He should keep the promise of good service to his employer that was implicit in his employment contract. He should respect the property rights of the company that employs him. It is unfair that he receive the $500 instead of everyone receiving holiday bonuses. The happiness he brings to his children will not outweigh the happiness that he takes from the children of the other employees. From the

Figure 2.1: Usually, more than one reason contributes to our judgment of what is best and to our decision about how to act.

point of view of ethical reasoning, this is a simple decision; all of these are reasons against taking the money. The only ethical theory that might support taking the $500 is ethical egoism, which would tell Ben always to act in his own self-interest. But ethical egoism, as we shall see in the next chapter, has many weaknesses. The balance of ethical reasons is thoroughly against the judgment that Ben should take the money. Furthermore, the ethical reasons apparently outweigh all Ben's selfish and strategic reasons. Unfortunately, not all ethical decision-making is this uncomplicated.

This discussion has assumed that ethical reasons apply universally in all contexts. Perhaps this assumption is wrong. Suppose that Ben's company has a dog-eat-dog corporate culture. All the people working there, from the CEO to the typists, share a view that life is "every man for himself," and that "he who dies with the most toys wins." People expect each other to lie, cheat, and even steal when they can get away with it. The prevailing ethical climate of the firm is that of ethical egoism. Within this corporate culture, would it not be permissible for Ben to take the $500 from the bonus fund?

Some people believe that what is right or wrong is relative to the culture in which people make decisions. In many hunter-gatherer societies, for example, cultural norms require clan members to share the proceeds of their work with the whole clan, whereas in a capitalist society, this is not morally required at all. The ethical climate we have just imagined in Ben's company is rather extreme. However, there is still a question whether the business community has a distinct ethical culture. Should we hold business people to ethical standards at work that are different from the ethical standards we would expect of them at home or in the wider community? This is part of the general question of whether ethical standards are relative to one's culture. **Ethical relativism** is the metaethical view that the truth or falsity of ethical judgments is relative to the traditional practices of a cultural group. It contrasts with the view that ethical judgments are universal and apply to everyone no matter what their cultural membership. Philosophers call these views "metaethical" because they are views about the nature of ethical reasoning. They are not themselves ethical judgments. Ethical relativism does not tell us what ethical judgment we should make; instead, it purports to tell us something about what an ethical judgment means.

In this chapter, we will look at some properties of ethical reasoning and at the implications of these properties for the nature of ethics. We will look at the strengths and weaknesses of the notion that ethical judgments and ethical reasons are relative to

THE NATURE OF ETHICAL REASONING

membership in a culture. Then we will look in more detail at how to apply the whole plurality of ethical theories to making an ethical judgment.

TWO IMPORTANT PROPERTIES OF ETHICAL REASONS

In English, the word "reason" is ambiguous. A reason can be a motivation for acting in a certain way, or a reason can be a justification for believing one thing rather than another. Ethical reasons, unlike many other reasons, embrace this ambiguity, and have both of these properties simultaneously. Ethical reasons are **action-guiding** because they motivate us to act in ways that we think are morally right, or at least ethically permissible, and to refrain from morally wrong actions. Ethical reasons tell us something about the attitudes of the person who holds them and about the effect the person intends to have on the actions of others by expressing them. At the same time, ethical reasons are **agreement-seeking** because we offer them as justifications to others for acting in a certain way. They are reasons about which there can be argument and debate. When we offer ethical reasons, our goal is to get others to agree with us about which ethical reasons are important, and about what they should do.

We gained an intuitive understanding of these properties of ethical reasons when we were children. We came to understand that when our mothers told us that some action was wrong that she meant for us to stop doing it. In other words, she meant for her ethical judgment to guide our action. At the same time, we came to understand that her ethical judgments had justifications, that we could sometimes argue with her about those justifications, and that she sought our agreement with her judgments.

Descriptive and scientific reasons are agreement-seeking, but not action-guiding. When someone asserts that the climate is changing because human beings are burning fossil fuels, she is asserting something about which there is controversy and debate. She can justify her claim by pointing to scientific evidence about atmospheric carbon dioxide concentrations and to scientific theories about how the greenhouse effect works. Such scientific evidence alone does not provide her with motivation to act in any way. She can easily believe that burning fossil fuel causes climate change without being motivated to buy a bicycle or become an environmental activist. Scientific reasons are motivationally inert; by themselves, they do not provide reasons for action.

In contrast, people's wants and desires are action-guiding, but are not agreement-seeking. When Keith asserts that he prefers chocolate ice cream, he does not expect that everyone else will agree with him. He will not seek to get others who prefer vanilla to agree with him. His desire for chocolate ice cream, however, will guide his actions. When confronted with a choice of flavours in the ice cream parlour, he will choose chocolate, but he does not care if others do not.

Ethical judgments and the reasons we have for making them both guide action and seek the agreement of others. They move us to action, but at the same time, we care about the agreement of others. When we say that an action is wrong, we would like others to agree with us and to stop doing this ethically wrong action. When we make ethical judgments and give ethical reasons, we intend that these reasons apply not only to our own actions, but also to the actions of others. We want others to agree with this so that they will do the right thing.

These two abstract properties of ethical reasons, that they are both action-guiding and agreement-seeking, have important consequences. We will see that, because ethical reasons are action-guiding, they cannot be directly derived from purely descriptive scientific reasons. We will see that, because ethical reasons are action-guiding, they cannot require people to perform actions that they are unable to perform. As well, we will see that, because ethical reasons are agreement-seeking, they apply to everyone. No individual can expect everyone else to agree that she alone is somehow special and exempt from obeying a moral principle.

THE "IS/OUGHT" GAP

Because ethical judgments have action-guiding force and factual or scientific statements do not, then we cannot logically derive ethical judgments from scientific judgments. There is a logical gap between statements about how the world is and statements about how the world ought to be. Philosophers refer to this important conclusion as the "is/ought" gap, the fact/value distinction, and the naturalistic fallacy. The **"is/ought" gap** means that we cannot derive an ethical conclusion from an argument consisting of purely scientific or factual premises.

The first philosopher to draw attention to the "is/ought" gap was the eighteenth-century Scottish philosopher, David Hume. He wrote the following passage about the work of other philosophers of his time.

> In every system of morality, which I have hitherto met with, I have always remarked, that the author proceeds for some time in the ordinary way of reasoning, and establishes the being of a God, or makes observations concerning human affairs; when of a sudden I am surprized to find, that instead of the usual copulations of propositions, is, and is not, I meet with no proposition that is not connected with an ought, or an ought not. This change is imperceptible; but is, however, of the last [i.e., the greatest] consequence. For as this ought, or ought not, expresses some new relation or affirmation, it is necessary that it should be observed and explained; and at the same time that a reason should be given, for what seems altogether inconceivable, how this new relation can be a deduction from others, which are entirely different from it. But as authors do not commonly use this precaution, I shall presume to recommend it to the readers; and am persuaded, that this small attention would subvert all the vulgar systems of morality ... (Hume 1740: Book III, Part I, Sect. I)

Hume points out the fallacy of reasoning directly from scientific facts to ethical judgments. His advice will lead us to chop off the ethical conclusion of an argument from its purely factual premises. Hence, philosophers sometimes referred to the "is/ought" gap as Hume's Guillotine.

For example, some people believe that business is, as a matter of fact, a ruthless and competitive game played according to a certain set of rules differing from those of ordinary life. Without committing a logical fallacy, such people cannot conclude simply from this description of the facts that business *ought* to be a ruthless and competitive game played according to a certain set of rules differing from those of ordinary life. To argue this way would be to neglect the logical distinction between facts and values and the logical gap between "is" and "ought."

The "is/ought" gap entails that any argument in favour of an ethical judgment must contain at least one ethical premise. In other words, at least one of the reasons for an ethical decision must be an ethical reason. For example, suppose it is the case that a firm can reduce its emissions of greenhouse gasses by using Carbon Capture and Sequestration (CCS) technology. This fact is not enough, by itself, to entail that the firm ought to install CCS. For the reason Hume pointed out, the following argument is invalid:

1, CCS will reduce emissions.
2, Therefore, the firm ought to install CCS.

The firm needs an additional ethical reason, such as the ethical principle that, in order to maximize the welfare of future generations, firms ought to reduce greenhouse gas emissions. The following revised argument is valid:

1*. For the sake of future generations, all
    firms ought to reduce emissions.
2*. CCS will reduce emissions.
3*. Therefore, the firm ought to install CCS.

Then the firm will have an ethical reason why it ought to install CCS. Identifying and analyzing such implicit ethical principles is the role of business ethics.

"OUGHT" IMPLIES "CAN"

A second important implication of the action-guiding nature of ethical judgments is that we are not ethically required to do an action if we are unable to perform it. Ethical judgments guide us to perform certain actions, and if we physically cannot perform any of those actions, then we are not obliged to do them. It is a necessary condition of being ethically obliged to perform an action that we are actually able to perform that action. For example, we are not ethically obliged to bring about world peace all by ourselves because it is not something that any one person like us is able to do. The metaethical principle that **"ought" implies "can"** means that a person cannot be morally obligated to perform an action or bring about a consequence if he or she is unable to do so. Even to save the world, we cannot be ethically obligated to walk across water or to fly unaided over a mountain.

To put the point less dramatically, ethical obligations can be demanding but not too demanding. The judgment that we should do everything we can to eradicate world poverty implies that we should give money to charity. It does not imply that we should give everything we own to charity and thereby make ourselves destitute and worse off than the people that we are trying to help. The latter implication is too demanding; it is not something that we can do.

For example, though there is a strong ethical reason why a firm should install Carbon Capture and Sequestration technology, suppose the firm cannot afford to do so. If the cost of CCS is too demanding, then the firm cannot install CCS. If the firm cannot install CCS, then there is no overall ethical reason that it ought to install CCS. Since "ought" implies "can," we will not hold the firm morally accountable for not installing CCS. The principle that "ought" implies "can" is important when we think about holding people morally accountable for their decisions. For example, if someone acts under the threat of physical violence, then we may say she cannot do otherwise. If she cannot do otherwise, then we should excuse her from moral accountability for what she did, and blame those who threatened her instead.

We must be careful, however, when we apply the "ought" implies "can" principle. Just because something is an inconvenience does not mean that it is too demanding. If one of us were able to eradicate world poverty by getting up from in front of the television and pressing a button on the wall, then we would not think it too demanding to say that he or she was obliged to do so. If government regulations changed, so that all firms were obliged to install CCS, allowed to pass the additional costs on to their customers, and provided with government financing, then installing CCS would be inconvenient, but no longer overly demanding. As it is, installing CCS is not merely inconvenient; it is quite demanding for some firms. The question is: is it *too* demanding?

ETHICAL RELATIVISM: STRENGTHS

Ethical relativism claims that what is right or wrong depends on a person's cultural membership. According to ethical relativism, we should not expect that the members of a different culture will have the same moral standards that we do. Nor should we expect that we can get them to agree to our moral standards. If there are ethical disagreements between different cultures, and if there seems no way to resolve these disagreements in a rational way, then it seems that we should abandon the principle that ethical judgments are always agreement-seeking.

Much of the motivation for adopting a relativist stance in ethics comes from the study of radically different cultures. Cultural anthropologists have shown that cultures differ drastically regarding the duties of members to their kin, on what members of the culture may eat and how they should eat it, on how and with whom people may have sexual relations, and on how people should worship a god or gods. Cultures also differ drastically in what they judge to be ethically permissible behaviour. Some cultures practice polygamy, some countenance the killing of family members to preserve the family's honour, and some cultures regularly mutilate the genitals of young girls. In the face of widespread cross-cultural disagreements regarding ethical judgments, and in the absence of any method of resolving these ethical disagreements in a rational way, it may appear that ethical relativism is the appropriate philosophical theory of ethics.

Ethical relativism appears attractive because it seems to epitomize toleration for other cultures. In its imperial past, the English-speaking world had little respect for the cultures that it colonized. Colonizers mostly assumed that their moral beliefs were far superior to those of the aboriginal peoples whom they had conquered. Anthropologists, such as Margaret Mead, reacted against this cultural imperialism by formulating the doctrine of cultural relativism. The ethical beliefs of aboriginal people were just as true for the aboriginal people as the ethical beliefs of the anthropologists were for the anthropologists. Cultural relativism seemed the proper way to show respect for other cultures, and ethical relativism provided a philosophical justification for cross-cultural tolerance.

ETHICAL RELATIVISM: WEAKNESSES

1. *Cultural Diversity:* Ethical relativism apparently follows from the fact of cultural diversity. However, this argument conflicts with Hume's Guillotine. Suppose it is the case that members of another culture do accept a particular morally repugnant practice. We cannot argue from this premise to the conclusion that it ought to be the case that members of the other culture accept this morally repugnant practice. To argue like that would be to cross the "is/ought" gap without a supporting ethical principle.

We should remind ourselves that the respect and toleration of others does not require uncritical acceptance of their beliefs. Proper respect for others requires an engagement with their views. We have to take their views seriously, and not simply dismiss them as true-for-them but not true-for-us. We show respect for others only when we take their arguments seriously. We do not take the arguments of members of another culture seriously when we simply label their arguments as true for people in that culture but not true for members of our culture. Ethical relativism can be a disguise for intellectual laziness, and can actually show disrespect for the views and arguments of members of other cultures.

There are limitations to the idea that tolerating and respecting other cultures implies that we should become ethical relativists. Some practices that are customary in other cultures are just too ghastly to tolerate. The killing of a young woman by her father and brothers in order to preserve the family honour is just wrong. Honour killing is wrong both for us and for members of that other culture. We are more certain of the wrongness of honour killing than we are of the truth of ethical relativism. If ethical relativism implies that honour killing is ethically permissible in the other culture, then ethical relativism must be false.

2. *Intolerant Cultures:* We should also note that toleration is not a virtue in all cultures. Members of extremely fundamentalist religious cultures, for example, are not at all tolerant of the different ethical beliefs of members of other cultures. Intolerant cultures hold that tolerating and respecting

the customs and practices of members of other cultures is a vice, not a virtue. In such cultures, the toleration is not a virtue, and so toleration gives people no reason to be ethical relativists. To members of an intolerant culture, the diverse ethical beliefs of other cultures will simply be false, not true for members of those other cultures.

3. *Cultural Conservatism:* Ethical relativism apparently defines what is right or wrong according to the accepted practices of the culture of which someone is a member. Therefore, ethical relativism implies that if any member of the culture disagrees with the accepted practices of her culture, then her dissenting view is false, by definition. If the accepted practices of a culture define what is right and wrong for its members, then how can people criticize their own culture's ethical practices? How can a member of an honour-killing culture criticize this accepted practice without contradicting herself? Ethical relativism potentially leads to a very strong cultural conservatism that makes critical reflection or cultural reform ethically impossible. This position is incompatible with ethics in general. The essence of ethics is to think critically about our accepted moral practices. Ethics, as practiced by philosophers, does not merely describe the ethos of a culture and the mores of its members. It subjects accepted cultural practices to critical reflection.

4. *Cultural Homogeneity:* Ethical relativism apparently assumes that the ethical beliefs and practices of a culture are homogeneous. This is unlikely to be the case. In any honour-killing culture, doubtlessly many members of the culture do not accept the practice. If cultures are internally diverse in their ethical beliefs, then how do we determine which of these ethical beliefs defines what is right and wrong for members of the culture? If we are to say that what is right or wrong is relative to cultural membership, then we need a way to determine which of a culture's ethical beliefs are authoritative for members of each culture. It is unlikely that we will be able to do so.

5. *Multiculturalism:* Ethical relativism does not tell people what to do when they are simultaneously members of different cultures with conflicting ethical practices. In multicultural societies, people are often members of different cultures at the same time, and have no particular cultural membership that is morally authoritative for them. For example, imagine a businessperson of mixed Sikh and German descent, a citizen of Hong Kong, but educated in an English public school with an MBA from Harvard, and married to a Thai. She does not have any one cultural membership that is always authoritative for her. There is likely no answer as to which ethical principles she should follow.

There is a temptation at this point for a cultural ethical relativist to argue instead for individual ethical relativism. Individual ethical relativism is the metaethical view that the truth or falsity of ethical judgments is relative, not to the culture of the speaker, but to the individual speaker himself. On this view, a speaker could claim that an action is right for him, even if it is wrong for everyone else. However, it is next to impossible to justify such a view. A cultural ethical relativist can point to the fact that the culture of which she is a member generally believes that her action is morally right. This cultural fact carries some rhetorical force that gives others some justification, albeit weak, for accepting her relativism. The individual ethical relativist, however, can only point to the fact that he believes that his action is morally right. His individual belief carries little rhetorical force. His mere assertion gives no justification whatsoever to others for accepting his relativism.

6. *Ethical Disagreement:* There is much genuine ethical disagreement in the world. Reasonable people can disagree on the morality of abortion, assisted suicide, eating animals, or imposing a carbon tax. Ethics is agreement-seeking, but not always agreement-finding. Sometimes people disagree because they have different beliefs about the facts of the case, sometimes because they hold different ethical theories, sometimes because they place different weights on the same ethical considerations, and sometimes because they come from different cultural backgrounds. The idea that ethics is agreement-seeking implies that we should not just accept moral disagreements uncritically, but should instead try to resolve disagreements by carefully clarifying the issues in dispute and discussing these issues respectfully.

Ethical disagreement between cultures may not be as rampant as ethical relativists assume. We should be careful not to assume that ethical disagreement about a particular case implies ethical disagreement at a deep level. The disagreement may be about the facts of the case, not the ethical principles involved. Consider the attempt by members of the Spanish Inquisition to use torture and execution to stamp out heresy during the Counter Reformation in the sixteenth century. We cannot immediately infer that they had radically different ethical beliefs from our own, and that we believe in promoting human welfare whereas the inquisitors did not. The inquisitors had particular factual beliefs that are uncommon today. They believed in an afterlife that included eternal hell for heretics who did not repent, and they believed that coerced repentance was a way for heretics to avoid this hell. The inquisitors probably believed in the importance of human welfare, where avoiding hellish torment in the eternal afterlife easily outweighed some days of pain in this life. We can interpret the inquisitors as holding similar principles regarding human welfare as we do, but differing in their application of these principles because of their different beliefs about the facts of the world.

This point about ethical relativism is relevant when we think about the differing ethical behaviour of people in their workplace and at their homes. People who are ruthless competitors in the business world are often loving spouses and parents when at home. Do these businesspeople need to be ethical relativists to justify this disconnection between their ways of acting? Do they need to say to themselves that a particular way of acting is right-at-work and wrong-at-home? For example, the ethical obligation to make full disclosure is different for a salesperson at work and at home. At work, she would never tell a potential customer that an equivalent product was available across the street at a lower price. At home, however, she would always tell her domestic partner where to get the product most cheaply. Is this because full disclosure is wrong-at-work and right-at-home? An alternative explanation is that the salesperson faces additional, but different, ethical demands in the two aspects of her life. At work, she has an obligation to promote the interests of her employer that she must balance against the interests of her potential customer. At home, she has an obligation to promote the interests of her domestic partner that she does not have at work. It is much more likely that the salesperson holds the same ethical principles about honesty and the requirements of disclosure at both work and at home, but that she decides how to act based on balancing other ethical considerations with the requirements of honest disclosure. There is no reason to suppose that people in the business community should have different ethical standards than everyone else; they just face different ethical constraints because of the complexity of the decision that they must make.

Ethical relativism suggests, but does not entail, that when we are visiting in a culture with different moral standards from our own, then we should adopt the moral standards of that culture. The old adage, "When in Rome, do as the Romans do," exemplifies this thought. This thought suggests, for example, that it is ethically permissible for businesspeople to pay bribes when doing business in a bribe-paying culture. This last suggestion actually does not follow from relativism because people do not become members of a different culture simply by visiting it. An American does not become a Roman simply by visiting Rome. If the ethical standards of a businessperson's own culture forbid corruption and bribery, and if she does not become a member of the bribe-paying culture by making a business trip to visit it, then she is still bound by the norms of her own culture not to pay bribes during her visit.

The role of cultural background in ethical decision-making is important for another reason. Some cultural backgrounds can supply powerful, but invisible, ethical conceptual frameworks to the thinking of their members. For example, someone raised in a fundamentalist, religious framework will bring an authoritative code of right and wrong to his ethical decisions that he has never examined critically. This ethical code may seem so natural and normal that he never sees reason to question it. His fundamentalist ethical code may thus be effectively invisible to him, and it may not be possible for him to think otherwise. Suppose now that his fundamentalist ethical code is false. Since "ought" implies "can," and he cannot decide otherwise, the question arises of whether we should hold him morally accountable for his decision. In some cases, it may be possible for cultural membership to lead to ethical brainwashing and loss of moral accountability.

Figure 2.2 summarizes the conclusions that we have drawn from the simple, but abstract, notion that ethical judgments are both action-guiding and agreement-seeking.

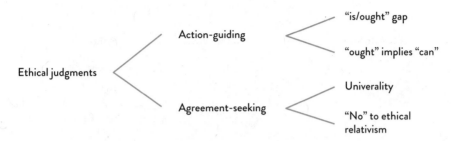

Figure 2.2: The consequences of ethical judgments being both action-guiding and agreement-seeking.

We have concluded that the motivating aspect of ethical judgments means that there is a logical gap between facts about the world and ethical judgments about the world. Crossing the gap requires reasoning based on ethical theory. We also concluded that people must sometimes do ethically demanding actions, but not actions that are too demanding or practically impossible. Finally, we saw that the agreement-seeking aspect of ethical reasons made it difficult to justify believing in ethical relativism.

ETHICAL PLURALISM

As we have seen before, people usually do not make a decision for just one reason. They consider, weigh, and balance many different reasons when deciding what to do. The same is true in ethical decision-making. We should not make an ethical decision without considering all the relevant ethical reasons. We should decide what to do by weighing the strengths and weaknesses of these reasons and then adjudicating among them.

There are many different sorts of ethical reasons. We started to classify them in the previous chapter. Some types of ethical reasons pertain to the identity and character of the decision-maker. Some types pertain to the motivation of the decision-maker and the principles that she follows. Other types pertain to judging the consequences of implementing the decision. All of these types of ethical reasons can provide reasons for or against a particular decision. Each of these general approaches to an ethical decision further subdivides into different ethical theories, as shown in Figure 2.3, which we saw before in the previous chapter.

These **ethical theories** are ways of systematizing ethical reasons that philosophers have developed over the many centuries during which philosophers have been thinking about ethical problems. Philosophers formulated each type of ethical theory in response to weaknesses that they discovered in other theories. In academic philosophy, philosophers generally hold that one of these theories is better than all the others, and then spend their careers thinking of ways to avoid its weaknesses and defending it against

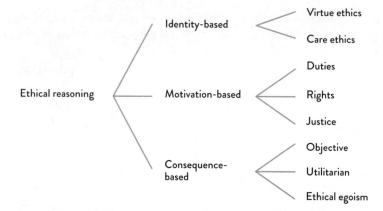

Figure 2.3: A taxonomy of ethical reasoning showing some of the different ethical theories that philosophers have developed to systematize ethical reasoning.

proponents of other theories. In applied philosophy, we will avoid focussing on just one theory and instead use all of these theories to get a complete picture of the ethical issues facing a decision-maker. We can make use of the discoveries made in the course of academic debates to help us assess the strengths and weaknesses of the different theories and to adjudicate between the ethical reasons for and against a particular decision.

Ethical pluralism is the view that we should make ethical decisions by considering and weighing the (often-conflicting) ethical reasons that follow from all ethical theories, and then judging how to proceed. It contrasts with the ethical monism of an academic philosopher who, for example, thinks that we should make all ethical decisions by applying just one particular theory such as utilitarianism. Ethical pluralism gives us a picture of ethical decision-making in which different ethical theories give the decision-maker ethical reasons of varying strengths that point for and against a final judgment of "Yes, do it," or "No, don't do it." By reflecting critically on the strengths and weaknesses of these reasons, weighing them, and balancing them, the decision-maker can decide what to do.

Unfortunately, philosophy does not provide a recipe for how exactly to balance the various ethical reasons affecting the decision. Making a final judgment is a high-level skill analogous to the skill shown by a judge balancing the evidence and arguments presented in a courtroom trial.

A useful comparison is to the way a large business makes a decision about, for example, launching a new product. The Chief Executive Officer is responsible for making the decision, but the CEO does not make it alone. The CEO solicits advice from other high-level managers. The Vice President of Research and Development advises on the technical feasibility of the product. The VP Production advises on how to produce it. The VP Marketing advises whether the product will sell and on what price to ask for it. The VP Finance gives advice on the potential new product's likely effect on the profitability of the firm. It would be foolish of the CEO to fail to solicit or to ignore

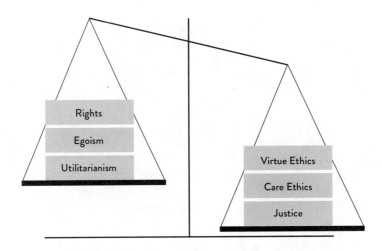

*Figure 2.4: The decision-maker must balance ethical reasons for and against
that are from various ethical theories and of different strengths.*

this advice. The advice of the different managers may be more or less favourable to
launching the product. The CEO must weigh all this advice and make the final decision
regarding the new product. The CEO has no recipe or algorithm for making the decision. The CEO must use his best judgment. Nevertheless, this decision will be a better
one for the CEO having listened to the advice of all the various experts.

The analogous picture of ethical pluralist decision-making is to imagine the Chief
Ethics Officer calling a meeting of representatives of all ethical theories and hearing
their advice. Each representative looks at the situation from the point of view of her ethical theory and gives reasons for and against potential decisions. The "CEO" weighs the
reasons advanced from each point of view, and makes a judgment about the best action
to take. Again, the "CEO" has no fixed decision procedure to follow, no algorithm that
will give the best answer in every case. Instead, the "CEO" must use experience and
judgment to make a decision. The decision will be a better one because of the input
from all the various ethical approaches.

If we apply this picture of ethical decision-making to the case of Ben, the potential
office thief, then we should cast Ben in the role of Chief Ethics Officer. His VP Virtue Ethics
will point out that an honest person will not steal from his office. His VP Care Ethics will
advise him not to poison the work relationships within his department. His VP Rights
will advise that his employers have a right to expect good service and respect for their
property. His VP Justice will advise Ben that he would justly deserve punishment for his
theft and that taking the money is unfair to his coworkers. His VP Utilitarianism will point
out that the loss of happiness to the children of the other employees will outweigh the
increased happiness of his children. Only the VP Egoism will advise taking the money, but
then only if the risk that his employer will find out is low enough. The balance of ethical
reasons is clearly against the "CEO," Ben, deciding to steal the money.

Figure 2.5: The chief ethics officer ("CEO") makes a decision after hearing from all divisions of ethical theory.

In the world of business, ethical decision-making should happen in tandem with commercial decision-making. The overall, final decision should incorporate both ethical and strategic considerations. Business decisions should be informed not only by considerations of finance, marketing, production, and human resources, but also by considerations of welfare, justice, human rights, and corporate character.

We should notice that this picture of ethical decision-making is ethical pluralist, not ethical relativist. Ethical pluralism does not say that the decision is the right one relative to one ethical theory, the wrong one relative to another, and that the disagreement has no rational resolution. It does not say, for example, that a decision may be right according to utilitarianism and wrong according to virtue ethics, and that we can never resolve the issue. Instead, ethical pluralism says that, though there is no explicit decision procedure or algorithm for making a final judgment, we can nonetheless make such a judgment, and it will be a better one for having considered the situation from all ethical points of view. The various ethical considerations sometimes conflict with one another. Nevertheless, we can claim that the particular ethical decision that we make is a better one than the alternatives. Furthermore, the claim that it is a better decision is universally true, not just true relative to some particular ethical theory.

SUMMARY

1. Generally, we consider not just one reason, but many reasons, when we make either strategic or ethical decisions.
2. Like preferences and desires, but unlike factual beliefs, ethical reasons motivate us to behave in certain ways. Like factual beliefs, but unlike preferences and desires, ethical reasons require justification and argument. Ethical reasons are both action-guiding and agreement-seeking.
3. Because ethical reasons are action-guiding and factual beliefs are not, we cannot justify an ethical judgment based on purely factual reasons.

There is a logical gap between assertions of how the world is and assertions of how the world ought to be. An ethical judgment requires at least one ethical reason.

4. Because ethical reasons guide our actions, they must not require that we perform actions that we are unable to do. Ethical reasons may be demanding, but not overly demanding.

5. People are attracted to the ethical relativism, the view that all judgments of right and wrong are relative to a person's cultural membership, because they think that ethical relativism expresses toleration of cultural diversity.

6. By making it too easy to agree to disagree, ethical relativism fails to do justice to the agreement-seeking aspect of ethical judgments. It encourages a sort of intellectual laziness that leads people not to allow members of other cultures to challenge their own moral views and not to respect their own moral principles. We can often explain cases of ethical disagreement between cultures as cases of different factual beliefs or as situations requiring a different balance between competing ethical considerations.

7. In applied ethics, ethical theories are useful ways of summarizing and systematizing ethical reasoning. Ethical pluralism applies the points of view of all types of ethical theories to get a complete analysis of an ethical decision. Even though there is no universal recipe for making a final decision, ethical pluralism is not the same as ethical relativism.

ONLINE LEARNING RESOURCES

You will find a collection of learning resources associated with this chapter on the book's website: http://sites.broadviewpress.com/businessethics/. Working through this material will help you understand and remember important concepts that we have discussed, and will help you apply them to issues in business ethics.

STUDY QUESTIONS

Answering the following questions will help you to understand the ethical theory in this chapter and will help you to create a set of review notes on the textbook.

1. Construct an example where someone makes a decision for many reasons, both strategic and ethical.

2. Suppose that businesses do show a ruthless disregard for the interests of their customers. Why is this not an argument that it is ethically permissible for businesses to gouge their customers?

3. Karl Marx summarized his theory of justice as, "From each according to his ability, to each according to his needs." How might this conflict with metaethical principles?

4. Why is toleration of cultural diversity not a strong argument for ethical relativism?
5. How can a businessperson avoid concluding that some actions are morally right towards customers, but morally wrong towards friends?
6. Suppose that Meghan is considering deflecting blame for a fiasco at work by telling her boss lies about a co-worker. Perform a simple ethical pluralist analysis of Meghan's decision.

DECISION QUESTIONS

The whole point of learning ethical theory is to understand and ask questions like the following when you are analyzing an ethically problematic situation or case.

- Have we been careful to distinguish factual, strategic, and ethical considerations?
- Are any ethical considerations overly demanding?
- Have we paid proper respect to different cultural backgrounds?
- Do any ethical considerations conflict?
- Can we resolve the conflict?
- On the balance of ethical reasons, are any of the alternative decisions ruled out?
- Do we face a situation where all decisions are ethically wrong?
- Do we have several possible decisions that are roughly equal, but better than the other alternatives?
- Is there just one decision that, on the balance of reasons, is best from an ethical point of view?

CASE STUDY

Analyze this case study using the ethical theory that you have learned so far. You will find a collection of learning materials applying to the case on the book's website: http://sites.broadviewpress.com/businessethics/. These materials will help you in your analysis.

Should Ben Take the Bonus Fund?

Ben Freeman has worked for three years with Jane Smith, Marc Dupré, Susie Wong, and Jim Dexter at the Provincial Power Corporation. He feels that PPC underpays him. His boss, Mary Jenks, recently passed him over for a promotion, and he would like revenge.

Ben is from a background that expected everyone to look out for him or herself. Ben's neighbours always locked their doors. Local people thought that anyone who did not lock up carefully was stupid and deserved to have their possessions stolen. Ben's parents were both from the neighbourhood, and brought up Ben to take care of himself first, and to take advantage of any opportunity for acquiring a little extra money.

The Provincial Power Corporation has a dog-eat-dog corporate culture. All the people working there, from the CEO to the typists, share a view that life is "every man for himself," and that "she who dies with the most toys wins." People expect each other to lie, cheat, and even steal when they can get away with it. The prevailing corporate culture is one of rampant self-interest.

Ben plays poker with some other men in a room above the local flower shop. He knows that that the people who organize the game are rather shady. Recently, he has gone behind and borrowed $500 from the game-organizers. He cannot borrow the money anywhere because he has reached the limit on his bank-overdraft. He knows that the ruthless characters who loaned him the money will hurt him if he does not pay his debt very soon.

Every holiday season, Ben's department collects a holiday-bonus fund by allowing department members to pay $5 to wear blue jeans to work on Fridays. Just before the holidays, everyone puts his or her name in a hat, and the boss gives the money to the department member whose name she draws. Ben is in a situation where he could easily steal $500 from this bonus fund. $500 is just enough to pay off his gambling debt. He may just act impulsively, but if he thinks before he acts, then he will find reasons both pointing toward taking his opportunity and pointing against doing so: He needs the $500 to stop the gangsters from hurting him. Someone might catch him, and then he will lose his job. On the other hand, he thinks that he can make everyone think that Susie took the money. When Jane, Mary, Marc, Susie, and Jim notice the loss and make inquiries, there will be an atmosphere of suspicion in his department for some months afterwards.

Should Ben take the money? Your moral gut reaction will tell you what Ben should do. Here, however, you should analyze Ben's situation as a way of practicing ethical analysis. Look at whose interests Ben's decision will effect, and find as many relevant ethical considerations as you can, both for and against him taking the money.

After you have done that, consider the interesting question of whether we should hold Ben morally accountable if he decides to take the money. Does either his cultural background or the threat from the gangsters imply that he cannot do otherwise than steal the money?

SELF-INTEREST AND THE DILEMMAS OF COOPERATION

Is self-interest our only motivation?

Should we always act only in our own self-interest?

What happens when purely self-interested people try to cooperate?

Popular culture often portrays high-powered businesspeople as ruthless, greedy egoists pursuing only their boundless self-interest. The model of rational choice used in economics reinforces this popular conception. Economic models assume that consumers and producers are rational maximizers of their own interests. This economic model of human beings as self-interested maximizers often leaks into people's ethical decision-making. Luckily, it is an only an abstraction. Both our common-sense knowledge of human psychology, and the experiments of behavioural economists, confirm that this model of human beings is over-simplified.

Doubtlessly there are infinitely acquisitive business tycoons, but their acquisitiveness is usually constrained by the rules of the game. Most do not steal from others in an outright fashion. Though they may skirt the edges of property law, they usually stay within its bounds. Though they may deal sharply with others, they mostly keep the contracts that they have made.

Self-interest is often more than a narrow concern for one's own welfare. People often have a sense of themselves as more than just the self within their skin. For example, even a very selfish person may work for the good not just of himself, but of his family too, seeing them, as it were, as extensions of himself. A person's narrow self-interest consists of an interest only in the welfare of that person's own ego and body. A person's broad self-interest includes the interests of other people and things with which the person psychologically identifies. Examples of broad self-interest include parents' identification with their children, business owners' identification with their companies, and employees' identification with their careers.

In this chapter, we will study the role of self-interest in ethics, by examining three abstract "games" that have been studied in game theory. The Ultimatum Game shows that people often do not behave as pure egoists. The well-known Prisoner's Dilemma Game and the lesser-known Centipede Game demonstrate that, paradoxically, a society of extreme egoists will not be in the best interest of its members. This will lead to an explanation of why egoists will be better off if they set up some enforceable rules of cooperation.

From an ethical point of view, it is fortunate that human beings are not extreme egoists. Compulsive extreme egoists are able to act only in pursuit of self-interest. Ethics, however, will sometimes demand that people set aside their self-interest in order to respect the rights or promote the welfare of others. If it were psychologically impossible for people to overcome their self-interest, then asking people to respect property rights or keep contractual promises would be too demanding. Since "ought" implies "can," these ethical judgments could not guide people's decisions and actions.

In the absence of overriding ethical reasons to the contrary, it is certainly ethically permissible that people may act for reasons of self-interest. Self-interest should be a consideration in ethical decision-making. Nevertheless, it is important to understand what limitations people face in the pursuit of their own interests.

PSYCHOLOGICAL AND ETHICAL EGOISM

Two types of theory stress the role of self-interest in ethics. **Psychological egoism** is the *scientific* theory that people always *do* act to maximize to their self-interest. Psychological egoism is a *scientific* theory, and scientific experiments can, in principle, confirm or disconfirm it. It underlies the view of producer and consumer behaviour in models of positive economics, and is the view that the new field of behavioural economics calls into question. On the other hand, **ethical egoism** is the *ethical* theory that people always *ought* to act to maximize their self-interest. Ethical egoism does not say that people always do act so as to maximize their self-interest, rather it says that people always should behave so as to maximize their self-interest.

Ethical egoism is a consequence-based ethical theory holding that only the self has moral standing. Decision-makers should consider only their own interests when they make ethical decisions. It is an extreme form of egoism. Figure 3.1 locates ethical egoism in our classification scheme for ethical reasoning.

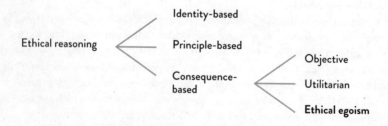

Figure 3.1: Ethical egoism as a form of consequentialist ethical reasoning.

It is important to note that ethical egoism is not the same as ethical relativism. The two theories operate at different levels of abstraction. Ethical relativism is a metaethical theory about the nature of ethical reasoning. Ethical egoism is an applied ethical theory about how people should behave. Ethical relativism says that right and wrong are relative to cultural membership, and many cultures are not ethical egoist.

Psychological egoism is an empirical theory about human nature. If psychological egoism were scientifically true, then people could not act except in their own self-interest. No other ethical theory but ethical egoism would work. Luckily, the evidence does not support psychological egoism. We can think of examples from common experience. For example, most people will leave a tip for the staff at an out-of-town restaurant that they will never visit again. They may do it because of habit or because of generosity, but they do not do it because it is in their own self-interest. Rationally maximizing self-interest, a psychological egoist would reason that because she is never coming back to the restaurant and because the meal is over and a tip cannot change the quality of the service, then the rational thing for her to do is to keep her money to spend on something else. People do not always rationally maximize their own self-interest.

The field of behavioural economics has the goal of testing the behavioural assumptions of economic theory. Psychological egoism is one of these behavioural assumptions. One empirical test of the assumption that people always maximize their self-interest is a test of how people play the Ultimatum Game. The rules of the Ultimatum Game are as follows: The game has two players and a referee. First, the Referee passes some amount of money, for example $10, to Player 1. Player 1 must then issue an ultimatum to Player 2 by offering Player 2 some amount between $1 and $10. If Player 2 accepts the ultimatum, then Player 2 keeps the offer and Player 1 keeps the balance. However, if Player 2 rejects the ultimatum, then the Referee takes back all the money and both players get nothing. For example, Player 1 might offer $3 to Player 2. If Player 2 accepts the ultimatum, then Player 2 gets to keep $3 and Player 1 gets to keep $7. If Player 2 rejects the offer, then neither player gets anything. The game is played just this one time.

The Ultimatum Game appears trivial, but the results are enlightening. Most people, if they imagine themselves in the role of Player 1, would probably offer $5 or a 50/50 split. Most people, if they imagine themselves in the role of Player 2 would probably reject anything but a roughly 50/50 offer because they would consider a lopsided offer to be unfair. Indeed, this is what usually happens when scientists do experiments on the Ultimatum Game. Nevertheless, it is not what the empirical theory of psychological egoism predicts.

If Player 1 is a true psychological egoist, and if Player 1 thinks that Player 2 is also a psychological egoist, then Player 1 will think: "2 is a psychological egoist, so 2 will accept a $1 offer, since $1 is more than $0." Therefore, Player 1 will offer only $1. If Player 2 actually is a psychological egoist, then Player 2 will accept the $1 offer since $1 is greater than $0. So psychological egoism predicts that Player 1 will offer the minimum amount that the rules permit, and that Player 2 will accept this offer. Empirical studies, however, show that players mostly offer an approximately even split, and players mostly reject offers less than an approximately even split. Perhaps ultimatum-issuing players feel ashamed to offer less than what seems fair, and ultimatum-receiving players feel indignant at unfair offers and punish the other players, even at some cost to themselves. Such experiments disconfirm psychological egoism, and show that other forms of ethical theory are psychologically possible.

ARGUMENTS FOR AND AGAINST ETHICAL EGOISM

It is not easy to think of strong arguments in favour of ethical egoism. Someone might be tempted to argue that ethical egoism is true because psychological egoism is true. Since it *is* the case that people act only to promote their self-interest, then it *ought* to be the case that people act only to promote their self-interest. However, such an argument is invalid because it ignores the "is/ought" gap.

Another justification of ethical egoism might argue from the premise that "ought" implies "can" and from the premise that people *can* only act to promote their self-interest, to the conclusion that no ethical theory other than ethical egoism can be true. However, the second premise of this argument is a restatement of psychological egoism, and we have seen that it is unlikely that this premise is a true one.

By definition, ethical egoists ought only to act in ways that promote their own interests. Also by definition, someone has moral standing if, and only if, people ought to consider their interests when they make ethical decisions. In other words, each ethical egoist must claim that he, and only he, has moral standing. How is an ethical egoist to justify this claim? We usually make claims to moral standing by pointing to some ethically relevant feature of individuals that justifies why those individuals' interests deserve ethical consideration. For example, an animal welfare advocate will point to the ability of animals to suffer pain and argue that the interests of animals in avoiding suffering deserve moral consideration just as do the interests of human beings. An ethical egoist would have to point to some feature of himself that explains why he has moral standing while others did not. It would have to be some feature that was both unique to him and relevant to the question of moral standing. However, there is no such feature. Any feature that picked out the ethical egoist uniquely, such as his passport number, is going to be morally arbitrary and irrelevant to the question of moral standing.

Ethical judgments, as we have seen, are fundamentally agreement-seeking. It is quite unlikely, however, that an ethical egoist could ever obtain the agreement of others that his interests, and his interests alone, deserve moral consideration. Ethical egoists might seek agreement in the sense of trying to convince others that ethical egoism is the right ethical theory; so, for example, Fred might try to convince Sally that she should look after only *her own* benefit. But real ethical egoists would not spread the word like this, because others' benefits will sometimes be their losses. Therefore, ethical egoism violates the agreement-seeking rule for ethical views.

EGOISM AND COOPERATION

The biggest problem for purely self-interested egoists is that they have difficulty cooperating. We can begin to see this difficulty by examining the paradox of egoism.

The **paradox of egoism** says that there exist states of affairs greatly in the self-interest of ethical egoists that these same ethical egoists cannot achieve because they ought always to act selfishly. Important relationships, like friendship, are greatly in the self-interest of everyone, including ethical egoists. However, personal relationships such as friendship or marriage are not available to people who only act to maximize their own interests. Friendship requires that people sometimes put the interests of their friends ahead of their own. Extreme ethical egoists, however, ought to betray their friends whenever such betrayal is in their own interest. Thus, extreme ethical egoists cannot have friends and so cannot maximize good consequences for themselves. Extreme ethical egoism is self-defeating because extreme egoists cannot cooperate.

More generally, cooperation dilemmas arise in situations where two or more egoists can maximize their self-interest by cooperating, but will be lead to cheat in order to promote their own interests. Extreme ethical egoists *ought* to cheat to maximize their self-interest. Extreme psychological egoists *will* cheat to maximize their self-interest. So both will cheat instead of cooperate in such situations.

We can illustrate the self-defeating cheating of ethical egoists using the tools of elementary game theory. Consider the following little game. There are two players, Don and Eve, and a referee. The referee places two piles of money, one containing $4, and the other $1, in front of Don. Don has two choices. One, he can stop the game, take the larger pile of money and give the smaller pile to Eve. Two, he can pass both piles to Eve, and the referee will double the money in each pile so that Eve has $8 and $2 in front of her. Now Eve faces a similar choice. She can stop the game and keep the larger pile, or pass both piles, which the referee will again double, to Don. The game keeps going until either player stops it. The game raises three questions: What is the best way to play this game? How will normal people play this game? How will ethical egoists who believe each other to be ethical egoists play this game?

We can more easily answer that last question if we draw the choice nodes of the game as shown in Figure 3.2. Each circle represents a choice node for Don or Eve. Each arrow represents an option to Stop and take the larger pile or to pass the choice to the other player. The boxes show the payoffs to each player. Game theorists call this the Centipede Game because they usually draw it with one hundred choice nodes. Our simplified version is a five-stage Centipede Game. If the players pass through all five stages, then the final payoff is $50 each.

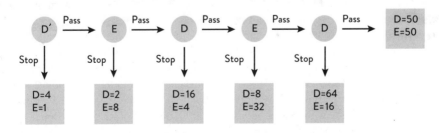

Figure 3.2: A five-stage Centipede game.

If we use Figure 3.2 and reason backwards from the end of the game, then we can see what will happen. Suppose that Don and Eve are both ethical egoists, and that they each know that the other is an ethical egoist. At the fifth and last stage of the game, Don will stop the game and take the pile of $64 because the $64 that he gets by stopping is larger than the $50 he would get by passing. At the fourth and second-last stage of the game, Eve will know that Don will stop at stage five, so she will stop the game to get $32 rather than the $16 she knows she will get if she passes and allows Don to stop at the final stage. Knowing this, Don will stop at the third stage rather than let Eve stop at the fourth. And so on back to the first stage of the game. What this adds up to is that Don will choose to stop the game at the first decision node. The solution to the Centipede Game is that Don and Eve, if they are ethical egoists who maximize their self-interest at every decision and who believe each other to be ethical egoists, will stop the game at the first stage, where Don will get $4 and Eve will get $1. However, if they could only have reached stage four, they would have both been better off, and if they could have played the game to the end, then they would have received $50 each. Both players make the cleverest choices that they can at each stage of the game, but the result is that they both do less well than they could have if they did not reason as egoists.

In a full one-hundred-stage centipede game, where the end is not in sight, regular people, such as college students, will generally assume the trustworthiness of the other player, and cooperate by passing the piles of money back and forth. They will continue until the piles become big enough that they start to wonder whether the other player will be tempted to stop the game. At this point, they will stop the game themselves and take the payoff. In a shorter game, like the five-stage game above, they will likely behave as they would in the ultimatum game, with both aiming at an even split of $50 each. Two expert game players, such as highly rational, super competitive, professional chess players, will generally see the backward induction immediately, and will stop the game at the first move. The interesting point is that regular, unsuspicious, and dependable people will usually receive higher payoffs than will expert game players because they will allow the game to continue longer. Regular, reasonably altruistic, and moderately cooperative people will do better in the Centipede Game than will selfish egoists who believe that others are also selfish egoists.

THE PRISONER'S DILEMMA

A more familiar game, the Prisoner's Dilemma Game, also demonstrates the cooperation dilemma for extreme egoists, and shows how more enlightened egoists might work their way around such dilemmas. Suppose that Fred and Gina are two extreme ethical egoists who work together on a project for their boss. Their boss has set up the following incentive structure for them: They each get a $2,000 bonus if they each claim to have done an equal share of the work. If one of them claims to have done most of the work and the other claims to have done an equal share, then the one who claims to have done most of the work gets a bonus of $3,000, and the other gets no bonus at all. If both employees claim to have done most of the work, then they each get a reduced bonus of $1,000. Fred and Gina promise one another that they will tell their boss that they each did an equal share of the work. Their boss, who is pleased with the project, interviews each of them separately in their individual offices, and asks each of them who did the work. Should Fred and Gina, who are extreme ethical egoists, keep their promises to one another and say that they shared the work equally?

We can see better what should happen if we represent their strategic choices in a payoff matrix as in Figure 3.3.

		Gina	
		Keep promise	Break promise
Fred	Keep promise	$2,000 UL $2,000	$3,000 UR $0
	Break promise	$0 LL $3,000	$1,000 LR $1,000

Figure 3.3: A payoff matrix for Fred and Gina who can each either keep or break their promises.

A **payoff matrix** for a game is a table that shows each player's payoff for every possible combination of strategies. In this case, the game has two players, Fred and Gina, who each have a choice of two strategies, either to keep their promise to the other player about what to tell the boss, or to break that promise. We represent Fred's two strategies as the two rows of the table, and Gina's two strategies as the two columns of the table. This gives four possible outcomes that we represent by the four cells of the table. Each of these cells shows the payoffs to Fred and Gina for a particular combination of strategies. We show Fred on the left side of the payoff matrix, so we show Fred's payoffs in the lower left of each cell. We show Gina on the upper side of the payoff matrix, so we show Gina's payoffs in the upper right of each cell. For example, if Fred keeps his promise and Gina breaks hers, then their payoffs are in the upper right cell (UR) of the payoff matrix. Fred will receive a $0 bonus and Gina will receive a $3,000 bonus. The payoffs in the matrix correspond to the payoffs given in the verbal description of the situation.

In order to see what will happen, we have to reason carefully through the options facing each player. Let us look at Gina's reasoning. First, what should Gina do if she thinks that Fred will keep his promise? We must consult the first row of the table. If Gina keeps her promise then her payoff in the Upper Left cell (UL) will be $2,000. If she breaks her promise, then her payoff in cell UR will be $3,000. Her payoff for breaking her promise is higher than her payoff for keeping it. Figure 3.4 shows the $3,000 payoff in bold. Therefore, Gina will reason that if Fred keeps his promise, then she should break hers. Second, what should Gina do if Fred breaks his promise? Her payoff of $1,000 in cell LR for breaking her promise is higher than her payoff of $0 in cell LL for keeping it. Therefore, Gina will reason that if Fred breaks his promise, then she should also break hers. Gina will now reason that no matter what Fred does, she should break her promise. Gina will see that she has a dominant strategy. A **dominant strategy** in game theory is a strategy that yields a higher payoff regardless of the strategy chosen by the other player. Figure 3.4 shows her dominant strategy in bold letters. Second, let us look at Fred's reasoning. Figure 3.4 shows that no matter which strategy Gina plays, Fred's payoff (also in bold letters) will be higher if he breaks his promise. Therefore, Fred too has a dominant strategy, shown in bold letters, which is to break his promise.

Gina

	Keep promise	**Break promise**
Keep promise (Fred)	UL $2,000 $2,000	UR $3,000 $0
Break promise (Fred)	LL $0 $3,000	LR $1,000 $1,000

Figure 3.4: This payoff matrix shows Fred and Gina's best responses bolded. Their dominant strategies are also bolded. The payoffs from both playing their dominant strategies are in cell LR.

If Fred and Gina, reasoning as egoists, both break their promises, then they will receive the payoffs of $1,000 shown in cell LR. Their dilemma is that this outcome is not the one that would maximize their self-interest. They would both be better off with the outcome shown in cell UL, where they each get $2,000. They can obtain this outcome if they both keep their promises, but, as we have seen, reasoning as self-interest maximizing egoists, they cannot reach this better outcome. In the language of economics, the outcome of their game is not Pareto efficient. A distribution of payoffs is **Pareto efficient** if no change is possible that will increase the payoff to one player without decreasing the payoff to another. In this case, a change from the outcome in LR to the outcome in UL will increase the payoffs to both players. By playing their dominant strategies, the two egoists arrive at a Pareto inefficient outcome. (We should notice that the payoffs in cells LL and UR are also Pareto efficient, because any change will result in a pay-off loss for one or the other of the two players. For example, a change from UR, where Gina gets $3,000 and Fred gets $0, to any other outcome will result in a smaller payoff for Gina. A Pareto efficient outcome is not always a fair outcome.)

A game is a **Prisoner's Dilemma Game** when both players have dominant strategies that, when played, result in an outcome with payoffs smaller than if each had played another strategy. It gets this name from a strategy sometimes employed by the police to get two criminal accomplices to inform on one another. Like the Centipede Game it shows that ethical egoists, doing what they should, or psychological egoists doing what they do, will be unable to achieve the benefits of cooperation.

THE BENEFITS OF COOPERATION

Cooperation is more important to businesses in a market economy than people often realize. People often think that it is competition between business firms that generates economic goods and services. Competition between firms is important in keeping down the prices of goods, but it is not what produces the goods. The main mechanisms behind the huge productivity of modern economies are the mechanisms of cooperation and organization that allow for gains from specialization and the division of labour. If people were too ruled by their own narrow interests to be able to cooperate, they would not be able to specialize in different tasks and divide the labour in ways that vastly increase productivity. A famous passage from Adam Smith describes the gains from specialization and the division of labour between ten employees in an eighteenth-century pin factory.

> To take an example ... the trade of the pin-maker; a workman not edu-
> cated to this business ... nor acquainted with the use of the machinery
> employed ... could scarce, perhaps, with his utmost industry, make one pin
> in a day, and certainly could not make twenty.... One man draws out the
> wire, another straights it, a third cuts it, a fourth points it, a fifth grinds
> it at the top for receiving the head; to make the head requires two or three
> distinct operations; to put it on, is a peculiar business, to whiten the pins
> is another; it is even a trade by itself to put them into the paper; and the
> important business of making a pin is, in this manner, divided into about
> eighteen distinct operations ... I have seen a small manufactory of this
> kind where ten men only were employed, and where ... they could, when
> they exerted themselves, make among them about twelve pounds of pins
> in a day. There are in a pound upwards of four thousand pins of a mid-
> dling size. Those ten persons, therefore, could make among them upwards
> of forty-eight thousand pins in a day. Each person, therefore, making a
> tenth part of forty-eight thousand pins, might be considered as making
> four thousand eight hundred pins in a day. (Adam Smith, *The Wealth of
> Nations*, 1776, I.1.3)

By specializing in work that they have learned to do quickly, by using specialized machinery, and by organizing and dividing the tasks required in pin manufacture, the workers cooperate in the factory to produce 4,800 times as many pins per worker as they could produce working alone. A major role of business managers is to organize production to take advantage of specialization and the division of labour.

We can better see how cooperation increases productivity in the small, abstract model of the Pin Factory shown in Table 3.1. Here there are only two workers, Jack and Jill, and only two stages in the pin production process. In this model, Jack is better at producing the heads for pins than he is at producing the points. He can produce 9 pinheads per hour of work, but only 1 point. Jill's skills are complementary. She can produce 9 points per hour of work, but only 1 pinhead. Working alone each can produce only 9 complete pins in a day. Jack, for example will have to work for 1 hour to produce 9 pinheads and then 9 more hours to produce 9 points in order to produce 9 complete pins. For simplicity, we will assume that the pins take no time to assemble from the parts. If Jack and Jill work alone, then they will produce 18 complete pins.

	Jack		Jill	
	Heads	Points	Heads	Points
Productivity per hour	9	1	1	9
Solitary pin production in a 10-hour day	9		9	
Total solitary pin production in a 10-hour day	18			
Specialized part production in a 10-hour day	90	0	0	90
Total cooperative pin production in a 10-hour day	90			

Table 3.1: Model Pin Factory: When Jack and Jill specialize in the production that they each do best, they can create cooperatively many more pins in a 10-hour day.

On the other hand, if Jack and Jill are able to cooperate, then Jack will specialize in what he does best and make 90 pinheads. Jill will specialize in what she does best and make 90 pinpoints. By dividing the labour of making pins, Jack and Jill can vastly increase their productivity and produce 90 complete pins. No more effort is involved for either of them. They achieve this productivity gain, not by working any harder, but by organizing their work differently. This raises two questions: One, how do we create cooperation between egoists? Two, how should we distribute the gains from cooperation, that is, the profits from the extra 72 pins? We will look at the first question now and reserve the second for later chapters.

CREATING COOPERATION

Arguably, most of the goods that people enjoy in a modern economy are the results of specialization and the division of labour. Even the sophisticated technology that people enjoy can only come about because some talented people specialize in inventing new things while other people specialize in producing their food. Only a colossally complex system of cooperation between workers in the energy industry is able to discover, develop, and distribute the energy that runs cars, homes, and factories. Without the ability to cooperate, human beings would not flourish. In the seventeenth century, the English philosopher Thomas Hobbes realized that extreme ethical egoists would always cheat on one another, and that life for a society of ethical egoists would be, in his words, "nasty, brutish, and short."

> Whatsoever therefore is consequent to a time of Warre, where every man
> is Enemy to every man; the same is consequent to the time, wherein men
> live without other security, than what their own strength, and their own
> invention shall furnish them withall. In such condition, there is no place
> for Industry; because the fruit thereof is uncertain; and consequently no
> Culture of the Earth; no Navigation, nor use of the commodities that may
> be imported by Sea; no commodious Building; no Instruments of moving,
> and removing such things as require much force; no Knowledge of the face
> of the Earth; no account of Time; no Arts; no Letters; no Society; and
> which is worst of all, continuall feare, and danger of violent death;
> And the life of man, solitary, poore, nasty, brutish, and short.
> (Hobbes, 1651, Chapter 13)

He proposed that enlightened ethical egoists should establish a government with the coercive power to punish cheating. State punishment would then give cheating a lower payoff than cooperating, and would make all the warring egoists better off.

We can see how this works if we develop the situation between Fred and Gina. Suppose that instead of making mutual promises, Fred and Gina sign legally binding contracts with state-enforced penalties for breach of contract. Suppose that if either party fails to fulfil the contract, then the party is liable to a $2,000 fine. We can represent the new situation of Fred and Gina in the payoff matrix of Figure 3.5. Now they each have two potential strategies consisting of either fulfilling their contract or breaching it. If they breach the contract, then the $2,000 fine will reduce their payoffs as shown.

		Gina	
		Fulfil contract	Breach contract
Fred	**Fulfil contract**	**$2,000** UL $2,000	$3,000-$2,000=$1,000 UR **$0**
	Breach contract	**$0** LL $1,000=$3,000-$2,000	$1,000-$2,000= -$1,000 LR -$1,000=$1,000-$2,000

Figure 3.5: Fred and Gina face a $2,000 penalty for breach of contract resulting an a pareto efficient outcome. Best responses and dominant strategies are bolded.

Now Gina will reason that if Fred were to fulfil his side of the contract, then she should fulfil her side because the payoff of $2,000 for fulfilment is higher than the sum of her bonus for claiming to have done all the work less the fine she would have to pay for breach of legal contract. She will also reason that if Fred breaches the contract, then she should still fulfil her side because the $0 she will get for fulfilment is still better than the new loss of $1,000 she will face for breach of contract. She will see that her best response to whatever Fred does is to fulfil the contract and that this is her dominant strategy. Similarly, Fred has a dominant strategy, which is to fulfil his side of the contract. When both play their dominant strategies, the outcome will be the payoffs in cell UL. This outcome is Pareto efficient because changing to any other outcome will result in a lower payoff for one or other of the players.

A **contractarian ethical theory** is a theory claiming that ethics consists in an enforced contract among ethical egoists designed to prevent dilemmas of cooperation, such as the Prisoner's Dilemma situation. State enforcement of contracts and property rights constrains the freedom of ethical egoists to pursue their self-interest as they see fit, but it allows for a system of specialization and the division of labour that will make egoists who obey the new rules of the game better off. For example, in a society of egoists who obey the rules of property and contract law, Adam Smith's invisible hand will make the whole society better off. By accepting rules of the game, egoists can avoid the war of all against all that Hobbes envisioned, and reap the benefits of cooperation.

Nevertheless, egoists will endeavour to break the rules of the game whenever doing so is in their own interest. Ethical egoists will do so because they think they should; psychological egoists will do so because it is their nature. Ethical egoists think they are obliged to cheat if they can. Psychological egoists will cheat if they can. Consequently, society will require legal enforcement of the rules of the game. There will need to be legal coercion of cheaters such as damage suits, fines, and prison time. This will require a large legal apparatus of police, lawyers, and judges. If cheating is widespread, then this legal apparatus will become expensive. The enforcement costs for preventing the theft of property and the transaction costs of using lawyers and the courts to enforce contracts will become huge.

Internal enforcement would be less expensive. A society of people who were able to punish themselves for breaking the rules of the game would be economically more efficient than one where a judicial system of punishment had to be funded by the tax system. People who were capable of self-punishment for rule-infractions—people who experienced feelings of guilt and shame when they took advantage of others—could cooperate more efficiently than could egoists who felt no remorse whenever they cheated. People who would regularly mete out informal punishment even at some cost to themselves—people who are outraged at cheating and indignant when they see advantage being taken—could also cooperate more efficiently than could egoists who were always calculating the costs and benefits to themselves of informally punishing others. People who had learned virtues of trust and trustworthiness could cooperate more efficiently than could people who had learned only to be selfish. In other words, a society of people who had internalized the rules of the game, learned a set of moral virtues, and cultivated a set of moral emotions such as guilt, shame, indignation, and outrage, would be more productive than a society of people who only functioned through calculations of self-interest. Paradoxically, ethical egoists who committed themselves to other ethical theories, and thereby ceased to be ethical egoists, might find doing so in their self-interest.

Despite all the foregoing problems with the pursuit of our own interests, self-interest should still be a consideration in ethical decision-making. Ethical egoism is correct to identify self-interest as an important part of moral decision-making, but it is wrong to suggest that self-interest is the *only* concern. However, we must remember its dilemmas, and pay attention to other ethical considerations that often outweigh or override self-interest.

Now that we have looked at the bigger picture of how the various ethical theories can work together to advise us in our business decision-making, we will examine each theory in greater detail. Each of the next few chapters is devoted to one of the major ethical theories—first we will take a closer look at utilitarianism, then rights-based ethics, justice, virtue ethics, and care ethics.

SUMMARY

1. Psychological egoism is the empirical theory that people always do act to maximize the satisfaction of their own interests. Ethical egoism is the ethical theory that people always ought to act to maximize the satisfaction of their own interests.

2. Psychological egoism is a basic assumption of economics, but behavioural economics experiments, such as the Ultimatum Game, suggest that it is not a good description of human nature.

3. Ethical egoism is difficult to justify. The single-minded pursuit of self-interest, when others are doing the same, can often be self-defeating. For example, two highly rational maximizers of self-interest will do less well playing the Centipede Game than will two average, trusting people who have the emotional makeup required for cooperation.

4. Another example of the dilemmas facing extreme egoists is the Prisoner's Dilemma Game. Here, both players have dominant strategies based on self-interest that, when played, result in an outcome with payoffs smaller than if each had played another strategy based on cooperative considerations. Achieving Pareto efficiency requires constraining extreme egoism.

5. Most of the wealth of modern economies arises from people cooperating with one another and organizing production according to principles of specialization and division of labour.

6. Societies can create cooperation between egoists by coercively enforcing the rules of the game, rules such as laws regarding property and contracts. However, if people internalize the rules of the game as ethical obligations, then they can achieve cooperation more efficiently.

7. Self-interest is still an important consideration in ethical decision-making, but other ethical considerations often outweigh it.

ONLINE LEARNING RESOURCES

You will find a collection of learning resources associated with this chapter on the book's website: http://sites.broadviewpress.com/businessethics/. Working through this material will help you understand and remember important concepts that we have discussed, and will help you apply them to issues in business ethics.

STUDY QUESTIONS

Answering the following questions will help you to understand the ethical theory in this chapter and will help you to create a set of review notes on the textbook.

1. Explain the difference between ethical and psychological egoism.
2. Why is psychological egoism not an accurate model of human behaviour?
3. Describe a situation in which extreme egoists will be unable to achieve the benefits of cooperation.
4. Why is it so important that human beings be able to engage in cooperative production through specialization and the division of labour?
5. How can a society create cooperation between its self-interested members by enforcing the rules of the game?
6. How can a society of ethical people be more efficient than a society of extreme egoists?

DECISION QUESTIONS

The whole point of learning ethical theory is to understand and ask questions like the following when you are analyzing an ethically problematic situation or case.

- Should the decision depend only on self-interest?
- Which decision is in the decision-maker's self-interest?
- Should we also consider family, friends, community, or more?
- Should we think of others as psychological egoists?
- Will the decision-maker's strategic decision involve a prisoner's dilemma situation?
- Would a decision to maximize self-interest lead to vice, injustice, utility loss, or rights violations?
- Would a decision to maximize self-interest lead to problems with cooperation?

CASE STUDY

Analyze this case study using the ethical theory that you have learned so far. You will find a collection of learning materials applying to the case on the book's website: http://sites.broadviewpress.com/businessethics/. These materials will help you in your analysis.

What Should Carol Do about Workplace Safety?

Carol Walters is a production manager for World Auto Parts, a large manufacturer of transmission components for cars and trucks. Transmission parts production is a very competitive sector. If WAP's production cost were to rise, then WAP's two main competitors would rapidly take over WAP's markets.

WAP has the advantage of a loyal and experienced workforce who have nearly all been with WAP for over ten years. WAP is not unionized, but it does pay well. One reason that the employees stay with WAP is that there are no other jobs available in the local area.

Technology, however, has not stood still. Most of the machinery that was up-to-date ten years ago has gone obsolete, and WAP has replaced many of the machines on which employees originally worked. One such machine is the Sterling Gear Press Mark IV, with which WAP recently replaced the slower Mark III model. This new machine is the mainstay of gear production in the factory, and many employees now run it. WAP has installed the new Mark IV on the factory floor beside the older Mark III machines. Both of WAP's competitors have also upgraded to the new Mark IV machine in the same way.

Carol and another production manager, Phil Thomas, have recently noticed that the injury rate on the new machines is higher than the injury rate on the old machines. There appears to be a defect in the design of the safety cover of the Mark IV. The new design causes workers who use the machine to strain their backs and left arms. Because the new machine is so much faster than the old version, production has gone up. The savings to WAP have outweighed the cost of downtime and time off for injured workers taking sick leave. WAP gives sick pay at 60% of regular wages, and only for 10 days per year.

The situation does not violate local Occupational Safety and Health regulations. Still, it is in Carol's interest to fix the problem because, as a production manager, she will likely end up being blamed by senior management. Carol and Phil discuss how WAP could do something about the situation. They believe that if they both independently talk to their boss, Joan Ross who is the VP of production at WAP, then Joan will believe them that there is a workplace-safety problem. Joan could order them to inform the operators of the new machines about the problem. Joan could also order the machine operators to slow down and be more careful. Alternatively, Joan could order the operators to resume using the Mark III machines, which still sit beside the new models. Any of Joan's possible responses will put WAP at a competitive disadvantage, unless Joan can convince both of WAP's competitors to do the same. Even if WAP's competitors verbally agree to follow one of these workplace-safety strategies, Joan would not be certain that she could trust them actually to implement the strategy.

Complicating the situation is the issue that Carol and Phil are competing for a promotion to Senior Supervisor. In the past, Carol has not always kept her word to Phil, or done her share of work on group projects. She does not think Phil trusts her. If Phil and she independently tell Joan about the safety problem, then Joan may do something, and Carol will still be in competition for the promotion. However, if one of them does not follow through and tell Joan, then Joan will likely do nothing about the safety issue, and Joan will likely not promote the seeming naysayer and troublemaker who did bring up the safety issue. If neither tells Joan, then nothing will happen and the competition for promotion will continue.

Analyze the ethical issues in the situation facing Carol, paying particular attention to any cooperation dilemmas. Should Carol tell Joan about the workplace-safety issue?

# Chapter 4

CALCULATING CONSEQUENCES AND UTILITARIAN REASONING

Is causing maximum happiness for everyone the way to make ethical decisions?

How can we measure and compare people's happiness?

What should we do when maximizing happiness leads to injustice?

Self-interested people make decisions by looking at their options, calculating the consequences of each option, judging which option will contribute the most to their welfare,
and choosing that option. Purely business-minded corporate managers, who look out
only for the interests of their company, make business decisions by estimating the financial costs and benefits of alternative projects. They discount these costs and benefits
to the present, and then decide on the project that offers the highest present value of
net benefits to their company. Socially responsible corporate managers make ethical
decisions by reasoning in a similar way, except that they consider the costs and benefits
to their customers, employees, suppliers, and community as well. In doing so, they are
implicitly assuming some form of the utilitarian ethical theory.

According to utilitarianism, the best decision is the one that causes the maximum
amount of utility for all those whose interests it affects. Utility is a philosophical term
of art that the originator of utilitarianism, the eighteenth-century English legal theorist,
Jeremy Bentham, defined as follows.

> By utility is meant that property in any object, whereby it tends to produce
> benefit, advantage, pleasure, good, or happiness, (all this in the present
> case comes to the same thing) or (what comes again to the same thing) to
> prevent the happening of mischief, pain, evil, or unhappiness to the party
> whose interest is considered.... (Bentham, 1789, Chapter I, Paragraph 4)

In its original formulation, utilitarianism claimed that people should promote those states of affairs that produced the best balance of pleasure over pain for everyone.

In a society that assumed the interests of aristocrats were more important than were those of everyone else, Bentham's utilitarianism was a radical doctrine. It treated everyone's interests as having equal importance in formulating public policy. Each was to count for one, and none was to count for more than one. In the hands of the economists who followed Adam Smith it led to the idea that the business activity under conditions of perfect competition is ethically justified because it maximizes overall welfare. Utilitarianism also promised a universal algorithm for making ethical decisions. If scientists could only find some way of comparing and measuring people's pleasures and pains, then utilitarianism suggested a recipe for ethical decision-making resembling the method of financial cost-benefit analysis: For each option, sum the pains and pleasures of everyone, and choose the option likely to cause the best balance of pleasure over pain.

Unfortunately, what works for individual, self-interested decision-makers, is difficult to implement for decisions concerning more than one individual. Firstly, single individuals can easily compare one pleasure to another and determine which one is more intense, but scientists have not found a way to make this comparison between different people. Without a way of measuring degrees of pain and pleasure across individuals, it is impossible to sum and maximize net pleasure. Secondly, when individuals trade off their own pain for their own pleasure to maximize happiness within their own lives, issues of fairness do not arise. On the other hand, when a utilitarian decision-maker trades off the pain of one person for the pleasure of another in order to maximize the sum total of happiness, significant issues of fairness do arise.

In this chapter, we will look in more detail at the problems of measuring human welfare, and at the issues of distributive justice and respect for individual rights that occur when utilitarians add up welfare across many individuals. We will also look at the utilitarian response both to these issues, and to the sheer complexity of the calculations that people must make in their ethical decision-making. This utilitarian response is to apply the theory indirectly, at the level of policy formulation, rather than directly to each case. Indirect utilitarianism justifies the implementation of policies, such as the following of rules or the inculcation of virtues, rather than the performing of a net benefit calculation. The justification is that people will create maximum happiness by implementing these policies rather than becoming mired in a detailed calculation of costs and benefits every time they must make an ethical decision.

CALCULATING CONSEQUENCES

Bentham defined utility as the property of an object whereby it tends to produce welfare or happiness, which he took to be synonymous with pleasure. Bentham took "utility" as another word for "usefulness." Modern-day economists and philosophers think of **utility** as an abstract measure of the welfare that people get from consuming something as a product or service. They think of it as an amount of pleasure or satisfaction, rather than as a property. To a utilitarian, then, a decision is the right one if, and only if,

1. it causes
2. the maximum
3. aggregate amount of
4. utility.

Component (1) makes the decision procedure consequentialist. Component (4) makes it subjective or psychological. Component (3) says to add up or sum the utilities of everyone whose interests are affected. Component (2) tells how to make the decision: Pick the option that causes maximum total utility.

Suppose that we have some way of measuring a person's net utility with a value in utiles. In the table below, if Hal is an ethical egoist, then Hal will decide on option A because under option A he will maximize his own welfare score at 30 utiles.

Hal's decision	Hal	Ira	Jan	Aggregate	Maximize?
A	30	15	20	30+15+20=65	No
B	10	25	40	10+25+40=75	No
C	25	20	35	25+20+35=80	Yes

Table 4.1: A table of welfare scores (utility) for Hal's three options.

If Hal is an **altruist** (that is, someone who maximizes positive mental states in others with little consideration of his own interests), then he will decide on option B because the combined welfare scores of the other two, Ira and Jan, is highest for option B (25 + 40 = 65). If Hal is a utilitarian, then he will decide on option C because the aggregated welfare score for everyone, including himself, is at a maximum for option C. Figure 4.1 represents Hal's utilitarian reasoning.

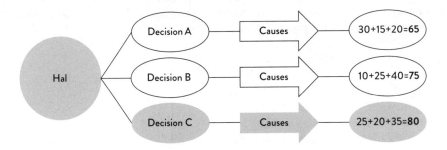

Figure 4.1: Utilitarian Hal chooses the option, shown in grey, which maximizes utility.

EXPERIENCE-BASED UTILITARIANISM

Utilitarians differ in what they think utility is. Proponents of experience-based utilitarianism believe, like Bentham, that utility consists in receiving pleasure and avoiding pain. Proponents of preference-based utilitarianism believe that welfare consists in having preferences satisfied, where a preference is a person's choice among all the states of affairs that a person might want or desire. Cost-benefit utilitarianism assumes a particular way of measuring intensity of preferences: willingness to pay.

Experiences are mental sensations of pleasure or pain, or of other feelings of enjoyment or suffering. They are action-guiding in that people mostly seek to find pleasure and avoid pain. For Bentham, pain and pleasure are also ethical. The first sentence of his important 1789 book, *An Introduction to the Principles of Morals and Legislation*, goes as follows.

> Nature has placed mankind under the governance of two sovereign masters, pain and pleasure. It is for them alone to point out what we ought to do, as well as to determine what we shall do. (Bentham, 1789, Chapter I, Paragraph 1)

Pain and pleasure govern what it is that we do as well as what it ought to be that we do. Experience-based utilitarianism bases itself on the ethical importance of feeling pleasure and avoiding pain. Even though we cannot argue from the fact that people avoid pain to the ethical value that people ought to avoid creating pain, the ethical value of avoiding pain is still an ethical intuition that most people share. Similarly, the fact that people seek pleasure does not entail that people should create pleasure, but the ethical value of pleasure is still a widely shared fundamental ethical intuition.

According to **experience-based utilitarianism**, the ethical value of the consequences of a decision resides totally in the mental experiences that it brings about. An agent's decision brings about a state of affairs in the world, and this state of affairs normally causes pleasurable or painful experiences. This is the picture Bentham had in mind when he wrote of utility as the property of an object that tends to produce pain or pleasure. Figure 4.2 shows this situation.

Figure 4.2: Ethically valuable mental experiences brought about by a state of the world that standardly brings about such experiences.

One problem is that we can imagine creating any mental experience in a non-standard fashion. Sensations are purely internal to the mind and do not depend on what happens in the external world. For example, amputees frequently report pain in phantom limbs, even though the real limb is no longer there. We can design thought-experiments to suggest that sensations, feelings, and experiences are not the only things with ethical value. Philosophers test conceptual claims, such as the claim that pleasurable experience is all that is valuable, with thought experiments, just as scientists test empirical claims with scientific experiments. One such thought experiment is the Experience Machine, invented by the twentieth-century American philosopher Robert Nozick.

> Imagine a machine that could give you any experience (or sequence of experiences) you might desire. When connected to this experience machine, you have the experience of writing a great poem or bringing about world peace or loving someone and being loved in return. You can experience the felt pleasures of these things, how they feel "from the inside." You can program your experience for tomorrow, or this week, or this year, or even for the rest of your life. If your imagination is impoverished, you can use the library of suggestions extracted from biographies and enhanced by novelists and psychologists. You can live your fondest dreams "from the inside." Would you choose to do this for the rest of your life? If not, why not? (Nozick, 1989, pp. 104–05)

If we would not choose to hook ourselves up to the experience machine, then we do not really believe that only pleasurable experience has ethical value. We do not value pleasurable experience if it comes about in a non-standard way. We also value the existence of the state of affairs that normally brings about each pleasurable experience.

Nozick's example suggests that what has ethical value for people is not just the experience, but also the state of affairs that brings about the experience. What one values is not only the mere feeling of writing a great poem, but also the fact that one really has written a great poem. In Bentham's terminology, what really matters to people is the existence of both the object that tends to bring about pleasure and the pleasure itself. Nozick's experience-machine example suggests that people want both an experience in their internal, mental world and a state of affairs in the external, real world.

PREFERENCE-BASED UTILITARIANISM

Experience-based utilitarianism aims at producing pleasurable experiences directly. **Preference-based utilitarianism**, on the other hand, aims instead at producing actual states of affairs that people want. By giving people the states of affairs that they want, utilitarians hope thereby also to make them happy. Most people prefer a state of affairs in which their friends love them. They do not want the fake love of pretend friends; they want the real love of real friends. Utilitarians also think that people want the love of their friends because loving their friends and being loved in return will make them happy.

Contemporary utilitarianism, and the economic thinking that it underlies, has concentrated on satisfying people's preferences. Preference satisfaction depends on the external world being a certain way, and preference satisfaction requires that we change the external world to fit our preferences.

People always have many future states of affairs that they want to have come about. Because their resources are finite, they cannot generally satisfy all of their wants and desires. They have to choose the wants that they can afford to satisfy. For example, at the corner store, a child may want both a chocolate bar and a bottle of soda pop, but having only one dollar in her wallet, she must choose which one of those treats she prefers.

Figure 4.3 represents the stages of preference satisfaction. A person starts with a set of states of affairs, A to E, that he wants because he thinks they will bring him pleasure. Unfortunately, he can bring about only one of these states of affairs. Of the five possible states of affairs, he chooses D, which is the one that he thinks will cause him the most pleasurable experience. He prefers D and acts to bring about D. State of affairs D satisfies his preference, and gives him a certain mental experience. If he has chosen wisely, then his preferred state of affairs will bring him a more pleasurable experience than will any of his alternatives.

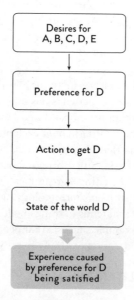

Figure 4.3: The stages of preference satisfaction.

The problem with using preference satisfaction to ground utilitarianism is that people do not always prefer wisely. We have all had the experience of wanting something, but finding that when we get it, it does not bring us any pleasure. For example, someone orders a slice of pepperoni pizza because she prefers it to the mushroom pizza and she anticipates the pleasure it will bring her. Unbeknownst to her the pepperoni has gone off, and the pizza tastes disgusting. We often do not have enough information to predict accurately the experience that we will have when our preference is satisfied. We get what we want, but it does not make us happy.

To make matters worse, it turns out that we do not prefer badly just because we lack information. Experiments in behavioural economics show that people systematically fail to predict the duration and intensity of experiences.

Behavioural economists have noticed mechanisms that systematically cause people to misjudge the ability of their preferred states of affairs to bring them pleasure and pain. People form preferences regarding future experiences based on their memories of past experiences, when such memories are available. Memories of past experiences are systematically inaccurate. People's memories are subject to a tendency to neglect duration in the evaluation of past experiences and to remember, not the overall intensity of past experiences, but only their maximum intensity and their final intensity. For example, experimenters asked subjects to hold their hand in cold water for 60 seconds, which caused the subjects mild pain. Then they asked the same subjects to hold their hands in water for 90 seconds. For the first 60 seconds the water was at the same temperature as in the previous experiment, and for the last 30 seconds it was slightly warmer and less painful. The second treatment involved more pain than the first, because while both included 60 seconds of the same pain, the second contained another 30 seconds of milder pain. The experimenters then asked the subjects which treatment they would prefer to have repeated. Wise judges of how future states of affairs would cause them pain would choose the first treatment because it involved less overall pain. Yet many subject preferred to repeat the second treatment because their memories were unable to store the actual duration of the pain, and because they remembered the intensity of the pain in the final 30 seconds of the treatment better than they remembered their experience during the rest of the treatment. Contrary to what made sense to Bentham, and contrary to what makes sense to us from the outside, subjects preferred pain of longer duration to pain of shorter duration, or more pain to less pain. Because people store memories of the experiences caused by past states of affairs in a biased way, they are liable to form preferences about future states of affairs in ways that systematically misjudge the psychological experiences that they will cause. People are bad at forecasting what will make them happy. (Kahneman 2011, Chapter 35; Gilbert 2006, Chapter 10)

INFORMED PREFERENCES

We noted earlier that our actual preferences are sometimes a bad guide to what will bring us happiness. We are quite often mistaken in our preferences about how we want the world to be. Perhaps a better guide to happiness is to follow only the preferences that we would have if we had true and adequate information about how the resulting states of affairs would work out for us. The **informed preference theory of value** holds that a state of the world is valuable if it would satisfy the preference that someone would have if she had full information and were reasoning rationally. To return to our previous example, we would not prefer the pepperoni pizza to the mushroom pizza if we had full information, that is, if we knew that the pepperoni had gone bad.

Sometimes our informed preferences are the same as our actual preferences. This happens when, in fact, we actually prefer the same state of the world as we would have preferred if we were fully informed. Quite often, we are right about what will make us happy. Sometimes, however, we are not, and then our informed preference for mushroom pizza is different from our actual preference for pepperoni pizza, which unbeknownst to us is rotten. What will promote our happiness is the mushroom pizza, the pizza we would have preferred had we known everything. The trouble is, our informed preference is not an actual preference that we have. Because it is a hypothetical preference and not an actual preference, we cannot measure its intensity using the techniques that we have surveyed. A subject will not be willing to pay anything at all to satisfy a preference that she does not actually have. Therefore, we cannot measure and aggregate those informed preferences that people do not actually have in the way that utilitarianism requires. We can only do a cost-benefit analysis over people's actual preferences, not over their hypothetical preferences.

Philosophers are also suspicious of using informed preferences in utilitarian calculations because world history is replete with examples of great harm done in the name of making people better, or giving them what their rulers think they truly want instead of what they actually want. Using hypothetical, informed preferences can lead to a form of objective consequentialism that no longer worries about people's actual mental lives.

MEASURING UTILITY: VON NEUMANN-MORGENSTERN

Utilitarianism also faces the problem of how to measure happiness, net pleasure, or utility. The utilitarian decision procedure involves summing the welfare of everyone affected by the decision, and this summing operation is impossible unless we can reliably measure people's welfare.

For experience-based utilitarianism, this involves measuring pleasurable and painful mental experiences. Experience-based utilitarianism treats everyone's pains and pleasures equally. When it adds up pains and pleasures it weights the pains of tenant farmers by the same factor as it weights the pains of landowning aristocrats. The problem, however, is measuring the intensity of people's pains and pleasures. Scientists do not have a pleasure-meter, a device which, when attached to someone's head, will tell the scientist the intensity of the subject's pleasures or pains. People can be asked to rank the intensity of a pain on a subjective scale of 0 for no pain to 10 for the most pain they can imagine. Nevertheless, we cannot know that the scales are comparable between the two individuals. For example, a peasant might rank the pain of his blisters at 5 while the Lady of the Manor might rank the pain of a prick from her embroidery needle at 7. Is what the Lady thinks as a 10 the same as what the peasant thinks of as a 10? We do not, and cannot, know. Yet, if we cannot compare the intensity of experiences between people, then we cannot measure utility in a way that would allow us to sum it up for different people.

Preference-based utilitarianism fares better in this regard. We can ask people what their preferences are. We can also observe the choices that people make, and from their choices, we can infer their preferences. We can observe that someone prefers A to B or that she is indifferent between B and C. This gives us an ordinal measure of utility, in which we can say that one outcome has more utility than another outcome, but in which we cannot say how much more utility the first outcome has than does the second outcome. We can then construct the science of microeconomics based on these observations. We can use these observations to create the whole apparatus of indifference curves and demand curves, and even define a notion of Pareto efficiency that can do duty as a maximization principle.

Once we have an ordinal measure of utility, there are two procedures for constructing a cardinal measure that will tell us how much more utility one outcome has over another. One procedure is the von Neumann-Morgenstern method from game theory. Another procedure is the willingness-to-pay method used in economic cost-benefit analyses.

Briefly, the von Neumann-Morgenstern method involves assigning a utility of 0 to the worst possible outcome that we can imagine and a utility of 100 to the best possible outcome that we can imagine. The experimenter then offers the subject a series of gambles, each of which gives a different percentage chance of winning the best outcome. To measure the utility of a particular outcome to the subject, the experimenter asks the subject to say where he would be indifferent between the outcome happening or receiving the gamble as a lottery ticket. For example, suppose the outcome in question is a promotion at work, and that table 4.2 shows the subject's responses.

Percentage chance of best outcome	10%	20%	30%	40%	50%	60%	70%	80%	90%
Prefers promotion to gamble	Yes	Yes	Yes	Yes	Yes	=	No	No	No

Table 4.2: The utility of a promotion is measured by the point where the subject is indifferent between the promotion and the gamble.

The subject prefers the promotion to gambles with a 50% or less chance of winning the best possible outcome, and prefers the gamble to the promotion for gambles with a 70% or more chance of winning the best outcome. He is indifferent between the promotion and a 60% chance of winning the best possible outcome, and this is a cardinal measure of the utility of the promotion to him. In principle, the von Neumann-Morgenstern method allows us to measure the intensity of someone's preference for an outcome.

MEASURING UTILITY: WILLINGNESS TO PAY

Another way of measuring utility uses the amount of money someone is willing to pay for a commodity as a measure of the intensity of her preference for it. **Willingness to pay** is the maximum amount of money that someone would be willing to exchange for an economic good. It is important to see that what someone is willing to pay is not necessarily the market price. The market price for a commodity is set both by what people in general are willing to pay for an additional item of that type and by what other people are willing to accept for giving up the item. When a market price exists for a commodity, no one will be willing to pay more for the commodity than the actual market price. Though most people would be willing to pay a great deal of money for a bottle of water in the middle of the desert, in the city, they will not pay more for the same bottle than the asking price at the nearest corner-store. What someone is willing to pay for an item is not its market price, but the person's reservation price. The reservation price is the maximum amount of money that someone would be willing to exchange for a commodity in the absence of a defined market price for that commodity. For example, someone's reservation price for a unique artwork is the most that she would pay for it at art auction. Willingness to pay has several severe problems as a measure of utility.

Willingness to pay is measured by reservation prices. Even though market prices are easy for economists to measure, reservation prices are not. Canny negotiators are very coy about revealing what is the maximum they would pay for an item. No sensible homebuyer offers $300,000 for a house and, at the same time, announces that the most she would be willing to pay for the house is $400,000. People conceal their reservation prices, and may even be deceptive and misleading about them as part of a negotiation strategy. People bluff about their willingness to pay. Consequently, even though someone's willingness to pay looks like it is a transparent measure of their preference intensity in currency units, in practice, it is actually very difficult to discover.

Willingness to pay is also affected by ability to pay. If a billionaire and a worker are both at an auction bidding on a rare coin, the reservation price of the billionaire will be far higher than the reservation price of the worker. This is not an indication that the billionaire desires the rare coin more intensely than the worker does. All it means is that the billionaire has more money than the worker has. We can only use willingness to pay to compare preference intensities among people with the same income and wealth. Since income and wealth vary widely across the population, willingness to pay will be a bad measure of preference intensity. Furthermore, if we do use willingness to pay as a measure of preference intensity, we will end up weighting the preferences of well-off people more highly than we weight the interests of low-income people. A billionaire with the same preference intensity as a worker will nonetheless be willing to pay (because able to pay) more to satisfy that preference than will the worker. This is unfair and contrary to a major attraction of utilitarianism, its equal consideration of interests, as in the slogan, "Each to count for one, and none to count for more than one."

ECONOMIC UTILITARIANISM

Economists use willingness to pay as a measure of utility when they do cost-benefit analyses. Economists are careful to distinguish when they are doing positive economics from when they are doing normative economics. **Positive economics** is a science that creates models describing the behaviour of economic markets and participants in those markets. **Normative economics** uses economic science to make policy decisions. It tells decision-makers what policies they ought to implement based on an economic analysis of the policy alternatives.

Decision-makers use willingness to pay as a measure of utility when they do a cost-benefit analysis (CBA). A **positive cost-benefit analysis** is an economic technique that measures the financial costs and benefits of different policy options according to people's willingness to pay for them, calculates the total net benefits of each policy, and uses the results as a factual input to a policy decision. A **normative cost-benefit analysis** is a decision-making technique that measures the financial costs and benefits of different policy options according to people's willingness to pay for them, calculates the total net benefits of each policy, and uses the results to justify a policy decision ethically. It is important not to confuse these two interpretations of a CBA. What starts off as a factual inquiry can easily become an ethical decision-making criterion. When this happens, the results of the initial inquiry become an ethical decision without anyone noticing.

Table 4.3 shows the results of a simple CBA. For each person and each alternative, the analyst calculates the benefits and costs and subtracts to find the net benefit. For example, if Kira's benefit under alternative A is $450 and her cost is $300, then her net benefit will be $150 as shown in the top left cell of the table.

	Alternative A	Alternative B	Alternative C
Kira	$150	$150	$100
Mike	$200	$150	$100
Nadia	$250	$150	$500
Aggregate:	$600	$450	$700

Table 4.3: A CBA will sum the net benefits of each alternative, and decide on the alternative with the highest total net benefits.

For each alternative, the bottom row shows the sum of the net benefits for all the three people. Alternative C maximizes net benefits, and is the one that a normative CBA tells us to choose. Someone might object that alternative B is fairer because it leads to everyone getting the same net benefits, but a normative CBA ignores fairness and looks only to maximizing net benefits.

If the analyst does not know for sure what will be the outcomes of an alternative, then the analyst can calculate an expected value for the alternative by multiplying the net benefits of each possible outcome by the probability that it will occur. For example, if some alternative has a 30% chance of producing an outcome with a net benefit of $1000 and a 70% chance of producing a net benefit of $100, then its expected net benefit will be (.3 x $1000 + .7 x $100) = $370. If the outcome produced by an alternative will not happen until some time in the future, then the analyst can discount the net benefit of the future outcome and compare its present value to the present value of the outcomes of the alternatives. For example if an alternative will produce an outcome with a net benefit of $110 in one year's time, and the rate of return for projects of a

similar risk is 10%, then the present value of the net benefit of this outcome will be
$100. Positive cost-benefit analysis is a sophisticated and elegant economic technique.

Clearly a positive CBA is on the "is" side of the "is/ought" gap, whereas a normative CBA is on the "ought" side. Proponents of normative CBA as an ethical decision-making technique can bridge this gap using an ethical theory as a premise. This
ethical theory will be a form of utilitarian reasoning that uses people's willingness to
pay (WTP) for outcomes to measure the intensity of their preferences for these outcomes.
The following argument is logically invalid.

1. Alternative Q is the one that maximizes net benefits, as measured
   by WTP.
2. Therefore, we ought to implement alternative Q.

The ethical ("ought") conclusion does not follow from the factual ("is") premise.
However, if we supplement the argument with a utilitarian ethical premise, then it
becomes logically valid. The following argument is valid.

0. Whatever alternative causes maximum net benefits, as measured by
   WTP, is the one we ought to implement.
1. Alternative Q is the one that maximizes net benefits, as measured
   by WTP.
2. Therefore, we ought to implement alternative Q.

The argument is logically valid, but whether it is a sound argument depends on whether
the ethical premise is true or not. If the ethical premise is false, then, despite the argument's logical validity, the argument lends no support to its ethical conclusion, the
decision to implement alternative Q.

The missing premise that we added to the above argument, Clause 0, is a statement
of economic utilitarianism. **Economic utilitarianism** is a form of preference-satisfaction utilitarianism where we measure the utility of a good or service to each person
according to his or her willingness to pay for it. It becomes a utilitarian ethical theory
when we add up the costs and benefits for each person affected by the alternatives, then
add up each person's total to discover which alternative maximizes the grand total of
financial net benefits for everyone, and then ethically justify our decision on the basis
that our chosen alternative causes maximum aggregate net benefits. One problem with
normative cost-benefit analyses is that decision-makers often apply them only in a limited context. For example, a cost-benefit analysis done for a firm may be limited just to
the interests of owners and employees. However, economic utilitarianism implies that
all people have moral standing. So any decision-maker using a normative cost-benefit
analysis should be careful to consider the costs and benefits for all parties whom the
decision effects.

UTILITARIANISM, RIGHTS, AND JUSTICE

Some of the worst difficulties with utilitarianism as an ethical theory arise because of the way that it adds up, or aggregates, everyone's interests and maximizes the total without regard to what happens to the individual human beings over whom it is summing. The requirement to aggregate interests is implicit in Bentham's description of the nature of a community.

> The community is a fictitious body, composed of the individual persons who are considered as constituting as it were its members. The interest of the community then is, what?—the sum of the interests of the several members who compose it. (Bentham, 1789, Chapter I, Paragraph 5)

Aggregating everyone's interests can lead to the violation of individual human rights, unfair distributions of welfare, and demands for people to behave in utility maximizing ways that are contrary to being a virtuous person. We have already seen an example of unfairness above, when a cost-benefit analysis favoured a maximizing distribution to an equitable distribution.

Our imaginations can provide more examples. It might be the case that we could maximize happiness in our society if we were to make members of a minority group into the slaves of the majority. The increased happiness of the majority group might outweigh the sufferings of the minority group, and the aggregate happiness would be at a maximum. If this were so, then utilitarianism would tell us to implement this slave-holding society. This conclusion is awful. All our ethical intuitions are against slavery. Drawing on other ethical approaches, we can articulate these contrary intuitions: Slavery violates the human rights of the slaves. Slavery violates the principle of the moral equality of persons; it unjustly subjugates some individual to others for morally arbitrary reasons. Slavery creates the exact opposite of the relationships that people should have to one another.

Another stock example of the problems that aggregation creates for utilitarianism is the case of the transplant surgeon. In the transplant ward of a hospital, two patients each need a kidney, two patients each need a lung, and one patient needs a heart. All five patients will die if they do not receive these transplants. Another patient is admitted to the hospital with a broken leg, but also with two healthy kidneys, two healthy lungs, and a healthy heart. The surgeon could save the first five patients by removing the healthy organs from the sixth one. She could satisfy the preferences of five people to continue living by frustrating the preference to live of only one person. Utilitarianism would approve this trade-off, but other ethical approaches would not. According to the rights approach, the surgeon would be violating the sixth patient's right to life. According to the justice approach, she would be treating the sixth patient unfairly, imposing a giant burden on him for the morally arbitrary reason that he happened to break his leg at the wrong time and place. According to the care ethics approach, the surgeon is undermining the sort of caring and trusting relationship that should exist between doctor and patient. According to the virtue approach, the surgeon is murderous and callous. Because it aggregates welfare without concern for individuals, utilitarian reasoning can violate our most basic moral intuitions as summarized in other ethical approaches.

INDIRECT UTILITARIANISM

As an ethical decision-making technique, utilitarianism suffers from two further difficulties. Firstly, applying utilitarian reasoning to every case is cumbersome, time-consuming, and expensive. This is apparent in the business technique of using cost-benefit analyses to decide on investment opportunities or to perform environmental impact studies. Such decisions are not simple ones, require a great deal of staff time, and are expensive if the organization hires outside consultants. Utilitarian reasoning is similarly demanding for individuals. Each time she makes an ethical decision, an individual must determine which people each of her alternatives will affect, predict the net welfare change of each affected person, decide on probabilities of outcomes, calculate the aggregate net welfare for each alternative, and finally pick the one that maximizes net welfare. This very complicated deliberation will be hugely demanding on the cognitive abilities of decision-makers. Because "ought" requires "can," if a direct utilitarian decision-making procedure is overly demanding on decision-makers, then it cannot be morally required.

Secondly, utilitarian decision-making is likely to neglect tiny consequences that, though insignificant by themselves, accumulate into important welfare effects. A stock example is the lawn-crossing problem. One person walking on the grass in a park will have no significant effect on the grass, or on anyone's enjoyment of the lawn. The growth of grass will soon fix any damage. Each person, when reasoning in a direct utilitarian way about what to do, will legitimately decide to walk on the grass. Nevertheless, many people walking on the grass over a short time period will destroy the grass and ruin everyone's enjoyment of the lawn. Another example is the effect of driving gas-guzzling automobiles on climate change. One person driving a gas-guzzler will have no effect on the climate, but millions of people doing so may have catastrophic consequences.

One solution to both of these problems is to say that we should not apply utilitarian reasoning to individual decisions and acts, but instead should use utilitarian reasoning to justify rules and policies, that if generally followed, would maximize overall happiness. It is clear that if people follow the rule, "Keep off the grass," then everyone will enjoy the lawn more than they would if people must make a decision whether to cross on every individual occasion.

We can extend this line of thought further to reduce, perhaps, some of the rights, justice, and character-based difficulties brought about by utilitarian reasoning's commitment to aggregation. Why stop with using utilitarian reasoning to justify rules? Why not use it to justify a whole suite of policies, including rules, human rights, principles of justice, and character education that, when implemented will maximize utility? **Direct utilitarianism** treats utilitarian reasoning as a *decision procedure* and judges each case according to a calculation of the utilities it causes. **Indirect utilitarianism** treats utilitarian reasoning as a *justification procedure*, and advocates obedience to rules, respect for rights, inculcation of virtues, and the creation of whatever policies are necessary to produce maximum aggregate utility. Instead of using utilitarian reasoning to decide what to do in each case, we should use utilitarian reasoning to determine a system of policies, rights, mechanisms of distributive justice, and methods of instilling virtue. The system is morally justified because the whole system maximizes utility.

For example, Adam Smith's famous metaphor of the invisible hand is an indirect utilitarian argument for people to behave as self-interested egoists. While Smith did not think that people were truly egoists, he did think that people generally behaved that way in commercial transactions.

> It is not from the benevolence of the butcher, the brewer, or the baker
> that we expect our diner, but from their regard of their own interest. We
> address ourselves not to their humanity, but to their self-love, and never
> talk to them of our necessities, but of their advantage. (Adam Smith,
> *The Wealth of Nations*, 1776)

Nevertheless, Smith claimed that if people did behave as egoists, then this would promote the welfare of everyone in the economy.

> [B]y directing that industry in such a manner as its produce may be of the
> greatest value, he intends only his own gain, and he is in this, as in many
> other cases, led by an invisible hand to promote an end which was no part
> of his intention.... By pursuing his own interest he frequently promotes
> that of the society more effectually than when he really intends to promote it.
> (Book IV, Chapter II, Paragraph 2.9)

In a market economy, a metaphorical invisible hand would lead egoists, looking out only for their own interests, to advance the aggregate interests of society as a whole. This is a forerunner of the economic argument that a free-market economy, under conditions of perfect competition, will maximally satisfy the preference of all participants. In this argument, indirect utilitarianism, which claims that we should promote everyone's interest, is the real justification for pursuing self-interest.

Employing utilitarianism indirectly may avoid the difficulty of the transplant surgeon case. Indirect utilitarian reasoning would likely justify assigning hospital patients a right to life, as well as educating surgeons in the Hippocratic Oath, "First, do no harm." These policies are justified because otherwise no one would use hospitals out of fear that a utilitarian calculation might cost them their lives. Indirect utilitarianism may have less luck with the slavery case. The slavery case incorporated the assumption that a system in which one class of people had no self-ownership rights, and another class of people had property rights in people in the first class, was the system that maximized aggregate utility. The system of slavery, by hypothesis, is the system that utilitarian reasoning justifies. Another system that assigns everyone full human rights will create less happiness.

Without changing the assumptions of the example, indirect utilitarian reasoning still conflicts with our considered moral opinions about this particular example.

SUMMARY

1. Utilitarian reasoning appears to be a very attractive ethical decision-making procedure. It says to maximize happiness, and happiness is widely agreed to be good. It treats everyone's interests equally, and it has a recipe that promises a decision in every case.

2. The recipe for utilitarian ethical reasoning says we ought to (1) cause (2) maximum (3) aggregate (4) utility. Our ability to apply the recipe depends on our ability to measure utility.

3. One major problem for utilitarian reasoning is seeing how to measure utility or happiness.

4. If we think of utility as being mental experiences such as pain and pleasure, then we will have trouble comparing the intensity of experiences between people. We will also reach the unattractive conclusion that we could lead the best possible lives in a virtual world.

5. It is likely better to think of utility as satisfied preferences for real states of the world. We can attempt to measure the intensity of people's preferences by comparing them to gambles or asking how much people will be willing to pay to satisfy them. Unfortunately, people are often bad judges of whether having their preferences satisfied will actually make them happy.

6. Utilitarian reasoning could try to avoid this problem by satisfying only informed preferences, but informed preferences are hypothetical and therefore not measurable.

7. When we do a financial cost-benefit analysis, we must be careful to distinguish between employing it as a source of information and employing it as a normative method of making an ethical decision. Willingness to pay is very problematic as a measure of utility because it is determined by people's financial resources or ability to pay.

8. A second major problem for cost-benefit or utilitarian reasoning is seeing how to aggregate, or add up, utility without violating human rights, distributing benefits unfairly, encouraging vice, and destroying human relationships. If we apply utilitarian reasoning, then we must always be alert for these sorts of problems.

9. A third problem for utilitarian reasoning is that finite human beings will be unable to perform all the required calculations of consequences.

10. A fourth problem for utilitarian reasoning is dealing with accumulative consequences such as harmful pollution brought about by many harmless individual acts.

11. To avoid some of these problems, it is likely better to use utilitarian reasoning to justify policies rather than to make individual decisions.

Indirect utilitarian reasoning may recommend policies such as respecting rights and treating people fairly because doing so will, on balance, cause maximum utility. It can also recommend following rules, which finite human beings can follow instead of performing complex calculations, and which will prevent accumulative harms by prohibiting some individually harmless acts.

ONLINE LEARNING RESOURCES

You will find a collection of learning resources associated with this chapter on the book's website: http://sites.broadviewpress.com/businessethics/. Working through this material will help you understand and remember important concepts that we have discussed, and will help you apply them to issues in business ethics.

STUDY QUESTIONS

Answering the following questions will help you to understand the ethical theory in this chapter and will help you to create a set of review notes on the textbook.

1. Describe the utilitarian algorithm for ethical decision-making.
2. How does utilitarian reasoning treat everyone's interests equally?
3. Describe how satisfying people's preferences can sometimes not make them happy.
4. What is a big problem with using people's informed preferences in utilitarian reasoning?
5. Distinguish carefully between a positive and a normative cost-benefit analysis.
6. Explain why willingness to pay has problems as a measure of the intensity of preferences.
7. Describe how utilitarian reasoning can lead to injustice and rights violations for individuals.
8. Why is it likely better to apply utilitarian reasoning indirectly, as a justification for policies, rather than as a case-by-case decision-making method?

DECISION QUESTIONS

The whole point of learning ethical theory is to understand and ask questions like the following when you are analyzing an ethically problematic situation or case.

- Should we consider everyone's suffering and enjoyment?
- Should we consider everyone's wants, desires, and choices?
- Is willingness to pay a good measure of the strength of people's preferences?

- Can we measure the strength of pleasures or preferences?
- Can we see how to maximize net utility?
- Can we measure the strength of these preferences?
- Should we perform a cost-benefit analysis of the alternative decisions?
- Is there a policy that we could follow that will maximize well-being?
- Should the relevant organization write a good policy to cover this decision?
- Should we follow a rights-based or virtue-based policy in order to maximize well-being?
- If people had full information, would they have different preferences?
- If we aggregated only informed preferences, would this change our decision?
- Would the decision to maximize aggregate utility lead to rights violations or unjust distributions?
- Would the decision to follow a utility-maximizing rule be overly harsh and authoritarian?

CASE STUDY

Analyze this case study using the ethical theory that you have learned so far. You will find a collection of learning materials applying to the case on the book's website: http://sites.broadviewpress.com/businessethics/. These materials will help you in your analysis.

Should Dan Blow the Whistle?

Dan Goldberg works as a cost accountant in the New York City headquarters of the Pear Tree Plastic Corporation. He had a degree from a well-known business school, and his credentials and experience made him a very desirable employee. His main task is to examine and assess the production cost figures for the various plastic factories the PTP has in North America. Dan is not happy with the corporate ethos of PTP, which he thinks focuses only on the bottom line and the related goal of creating value for shareholders. His boss, Sheila Dunsworth, PTP's vice-president for production, is part of the problem. It seems she will go to almost any lengths to have her department look good to the CEO and board of directors. In the past, she has questioned Dan's judgment regarding the assignment of costs, and ordered him to show production cost figures in a more positive light.

Recently, Dan examined the production cost figures for PTP's factory in Thornbrook, Ontario. Sheila has always pointed to the Thornbrook factory as an example for PTP's other factories to emulate. PTP recently awarded a bonus to the boss of the Thornbrook factory for his excellent performance. Dan noticed that the Thornbrook factory's costs for disposal of a mercury compound used in the manufacturing process were way below the figures for other PTP factories. It was this cost saving, more than any other factor, which contributed to the factory's success. He also noticed that the

Thornbrook plant spent much less on the catalytic compound used in the factory's smokestack scrubbers than did any other of PTP's plants.

Shocked, Dan realized what was going on. The Thornbrook plant was running without its scrubbers working to remove the mercury compound properly. Dan looked on Google maps and saw that the plant was located right in the centre of Thornbrook. The PTP plant was exposing ten thousand local residents to a high risk of mercury poisoning.

Luckily, Thornbrook is way out in the middle of nowhere, so the emissions were affecting no one else. Over time, however, the mercury emissions would likely end up in the rivers, with negative implications for the health of the fish in the nearby water system. PTP Co. is the only major employer in Thornbrook, and most of the residents either work at the plant, or provide services for people who do. If the plant were to close, the workers would have to leave, as would the teachers, nurses, and shopkeepers. No one would want to buy their houses, which would then be worth almost nothing.

Dan's first thought was to tell Sheila. His second thought was that Sheila would not want to hear about the problem. She would just give the Thornbrook assignment to one of the other cost analysts who was more of a team player than Dan was, and PTP would do nothing about the problem. His third thought was to threaten to resign unless Sheila ordered the Thornbrook plant to use its scrubbers, but that threat would likely not sway Sheila. Dan's fourth thought was to tip off the environmental authorities in Ontario. He could do this anonymously, but an anonymous letter would not have the same impact that a signed letter would.

What should Dan do?

Chapter 5

MOTIVATIONS, DUTIES, AND RIGHTS

Do we have moral duties, and what are they?

How should we respect the rights of others?

How do ethical obligations arise from promises and legal contracts?

We live our domestic lives within a web of ethical duties. Some of these duties are openly discussed and agreed to, such as keeping a promise or doing our share of the housework. Other duties are taken for granted, such as duties to our family members or to our friends. Still other duties are legal ones, such as our duty to drive only on the correct side of the road or our duty not to steal from other people.

We also live our business lives, within a web of ethical duties. When we go to work, we still have all the duties that we have in everyday life, and we have a host of new ones as well. Our everyday duties do not go away when we enter the business world. Instead, we take on additional explicit duties, such as keeping promises to coworkers, additional implicit duties, such as meeting the legitimate expectations of our local community, and additional legal duties, often embodied in legal contracts with employers, customers, and suppliers.

Legal contracts involve both law and ethics. A legal contract is a legally enforceable pair of promises: an offer and an acceptance. Because both an offer and an acceptance are promises, they can also give rise to ethical duties, the ethical duties to keep these promises. We can see this more clearly when the legal and ethical duties are different. In the case of a business contract that is legally enforceable yet somehow unfair or immoral, the parties to such a contract might have legal duties to one another, but they would not have ethical duties.

A modern business corporation is not a tangible thing like a factory building, but is rather an intangible nexus of contracts and other legal interests. A business corporation is the centre, or focus, of an interconnected network of contracts between owners, employees, suppliers, customers, the government, and the local community. Contracts depend on promises, and duties to keep promises are ethical duties. One of the tasks of business ethics is to assess contracts for unfairness and other ethical defects.

Our basic liberties depend on our basic moral rights. Our freedom to lead our lives as we ourselves judge best depends on our moral right to lead our lives without the interference of other people. Our liberties impose duties on everyone else not to interfere with our lives. However, these liberties have limits. We have no moral right to lead our lives in such a way that we caused harm to other people. This is a formulation of the Harm Principle. The Harm Principle puts limits on the freedom of action of both individuals and businesses. Peoples often think of business as a sort of game played according to a set of rules. Sometimes the rules of this game permit activities that are harmful to other members of society. In such cases, these rules need evaluation according to the ethical standards implicit in the Harm Principle.

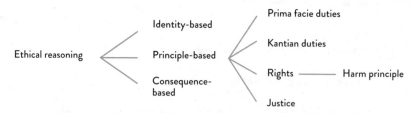

Figure 5.1: Shows a conceptual map of the types of principle-based ethical reasoning that we will look at in this chapter and the next.

There are different views regarding our principles and duties. One view is that our duties are the commands of God. **Divine command theories** of ethics hold that the commands of God create people's duties. Examples are the Ten Commandments given to Moses by the God of the Hebrews or the Golden Rule in the Christian New Testament. In what follows, though, we will look at secular theories of principles, duties, and rights. A second view is that we should simply list our duties according to our considered intuitions about the obligations that we have. These are our **prima facie** duties, duties that we have, but which can be overridden by stronger obligations. A third view is that our ethical duties are requirements of reason. Immanuel Kant thought that we have a duty not to do an action unless we can consistently claim that everyone can have a duty to do that action. A fourth view is that our ethical duties arise because other people have moral rights. A **right** is a justified claim by one person that other persons owe duties to her. A fifth view is that our duties arise from principles of justice. **Justice** is the requirement that we treat all persons fairly. We will look at the topic of justice in the next chapter and discuss duties, rights, and the harm principle in this one.

MOTIVATION AND ETHICAL REASONING

Ethical reasoning can evaluate (1) the consequences of a decision, (2) the motivation of the decision-maker, or (3) the character of the decision-maker. We have looked at self-interested and utilitarian ethical reasoning that evaluates the consequences of decisions. In this chapter, we will focus on motivation-based ethical reasoning. It is perfectly possible for people to produce good consequences for the wrong reasons, and for the best of intentions to result in bad outcomes. Ethical reasoning that emphasizes motivations and intentions will praise actions done according to good principles, even if the actions have bad consequences.

The motivation-based approach to ethical reasoning evaluates decisions according to the ethical principles that motivate the decision-maker. Motivation by ethical principles often consists in the decision-maker fulfilling her ethical duties, regardless of the expected consequences of her decision. An ethical duty is an ethical obligation that generally overrides considerations of maximizing good consequences or of personal virtue. **Duties** are overriding ethical obligations that agents have to act in certain ways. In ordinary English, however, we refer to almost any ethical obligation as a duty. For example, we sometimes call the ethical obligation to make everyone happy a "duty," and we sometimes say that the person who wishes to exemplify the virtue of honesty has a "duty" to tell the truth to other people. In what follows, however, our primary interest will be in duties as principles that are justified independently of their role in creating happiness or exemplifying virtue.

The German philosopher Immanuel Kant (1724–1804) thought that the consequences of an action did not matter. He thought that only the motivation of the moral agent matters in the ethical evaluation of an action. He believed a person's action, which might appear to be right according to self-interested or utilitarian reasoning, was actually right only if the person acted for the right reason. It was not enough for Kant that an action conformed to a person's duty; what was important was that the person performed the action because it was his duty to act that way. He gave the following example of a merchant who does not overcharge his customers.

> For example, it is in fact in accordance with duty that a dealer should not overcharge an inexperienced customer, and wherever there is much business the prudent merchant does not do so, having fixed a price for everyone, so that a child may buy of him as cheaply as any other. Thus the customer is honestly served. But this is far from sufficient to justify the belief that the merchant has behaved in this way from duty and principles of honesty. His own advantage required this behavior; ... (Kant, 1959, p. 13)

Even though the shopkeeper does the right thing, which is not to overcharge the child, if he does it for the wrong reason, such as for the sake of his reputation, his action has no moral worth. Only if the shopkeeper does not overcharge the child because he is motivated by his duty not to overcharge anyone, is his action morally right.

Suppose a business owner gives to charity because she thinks it would be good PR in her community. Even though this donation helped many people, Kant would not think that her action had moral worth. Kant would think that her self-interested motivation was morally worthless. By contrast, a utilitarian would judge her action morally good because it had such good consequences. Kant is concerned with the principles that motivate people, not with the results of their actions. For Kant, only people who act out of a sense of ethical duty can do morally right actions.

PRIMA FACIE DUTIES

One way to discover our ethical duties is to consult our considered moral judgments regarding our moral obligations. This will result in a list of duties that, on the face of it, are morally binding on us, but which other, more powerful, obligations may override. **Absolute duties** are over-riding obligations that people have no matter what happens. **Prima facie duties** are ethical obligations that people have, but which may yield to stronger obligations.

The early twentieth-century English philosopher, W.D. Ross, suggested such a list of prima facie duties. (Ross, 2002, p. 21) He thought this list of duties met our considered intuitions about the ethical obligations that we have. His list included seven prima facie duties. The duty of beneficence is the duty to benefit others. The duty of fidelity is the duty to keep promises. The duty of gratitude is the duty to be thankful for benefits received from others and to reciprocate if possible. The duty of justice is the duty to treat others fairly, reasonably, and impartially. The duty of non-maleficence is the duty to avoid harming others as much as possible. The duty of reparation is the duty to compensate others if we harm them unavoidably. The duty of self-improvement is our duty to be the best that we can be.

Ross's list of prima facie duties could form the basis for making ethical decisions in business. Prima facie duties provide us with a checklist of ethical considerations with which to examine a problematic case in the world of business. To make a decision in a case where prima facie duties conflict with one another, we then must determine our overall duty by seeing which prima facie duties are stronger and which prima facie duties get overridden. However, we can get a deeper understanding of the types of ethical reasoning at play in decision-making if we use our similar framework of ethical pluralism.

KANTIAN DUTIES

Kant formulated an important theory of ethical duties that is still influential today in business ethics. (Bowie, 1999) Kant distinguished between two types of moral principles, hypothetical and categorical imperatives. A **hypothetical imperative** is a strategic principle that will help someone get what he wants. A hypothetical imperative is a useful strategy that we can usually formulate in a conditional form. For example, the hypothetical imperative, "If you want people to trust you, then don't tell lies," is a useful strategy, but not a moral principle. A **categorical imperative**, on the other hand, is a moral principle of action that does not depend on anyone's wants or desires. A categorical imperative is an absolute duty, such as, "Don't tell lies," rather than a strategic principle.

Kant had a theory of absolute ethical duties. He thought that all absolute ethical duties stemmed from one main principle, the Categorical Imperative, "Act only according to that maxim by which you can at the same time will that it should become a universal law." (Kant, 1959, p. 39) Kant applies the Categorical Imperative to an illustrative business case, that of a man who

... finds himself forced by need to borrow money. He well knows that he will not be able to repay it, but he also sees that nothing will be loaned him if he does not firmly promise to repay it at a certain time. (Kant, 1959, p. 40)

According to Kant's Categorical Imperative, this man should notice that he is following a universal principle that says anyone who needs money can make promises he cannot keep. Then he should notice that it makes no sense for this principle to be a universal moral law.

For the universality of a law which says that anyone who believes himself to be in need could promise what he pleased with the intention of not fulfilling it would make the promise itself and the end to be accomplished by it impossible; no one would believe what was promised to him but would only laugh at any such assertion as vain pretense. (Kant, 1959, p. 40)

Because this principle, the moral law that people may make false promises to obtain loans, is self-defeating when we universalize it, the man has a duty not to act on the principle. That is, he has a duty not to make a false promise to obtain a loan. We cannot hold that people have no duty to repay loans, because if everyone had no duty to repay loans, then the entire financial, banking, and credit system would fail to function. Likewise, business people cannot adopt the universal principle of always lying during negotiations because, if they did, business negotiations would become impossible. Similarly, we have a duty to respect other people's property because we cannot universalize the maxim that it is ethically permissible for us to steal. If we were to hold that it is permissible for anyone to steal, then the basis of the whole institution of private property would collapse.

Kant's theory tells us our ethical duties by asking us to universalize what we think are our duties and see if this leads to some sort of contradiction. Kant's Categorical Imperative looks like rule utilitarianism, but it is not the same. When a rule utilitarian tries to justify a duty, she tries to show that if everyone adheres to the rule, then the consequences will be better overall according to some measure of happiness. When Kant tries to justify a duty, he tries to show that if everyone follows this duty, then the overall consequences will be inconsistent with preserving the institution within which the duty has a place. For example, the duty not to repay loans is, if universalized, inconsistent with preserving the institution of money lending within which the idea of a loan makes sense. He does not need to argue, as the rule utilitarian would, that credit and money lending lead to greater happiness. Kant's view of duties is principle-based rather than consequence-based. Kant endeavours to find principles that are rational in the sense of being universal moral principles that everyone can follow. He is not concerned with producing happy consequences.

The weakness of the Kantian view of duties is that it creates implausible ethical duties in extreme cases. Consider the philosophically famous case of the Truth-teller and the Axe Murderer. Kant's Categorical Imperative tells us that we have an absolute duty to tell the truth. The duty to lie whenever it is convenient to do so is not universalizable, because if everyone were to lie when convenient, then conversation, which depends on people being able to believe other people, would be impossible. Suppose that an Axe Murderer comes to the door of a house looking for his intended victim who is hiding in the attic. He asks the person who answers the door if his intended victim is at home. According to Kant, the person who answers the door has an absolute duty to be a truth-teller and not lie to the Axe Murderer. However, Kant's duty-based theory just seems wrong in this extreme case whereas utilitarian ethical reasoning clearly works better. Lying has much better consequences than does truth telling. Virtue-based ethical reasoning also works better in this case. The Truth-teller appears to suffer from the vices of being overly rigid and inflexible regarding her actions. Kant's Categorical Imperative provides an instructive first pass at discovering our duties, but we must still weigh it against other sorts of ethical reasons.

RIGHTS AND DUTIES

People should be motivated not only to act in accordance with their duties but also to respect the rights of others. Rights and duties relate in the following way. A moral right is a morally justified claim on others. The possession by one person of a moral right creates a duty in others to respect that right, a duty that correlates to that right. If Miguel has a right that Lori does Φ, then Lori has a **correlative duty** to do Φ that she owes to Miguel. It also follows that if Lori owes Miguel a duty to do Φ, then Miguel has a right that Lori do Φ.

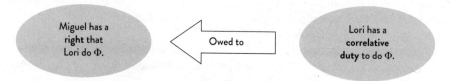

Figure 5.2: Miguel's right against Lori means that Lori has a correlative duty that she owes to Miguel.

The simplest type of right to understand is the sort of specific right created by a contract between two people. A **specific right** is one whose correlative duty only falls on a determinate person or group. If Miguel loans $100 to Lori for 30 days, then the loan contract will give Miguel the right to claim $100 from Lori in 30 days, and impose a correlative duty on Lori to repay the $100 at that time. Only Miguel has this right, and only Lori has the correlative duty to repay Miguel. No other people besides Lori have the duty to repay Miguel. On the other hand, a **general right** is a right whose correlative duty falls on everyone. Like everyone, Miguel has a general right to his life. His right is a general one because everyone, not just Lori, has a correlative duty not to kill Miguel, a duty that everyone owes to him because his life is ethically so important.

Specific rights and duties may arise voluntarily when people make promises and enter into contracts. Specific rights and duties may also arise involuntarily through people's friendships, and family and community memberships. General moral rights are sometimes derivatively justified by non-rights-based ethical theories such as indirect utilitarianism or theories of justice. General moral rights are sometimes justified as natural rights either because they protect people's autonomous choices or because they protect people's crucial interests.

We use the concept of a right in both ethics and law. **Moral rights** are rights that are justified by moral theories. Some moral rights are also legal rights, such as Miguel's right that Lori repay his loan or Miguel's right to life. **Legal rights** are legally enforceable rights. Some moral rights may not be legal rights because they are not legally enforceable under the laws of the applicable legal jurisdiction. For example, if Miguel promises to mow Lori's lawn on the weekend, Lori's moral right that Miguel do what he said he would do will not be a promise that Lori can enforce in the courts.

Rights can be either positive or negative. A **positive right** imposes a duty on others to assist the right bearer in some way. Some examples are the right to disaster relief, the right to an education, the right to unemployment insurance payments, and, in many countries, the right to medical care. One problem with the notion of a positive right is deciding on whom the correlative duties fall. For example, we must determine who has the duty to satisfy the right to an education. We would usually say that the positive right to an education imposes a duty on the state to provide an education for everyone, and that the state must find a fair way to spread the cost of providing education across all its citizens.

A **negative right** imposes a duty on everyone else not to interfere with the right holder's activities. It gives the right bearer a liberty or freedom from the interference of others. Examples include the right to life, which protects each person by imposing a duty on everyone else not to kill him or her, and freedom of expression or freedom of association, which give people freedom from the interference of the government. The existence of negative moral rights is less controversial than the existence of positive rights, because it is easier to see who has the relevant correlative duties. People often suppose that negative rights, like the right to personal security, are on a stronger ethical footing than positive rights, like the right to welfare. However, it is worth noting that a negative right, such as the right to personal security, requires enforcement. The enforcement of the negative right to personal security imposes a duty on others to assist the person whose security is in jeopardy. The enforcement of negative rights requires positive rights, and raises the question of determining who bears the correlative duties. We would usually say that the positive right to the enforcement of a negative right to personal security imposes a duty on the state to protect its citizens, and that the state must find a fair way to spread the cost of protecting personal security across all its citizens.

Negative rights, freedoms, and liberties protect people from interference by others, but rights and freedoms have limits. The Harm Principle that John Stuart Mill first formulated in his book, *On Liberty* (1859), sets these limits.

> ... the sole end for which mankind are warranted, individually or collectively, in interfering with the liberty of action of any of their number, is self-protection. That the only purpose for which power can be rightfully

exercised over any member of a civilised community, against his will, is to prevent harm to others. His own good, either physical or moral, is not a sufficient warrant. (Mill, 1859, p. 18)

The **Harm Principle** says that people (or the government) may interfere with people's freedom, liberty, or exercise of their rights only in order to prevent harm to others. For example, people have a negative right to freedom of movement. This freedom is not absolute or unlimited but may be limited to prevent people from hurting others; so it does not extend to my right to drive my car on the wrong side of the road.

In the law, the criminal law and tort law prevent harmful conduct by legitimately limiting people's liberties. Criminal law aims to punish harmful conduct. Tort law aims to compensate the victims of harmful conduct. Generally, someone who does harm is liable to paying compensation to her victim if her action is faulty and causes the harm to the victim. She is at fault if she owed the victim a duty of care not to harm him and if she broke this duty. She caused the harm to the victim if, but for her actions, there would be no harm to the victim. However, cause and fault are not always required for liability. For example, the law will sometimes hold an employer vicariously liable for harms caused by her employee, even though the employer did not herself cause the harm.

CONTRACTUAL RIGHTS AND PROMISES

Contractual rights and property rights are common types of rights in the business world. In this section we will examine the structure of contractual rights. We all occupy nodes in a network of legal contracts. For example, we enter into a sales contract whenever we shop and the sales clerk hands us our groceries in return for our credit card number. In the business world, this network of legal contracts becomes much larger. Businesses work through production and exchange, and contracts govern all of this. This new network of business contracts adds to our network of personal contracts, but it does not replace the old one, just as going to work does not absolve us from paying our personal credit card bills.

It is important to understand the structure of legal contracts. A legal **contract** is composed of two legally enforceable promises. The first party makes an offer, which is a legally enforceable promise to supply some good or service, X, in return for fulfilment of some condition, Y. The second party indicates acceptance, which is a legally enforceable promise to fulfil condition Y. A legal contract consists in a legally enforceable offer plus a legally enforceable acceptance. Legal contracts create two specific, legal rights. These rights are legal rights because they are right enforceable by the legal system, and they are specific rights because they affect only the parties to the contract. The first party now has a specific legal right that the second party fulfil condition Y, and the second party has a specific legal right that the first party supply good or service X. For example, a contract between Lori and Miguel might start with Lori offering to loan Miguel $100 on condition that Miguel repay her $110 in one year's time. The contract comes into existence when Miguel accepts by promising to repay Lori.

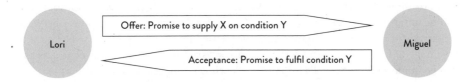

Figure 5.3: A contract between Lori and Miguel consists of two promises. Lori offers to supply $100 (X) on condition (Y) that Miguel repays her $110 one year later. Miguel accepts by promising to fulfil the condition (Y) that he will repay Lori $110 one year later.

A promise is a pledge to someone to supply some good or service. An ethically permissible promise creates a moral duty and a moral right. The promisor has a moral duty that he owes to the promisee to fulfil his promise. The promisee has a right against the promisor that the promisor fulfil his promise. Since forming a contract involves an offer and an acceptance between two parties, and since offers and acceptances are promises, forming a contract is an ethical action as well as a legal action. Of course, many ethically binding promises are not legally binding, so not all promises create legal contracts. On the other hand, all legal contracts involve promises that we must evaluate from an ethical perspective. If an offer and acceptance are both ethically permissible, then the contract creates two specific, moral rights. Contracts that are not ethically permissible are either morally void or immoral. For example, a contract where one party deceives the other into acceptance will be both legally and morally void. A promise induced by deception is not an ethically binding promise, which means that the contract is not ethically binding. Likewise, a promise to commit murder would not only be morally void, but also immoral.

Promises have an ethical dimension. We can see this by applying the framework of ethical pluralism to our obligation to keep promises. As we have just seen, Kant would argue that we have a duty to keep promises because if we tried to make the principle of not keeping promises into a universal principle, then we will destroy the whole institution of promising. To fail to keep a promise, is to deceive another person and undermines their ability to make authentic and autonomous choices. Persons concerned only with their own self-interest might still keep promises in order to avoid prisoner's dilemma type situations. From the perspective of virtue ethics, we should keep promises because we should develop an honest, truthful character. Promises are involved in building good, trusting relationships and therefore we should keep promises according to a feminist ethics of care. Indirect utilitarians argue that if everyone kept their promises, then everyone would be better off than if people did not. Direct utilitarians, on the other hand, recommend keeping promises only if the net benefits of keeping the promise outweigh the net benefits of breaking it.

Because business contracts involve promises, and promises are subject to ethical valuation, then business ethics must examine business contracts critically. Business contracts can be unconscionable if one party benefits unreasonably at the expense of the other, or if one party exercises undue influence over the other. Business contracts can also be unfair if there are unreasonably large differences in bargaining power between the parties or if there is a situation of asymmetric information, where one party takes advantage of having information that the other party does not. Business contracts can also be immoral if they involve promises to perform wrongful actions, such as stealing.

Joint stock corporations have the legal capacity to make contracts, but must make them through their agents. An agent is a person whom a second party, the principal, authorizes to make contracts between the principal and third parties. For example, a storeowner may authorize her sales staff to enter her store into sales contracts with customers. The officers of a joint stock corporation can bring the corporation, which is a legal person but not an actual person, into contractual relations with suppliers, customers, and employees. An incorporated business is not a tangible thing, like a factory, nor is it a human person. It is an intangible thing, a nexus of contracts and other legal interests.

Agents may make contracts that are binding on their principals, but not just any contracts. Agents owe their principals **fiduciary duties**—that is, duties to act for the benefit of their principals and to put the interests of their principals ahead of the interests of themselves and others. People usually create agency relationships by contract. For example, a principal might contract with an agent to sell the principal's goods on consignment. Agency relationships can also arise within a contract of employment. Some employees are also their employer's agents and some are not. The CEO can enter into contracts with suppliers on behalf of the corporation that employs her, whereas the janitor cannot. An agency relationship may sometimes exist without any explicit contract. This happens when third parties might reasonably expect that a putative agent can make contracts binding on the principal, and where the principal has not explicitly repudiated this relationship. For example, third parties may reasonably expect that two married people are able to make contracts on behalf of one another.

Another familiar contract is the contract of employment. Employment contracts can be very complete when they explicitly include all details of the offer and the conditions of acceptance. Employment contracts can also be incomplete, with many details of the contract left unspecified. Government regulations will partially govern the content of an employment contract. In law, the employee owes a duty of loyalty to the employer. This duty of loyalty is not the virtue, or character trait, of loyalty. Instead, it is a legal term meant to indicate a legal duty that includes both the duty to obey the employer and the duty not to harm the employer's interests. As in other contracts, mutual promises create specific moral, as well as legal, rights between employer and the employee.

PROPERTY RIGHTS

The other major type of moral rights that emerge in business transactions are property rights. Property rights are general moral and legal rights, not specific contractual rights, because they involve everyone owing duties to the property owner. These duties are mostly duties not to interfere with the owner possessing, managing, and benefiting from her property, so property rights are mostly negative rights.

When we think of owning personal property, like a toothbrush, ownership appears to be a very simple concept. However, the concept of ownership is actually very complex and abstract. We can own not only tangible objects like toothbrushes, cars, houses, and factories, but also intangibles such as stock in a company or even contracts. People can buy and sell many contracts in the same way that they can buy and sell machinery and factories. For example, a lender can sell a loan contract to a debt collector. Purchasing contracts, customer contracts, and employment contracts can transfer the new owners when the old original contractors sell their business.

Ownership is also complex because there is not such thing as a unitary private property right. **Ownership** of a tangible or intangible thing consists in a bundle of rights and liabilities. In simple cases, such as ownership of a lawnmower, all of these rights and liabilities go together in what appears to be a single property right of the lawnmower owner. The lawnmower owner has the right to manage how the mower is used, and to receive any income that he earns from using it to mow other people's lawns. Yet, in many important cases, different parties split the bundle of rights between themselves. For example, in ownership by a trust, the beneficiary of the trust has the right to receive the income generated by the trust assets, but the trustee has the right to manage these assets.

The legal scholar, A.M. Honoré, identified eleven types of rights and liabilities in the bundle that would constitute full, unshared ownership of a tangible or intangible thing. (Honoré, 1961, pp. 107–47) We shall list the components of this bundle of rights and liabilities to give a sense of just how complicated ownership really is.

#	Legal Rights or Liabilities
1	Rights to possess
2	Rights to use
3	Rights to manage
4	Rights to the income
5	Rights to the capital
6	Rights to security
7	Rights to bequest
8	Rights to absence of term
9	Liabilities under tort law
10	Liabilities to execution for debt
11	Rights to residue after termination

Table 5.1: Components of the bundle of rights and liabilities that is full, unshared ownership.

The first components of the bundle are rights to possess or be in physical control of a thing. Second are rights to use and enjoy the thing. Third are rights to manage the thing, to decide whom will use the thing, and how, and when. Fourth are rights to receive any income, such as rent or profit, which the thing generates. Fifth are rights to the capital, which include the right to consume, destroy, or sell the thing. Sixth are rights to security, which are rights not to have others take away or expropriate the thing. Seventh are rights to bequeath the thing to someone else after death. Eighth are rights to the absence of term, which include rights of an owner, as opposed to a renter, not to have the other rights cease at any particular date. Ninth are liabilities under tort law to compensate victims of the harmful use of the thing. Tenth are liabilities of the owner to lose the other rights if the legal system seizes some rights in the thing for repayment of the owner's debts. Eleventh are residuary rights always to receive back any temporarily transferred rights such as, for example, the right to recover possession when a lease expires.

The most common form of business organization, the joint-stock company, is an important example of the complexity and divisibility of ownership. A stockholder does not own any tangible things like machinery or warehouses. Instead, she has a marketable right to an intangible, a share of only some components of the whole bundle of rights and liabilities over the tangible and intangible assets of the company. She does not have the right to possess, use, or sell any of the company's assets. Her management rights are limited to a vote at the company's annual general meeting. She has a right to a defined share of any income the company may generate. In addition, the law limits her liability for the debts of the company to the value of her stock. The managers of the corporation hold the other components of the bundle of rights over the company's assets. Managers buy and sell the assets of the company and decide how to employ the assets of the company in the interests of the stockholders and other stakeholders.

Property rights are moral rights that need ethical justifications. Philosophers have offered a plurality of ethical justifications. Some, such as the eighteenth-century English philosopher, John Locke, argue that property rights are natural rights initially acquired through labour on the un-owned world. Indirect economic utilitarianism justifies a system of property rights by the success of the capitalist economic system in delivering maximum overall prosperity and welfare. Various theories of justice distribute property rights according to criteria of fairness and equal treatment. We will look at some of these theories of justice in the next chapter.

We now have a better view of the moral network which businesspeople inhabit. Overlaying their personal moral network of family, friendship, and community obligations is another network of contracts and ownership rights. Specific rights and duties regarding owners, customers, suppliers, governments, and other employees have an ethical foundation in the explicit promises that ground contracts. Specific duties also have an ethical foundation in the implicit expectations of owners, suppliers, governments, the local community, and other employees that arise from a person's role in the firm. General rights regarding the assets of owners, customers, suppliers, governments, the local community, and other employees have an ethical foundation in the just distribution of bundles of property rights. The ethical aspect of the world of business can be extremely complex.

SUMMARY

1. The ethical assessment of a business decision requires examining the motivations of the decision-makers as well as the consequences of the decision and the character of the decision-maker. Someone can make a decision with good consequences for bad reasons, or a decision with bad consequences for good reasons.
2. Good ethical motivations include applying moral principles, fulfilling ethical duties, respecting moral rights, and treating others fairly.
3. Kant thought that all rational agents have a duty not to perform an action if the universal moral principle that everyone may perform the action is self-defeating. For example, we have a duty not to break promises because if it were ethically permissible for everyone to break promises, then the whole activity of promising would be undermined and would cease to exist.
4. Someone's moral right always correlates with a duty owed to him by either some specific person, or by everyone in general.
5. A positive right imposes a duty on others to provide aid, while a negative right imposes a duty on others not to interfere.
6. The harm principle, which is a general obligation not to harm others, puts limits on the extent of people's negative rights.
7. Contractual rights are specific rights that are created by two interrelated promises: an offer and an acceptance. Most business transactions involve contracts, and contracts involve the ethical duties of promise keeping.
8. Ownership is not a unitary right. Instead, it involves a bundle of rights and liabilities in either tangible or intangible things. Different components of the bundle may belong to different persons, as in the separation of management and stockholding in business corporations.

ONLINE LEARNING RESOURCES

You will find a collection of learning resources associated with this chapter on the book's website: http://sites.broadviewpress.com/businessethics/. Working through this material will help you understand and remember important concepts that we have discussed, and will help you apply them to issues in business ethics.

STUDY QUESTIONS

Answering the following questions will help you to understand the ethical theory in this chapter and will help you to create a set of review notes on the textbook.

1. Give an example of a decision with good consequences, but made for bad reasons. Give an example of a decision with bad consequences, but made for good reasons.

2. How could Kant use the Categorical Imperative to argue that we have reciprocal duties to help our friends?
3. What is the conceptual relationship between rights and duties?
4. Why are property rights negative general rights while rights to the enforcement of property rights are positive general rights?
5. Someone cries "Fire!" in a crowded cinema that is not on fire. Why is punishing her not an infringement of her freedom of expression?
6. S&S Builders contract to renovate Ann's house next month in return for $50,000.00 plus tax. What is the offer promise? What is the acceptance promise? What are the specific contractual rights that come into existence at the time of acceptance?
7. Explain what it means to say that ownership is a bundle of rights and liabilities.

DECISION QUESTIONS

The whole point of learning ethical theory is to understand and ask questions like the following when you are analyzing an ethically problematic situation or case.

- What are the decision-maker's motives?
- Are the decision-maker's motives in accordance with justified ethical principles?
- What duties should the decision-maker fulfil?
- Can everyone consistently fulfil these duties?
- Is the decision-maker treating anyone as a means rather than an end?
- Does the decision-maker have any correlative duties arising from the general rights of others?
- Does the decision-maker have any general rights that others must respect?
- Does an obligation not to harm others limit the decision-maker's liberty of action?
- Does the decision-maker have any correlative duties arising from the specific rights of others?
- Do any promises arise from contracts involving offers and acceptances?
- Are these legal contracts ethically free and fair?
- Do any promises arise from customary expectations and practices?
- Would the decision to respect rights lead to unjust distributions or to utility reductions?

CASE STUDY

Analyze this case study using the ethical theory that you have learned so far. You will find a collection of learning materials applying to the case on the book's website: http://sites.broadviewpress.com/businessethics/. These materials will help you in your analysis.

Should Eve Reveal Trade Secrets?

Two months ago, Eve Duplessis left her job as an information technology professional at Banana Co. to take a similar, but better paying, job at Orange Co. Both Banana and Orange are huge corporations producing wireless mobile devices for consumers around the world. Her employment contract with Orange obliges her to use all her skills and knowledge in the service of improving Orange's products. Her employment contract at Banana contained a clause obliging her not to reveal any of Banana's commercial information, processes, and techniques to anyone else for one year after the end of her contract with Banana.

Banana treated Eve very well, and she has many friends who still work there. Some days she regrets her move to Orange, despite the higher salary, because the tenor of the workplace at Orange is more competitive and less cooperative than it was at Banana, and managers at Orange seem to have little empathy for their subordinates. She is finding it difficult to make friends at Orange, even among the members of her project team.

Orange has assigned Eve to a project that is developing a more efficient way for Orange's devices to connect to the correct signal from a cellular network. As Eve gets up to speed on the project, she realizes that engineers at Banana had solved a similar problem by applying the Kalashnikova algorithm to the signal selection. The Kalashnikova algorithm is in the public domain, but the technique of using it to speed up cellular connections took a large team of engineers at Banana half a year to develop.

Eve also realizes that she could significantly contribute to her project at Orange if she were to point out to her development team how to use the Kalashnikova algorithm in its new design. Making this contribution would be a big boost to her career at Orange, and put her in line for promotion to team leader next year. She would not have to reveal that she learned the technique at Banana Co. because Orange engineers have been unable to reverse engineer the Banana design.

Both Banana and Orange have gigantic and expensive legal teams who are in continuous legal battle with one another. The two legal teams try to protect the intellectual property of their respective firms from what they deem to be the other firm's infringements. Eve does not think that making this suggestion to her team will get her in any legal trouble, but she would have lots of legal backup if it did. She also doubts that Banana will be able to reverse engineer Orange's solution to discover that Orange uses the technique, let alone when Orange started using it, or that she, Eve, was the one who suggested using it.

What should Eve do?

Chapter 6

FAIRNESS AND DISTRIBUTIVE JUSTICE

How should we treat people in order to treat them fairly?

What does an ethically justifiable distribution of income look like?

When does justice require us to respect people's property rights?

In 2012, the average CEO of a corporation listed on the S&P 500 index received a total compensation of about 12 million dollars, which was 354 times as much as the yearly salary of an average US worker. (AFL-CIO, 2013) This 354:1 ratio rose from a ratio of only 42:1 in 1980. (Institute for Policy Studies, 2012) Table 6.1 shows the situation in other countries around the world.

Country	Stock index	Average CEO compensation	Average worker compensation	Pay ratio CEO:worker
USA	S&P 500	$12,259,894	$34,645	354:1
Canada	TSX 60	$8,704,118	$42,253	206:1
Australia	ASX 100	$4,183,419	$44,983	93:1
UK	FTSE 100	$3,758,412	$44,743	84:1
Japan	Nikkei 225	$2,354,581	$35,143	67:1
Norway	OBX	$2,551,420	$43,990	58:1

Table 6.1: CEO-to-worker pay ratios in selected countries 2012. (AFL-CIO, 2013)

Is this situation fair? Arguments about the fairness of executive compensation are the concerns of distributive justice. Principles of distributive justice are ways of treating people as moral equals. Treating people as moral equals, however, does not mean treating everyone the same. Sometimes there are good moral reasons why some people should have more than others have.

Some argue that CEOs of large corporations deserve higher compensation relative to workers because of their higher productivity; the CEO makes a much larger contribution to the firm's output than does the worker. Because everyone has an equal opportunity to compete for CEO positions, the system gives equal treatment to both those who become CEOs and those who become workers. As we shall see, however, there are problems measuring individual contributions to corporate output.

Others base their argument on the moral justification of the free-market. The free-market system is fair because it respects everyone's property rights equally. Very able individuals own their talents and their time, and they are entitled to sell their talents and time for whatever other people are willing to pay for them. If the pay of those who become CEOs is higher than the pay of those who work on the shop floor, then this is fair. As we shall see, however, there are problems with this Libertarian theory of ownership.

Others offer a utilitarian argument, claiming that the free-market system is the most efficient way to produce and distribute goods and services, and that maximizing the production of goods and services will maximize human welfare. Even though the free-market offers higher compensation to those who become CEOs than to those who become workers, the market still maximizes total human welfare. Because a utilitarian argument weights everyone's interests by the same factor, it considers everyone's interests equally. As we shall see, however, there is another way of thinking about utilitarian justice that argues for equal compensation for everyone.

Yet others might offer an argument based, surprisingly, on the idea that everyone should have an equal share of society's resources. They would argue that giving incentives to the talented to work extra hard will increase the total amount of goods and services produced by the economy. Because there will be more economic goods to go round, even the least well off will be better off than they would have been if everyone had received a strictly equal share. This argument still treats everyone as moral equals in the distribution of resources, even though it does not treat everyone in the same way. However, this argument only works if there is some system of redistributive taxation in place that ensures the least well off do benefit.

In this chapter, we will examine these sorts of arguments about justice. Ethical reasoning about distributive justice is very complex. We will survey some of the approaches and issues that are relevant to business decision-making.

THE MORAL EQUALITY OF PERSONS

We treat people fairly by not favouring one person over another for arbitrary reasons. Business firms treat customers, suppliers, owners, and employees fairly by giving them equal treatment. Justice requires that we treat people as moral equals, yet justice does not require that we treat everyone exactly the same way. What moral equality requires is that governments, business firms, and individuals do not treat people differently based on morally arbitrary features. Race, sex, age, religious preference, sexual orientation, and family background are morally arbitrary features of people. At the most basic level, justice requires that we not favour one person over another based on such features. Paradigm examples of injustice include aristocratic societies, where positions in society go to those who are born to privileged parents, and caste societies, where people are born into their positions in society and coerced into staying there for religious reasons.

On the other hand, treating people as equals requires that we also recognize morally relevant differences between people. Society treats disabled people equally by treating them differently when it gives disabled people reserved, convenient parking spaces. Businesses reward workers who put in more effort. Society allows only women to take pregnancy leave, and requires that high earners pay income tax at a higher rate than low earners do. Justice is not as simple as treating everyone in the same way.

Ethics commonly deals with three types of justice. Corrective or **retributive justice** ensures that society holds people accountable for harming others or violating their rights. **Compensatory justice** ensures that people who infringe the rights of others without consent fairly recompense those who they harm. **Distributive justice** ensures that society allocates benefits and burdens in a way that treats people as moral equals. A theory of distributive justice does not actually take physical economic goods or services and pass them around. Rather it justifies a particular system of legal rights regarding economic goods and services. Distributive justice criticizes or justifies schemes of property rights, such as the legal rights to possess or sell economic goods and productive resources. This chapter will focus on theories of distributive justice.

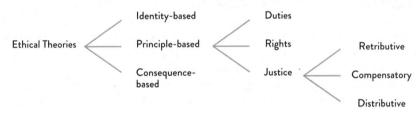

Figure 6.1: A conceptual map locating the different types of justice.

Distributive justice involves treating people as moral equals when assigning property rights to economic goods and services. However, different theories of distributive justice interpret the moral equality of persons in different ways. One theoretical approach understands moral equality as requiring no more than giving everyone an equal opportunity to compete for ownership of resources. A second approach, the libertarian view, understands moral equality as requiring equal respect for the natural rights of persons to acquire and exchange private property. A third approach, based on a utilitarian concern for human welfare, understands moral equality as requiring giving equal consideration to the welfare interests of every person. A fourth approach understands moral equality as requiring that we employ a principle of equality in directly assigning property rights in resources. Figure 6.2 gives a conceptual map of the various theoretical approaches to treating people as moral equals, and shows the issues of distributive justice to which each approach gives rise.

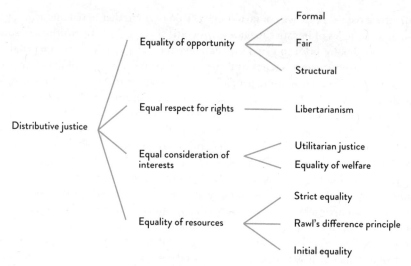

Figure 6.2: A conceptual map of the various approaches to treating people as moral equals, and the issues of distributive justice that these approaches raise.

EQUALITY OF OPPORTUNITY: FAIRNESS

Equality of opportunity says that a distribution is just if, and only if, it assigns positions in society according to morally relevant criteria such as ability or merit and not according to morally arbitrary criteria such as race or gender.

However, there are several different conceptions of the nature of equality of opportunity. **Formal equality of opportunity** requires that there be no legal impediment to a person with certain talents competing for a position that requires those talents. People should get the position they deserve based on ability and past performance, and no organization should deny them these positions because of their race or gender. Business decisions often employ this conception of equality regarding employees, suppliers, and customers.

From the point of view of the moral equality of persons, the weakness of formal equality of opportunity is that morally irrelevant factors often determine people's talents. People's family background, their luck in the genetic lottery for intellectual ability, and their receipt of a good education often determine the talents with which they compete for positions. Factors that are arbitrary from a moral point of view often determine people's abilities, their willingness to exert an effort, and their productivity in society. Even though formal, legal considerations do not block them from the opportunity to obtain positions, their level of talent does. If morally arbitrary factors, such as the social class from which they come, determine their level of talent, then the distribution of positions will still be unjust.

Fair equality of opportunity tries to rectify this weakness of formal equality of opportunity by requiring that society make a special effort to provide high quality education to those who would otherwise receive a poor education. **Fair equality of opportunity** requires both that there be formal equality of opportunity and that society provide a uniform quality of education for all to give everyone a fair chance to acquire the skills needed to compete for social positions. Unfortunately, it is difficult for education to compensate for bad luck in the genetic lottery for innate abilities. Fair equality is also not something that a single business firm can easily implement; it is something that only the whole society can create.

Feminists have pointed out that, even under conditions of fair equality of opportunity, there may still be structural inequality of opportunity. One example of the structural inequality of opportunity is that many positions in business and government are not really positions that people responsible for the care of small children can fill. Even if there are no legal impediments to a caregiver applying for the position, and even if these potential applicants are well trained and educated, the nature of the position and the demands it makes on the occupant's time, may mean that caregivers cannot fill the position.

Structural equality of opportunity requires that organizations design positions in such a way that persons doing the necessary work of society, such as those responsible for the care of young children, can still fill those positions. Structural equality of opportunity is something that businesses can implement in the design of jobs and in the provision of services such as daycare.

EQUALITY OF OPPORTUNITY: MEASURING CONTRIBUTION

Equality of opportunity in its various forms is not yet a theory of distributive justice. It removes various types of impediments to people applying for positions, but it does not say anything about what is the appropriate compensation for various positions. How should organizations distribute benefits to positions? The usual answer is that compensation should correspond to marginal productivity, or the marginal contribution that a person in this position makes to the firm. The CEO arguably makes a larger contribution to the profitability of a firm than does the janitor, and so her compensation should be correspondingly larger.

The problem with using marginal productivity to determine compensation is that we cannot easily measure marginal productivity, and when we can it will often appear unfair as a gauge to compensation. In the modern world, production is seldom carried out by a solitary artisan, but is instead the joint product of many people working together. It is through specialization and the division of labour that large firms are able to achieve high levels of productivity. Adam Smith pointed this out in his example of the pin factory, and all introductory economics textbooks reiterate Smith's point. As we saw in an earlier chapter, Smith claimed that a solitary pin maker could scarcely produce 20 pins a day, but that 10 specialists working together in a factory setting could produce around 48,000 pins per day. (Adam Smith, *The Wealth of Nations*, 1776, I.1.3) The increased productivity of the factory arose from specialization, and the organized division of labour. However, there is no obvious way to attribute the increased productivity to the individual workers.

Nor does marginal productivity reasoning work in a model where just two workers cooperate. Together, as we saw, Jack and Jill produce 90 pins per day. Without Jill, Jack can produce only 9 pins per day. Jill's additional contribution to the factory appears to be 81 pins. (90 - 9 = 81) Therefore, if we distribute ownership of the pins according to marginal contribution, then Jill should receive 81 pins. On the other hand, without Jack, Jill can produce only 9 pins per day. Therefore, if we distribute ownership of the pins according to marginal contribution, then Jack should receive 81 pins. Unfortunately, their total entitlements, which are 81 + 81 = 162 pins, exceed their total production of 90 pins. This will not work. In joint production, marginal contributions are likely to exceed the total production of the firm.

Economists would think about marginal contribution financially, as the marginal revenue generated by the employee minus any marginal costs, other than salary, of adding the employee. Because of the law of diminishing marginal returns, in the short term, with a fixed supply of other factors of production besides labour, a firm's marginal revenue from an additional employee will decrease as it adds new employees. At the same time, the supply curve for the labour market will ensure that the marginal cost of each additional employee will gradually rise.

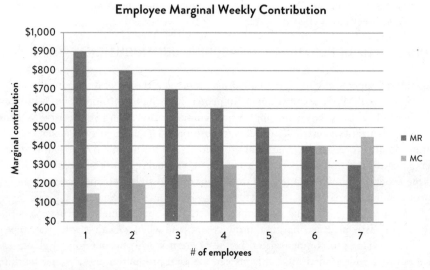

Figure 6.3: Weekly marginal contribution of additional employees in a firm.

For employees all doing the same work, the situation for a small firm will look like the model in Figure 6.3. The marginal contribution of each employee is the difference between MR, the marginal revenue generated by the worker, and MC, the marginal cost other than salary of employing the worker. A firm seeking to maximize profit will keep adding employees until the additional cost of employing a worker (MC) exceeds the additional revenue (MR) she generates. In this example, the firm will hire 6 workers.

This marginal financial contribution method of determining the appropriate level of compensation for positions also has a major weakness. By hypothesis, all of the workers are doing the same work, yet the method attributes to the employee designated as employee #1, perhaps the first one hired, marginal contribution of $900 - $150 = $750, and attributes to the employee designated as #2 a marginal contribution of $800 - $200 = $600, and so on. Compensation for identical work will be different, and will depend on the order in which the employees are hired. Paying people different wages based on the order in which they are hired is arbitrary from a moral point of view. It results in unequal pay for equal work. This would be unacceptable to the employees, and goes against our intuitions regarding distributive justice.

These models show how difficult it is to measure the contribution of a worker or a CEO to the total output of the firm. Yet if we do not have a plausible way of measuring contribution, then it appears that we need further arguments for why it is fair for a CEO to receive 354 times the compensation of the average worker.

EQUAL RESPECT FOR RIGHTS: LIBERTARIANISM

Libertarianism holds that a distribution of rights and responsibilities is just if, and only if, it respects people's natural rights to self-ownership. Libertarian political theory attempts to justify a system of unrestricted private property rights by tracking property rights back to a natural feature of human beings, their capacity for autonomous choice. The moral rights that protect the capacity for autonomy are the negative rights of self-ownership. Self-owners are the opposite of slaves. Self-owners have the maximum possible liberty compatible with other people having the same. In particular, self-owners have the right to manage and sell their own labour.

A libertarian system of property rights entails a minimally regulated, free enterprise economic system. A libertarian argument for justifying a system of private property rights and a free market economy goes as follows: All people have a natural right of self-ownership to their own labour. When people labour on things that are un-owned, they come to own them, so long as they leave enough of the un-owned things for others. Therefore, people have a natural right to things acquired in this way. Their property rights in these things include the right to give, sell, or trade them with others. Therefore, people have a natural right to any property that they have acquired either by initial acquisition or by just transfer from others.

The premise in this argument regarding the initial acquisition of property comes from the influential writings of the seventeenth-century English philosopher, John Locke (1632–1704). He formulated his theory in the following passage.

> Though the earth, and all inferior creatures, be common to all men, yet every man has a property in his own person: this no body has any right to but himself. The labour of his body, and the work of his hands, we may say, are properly his. Whatsoever then he removes out of the state that

nature hath provided, and left it in, he hath mixed his labour with, and joined to it something that is his own, and thereby makes it his property. It being by him removed from the common state nature hath placed it in, it hath by this labour something annexed to it, that excludes the common right of other men: for this labour being the unquestionable property of the labourer, no man but he can have a right to what that is once joined to, at least where there is enough, and as good, left in common for others. (Locke, 1689, Chapter 2, Section 27)

The notion of mixing self-owned labour with un-owned nature to create a privately owned economic good is a weak metaphor. Someone who pours his can of beer in the ocean and thereby mixes something he owns with something that is un-owned, does not gain ownership of the ocean. (Nozick, 1974, pp. 174–75) One libertarian response is to shift focus from the mixing metaphor to the idea of adding value. The new argument instead claims that, by her labour, the initial appropriator adds value to natural objects and thereby deserves to own these modified natural objects. The argument then makes the factual claim that, because of the productive efficiency of property-based economic systems, some of this value will accrue to those who missed the initial appropriation, leaving them better off than they would have been in a state of un-owned nature. Thus, the value added approach satisfies the requirement that enough, and as good, be left in common.

Nozick's reconstruction of Locke's argument goes like this: All people have equal natural rights of self-ownership to their labour. People who add value to something un-owned, thereby come to own it, as long as this process leaves others at least as well off as they were before this initial acquisition. Therefore, people have a natural right to their initially acquired property. This property right includes the right to give, sell, or trade with others. Therefore, people have a natural right to any property that they have acquired either by initial acquisition or by just transfer from others. Property rights are distributed justly only when they are acquired in these two ways. Libertarian justice gives equal respect to everyone's rights to their own labour and to their private property. However, it justifies an unrestricted capitalist economic system in which some people can receive large incomes while others have very little.

It seems to follow from libertarianism that the CEO of a large firm, who owns her talents and skills, is justified in receiving from her company whatever compensation she can negotiate with the company's board of directors. The company freely contracts with her for her services and she is entitled to charge what the market will bear. However, her compensation is fair and just only if the company's ownership of the resources that it transfers to her is fair and just. Libertarianism is a historical theory of justice, so it requires tracking down the title to each piece of private property to see if its present owner acquired it through a series of fair transactions from a fair act of initial acquisition centuries ago. For example, Locke's model for initial acquisition was the European appropriation of North America in the seventeenth century. Most land titles in North America will track to theft from Native Americans and most land titles in Europe will track to acts of conquest.

Therefore, in order to justify huge levels of executive compensation, the libertarian must trace how the company's shareholders acquired their assets either by adding value to something un-owned or by freely contracting with someone who did so. This is a daunting task. It is especially daunting because, as Adam Smith pointed out, the source of most value added is specialization and the division of labour, not individual labour. Attributing value added to the labour of a particular individual is mostly impossible. Yet, if libertarianism is to justify huge disparities in compensation, then it must be able to justify long chains of individual acquisition and transfer.

EQUAL CONSIDERATION OF INTERESTS

Utilitarianism is the ethical theory that people and organizations should bring the best consequences judged in terms of the sorts of mental states that they bring about in others. Having positive mental states, like pleasure or preference satisfaction, is always in a person's interest. Utilitarianism implicitly treats people as moral equals because it considers everyone's interests equally. For example, it does not weight the interests of men higher than the interests of women when it comes to maximizing human welfare. Its implicit theory of equality is equal consideration of interests. **Equal consideration of interests** holds that a distribution is just if, and only if, it assigns the same weight to everyone's interests in the aggregation of interests for purposes of utilitarian maximization.

Equal consideration of interests, however, does not imply any sort of equal distribution of resources. We have seen before the potential conflict between the maximizing concerns of direct utilitarianism and the fairness concerns of distributive justice. For the direct utilitarian, if an action that leads to the impoverishment of a minority happens to create the most happiness, then it is the action that a person should perform.

Indirect utilitarianism does not try to maximize welfare in each decision, but instead advocates whatever policies are necessary to produce maximum aggregate utility, including obedience to rules, respect for rights, or a system of distributive justice. It turns out that indirect utilitarianism has the potential to imply a theory of distributive justice in which everyone receives an equal income. An **indirect utilitarian theory of justice** claims that equal consideration of interests will lead to equality of resources because of the diminishing marginal utility of income.

Financial income is an all-purpose economic resource that people can use to purchase the goods and services that satisfy their preferences and bring them well-being. Utility is an abstract measure of people's well-being. The **total utility** of a group of economic goods or services is the sum of all the utility produced by the consumption of those goods or services. The **marginal utility** of an economic good or service is the additional utility gained through the consumption of one additional unit of that good or service. In economics, the **law of diminishing marginal utility** states that as the consumption of a given economic good increases, the marginal utility produced by the consumption of one additional unit of the good tends to decrease. For example, as someone consumes more and more candies, the total pleasure or utility that she receives from each candy will rise, but at a diminishing rate. Table 6.2 shows a simple model of this situation.

# of candies	0		1		2		3		4
Total Utility (TU) in utiles	0		3		5		6		6
Marginal Utility (MU) in utiles		+3		+2		+1		+0	

Table 6.2: Diminishing marginal utility of candy consumption.

We can see the same information if we graph this person's total utility as a function of her candy consumption.

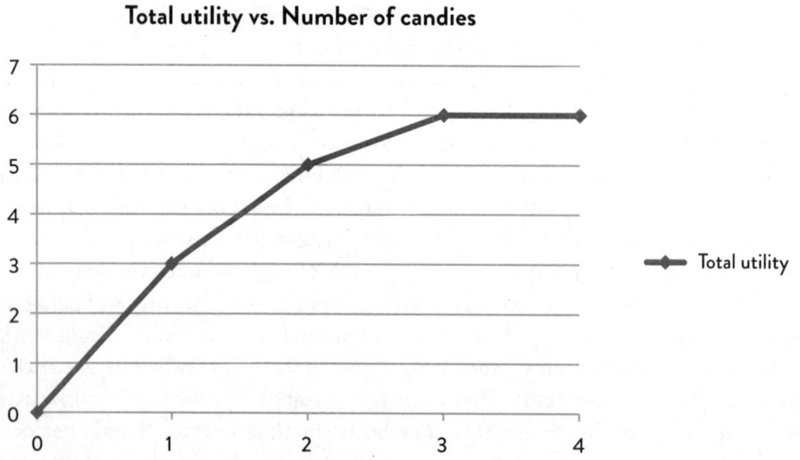

Total utility vs. Number of candies

Figure 6.4: Graph showing the diminishing marginal utility of candy consumption with total utility on the vertical axis and number of candies on the horizontal axis. Each additional candy brings the person less and less utility.

In general, poorer people get more satisfaction out of an extra dollar than do rich people. Therefore, we can maximize satisfaction by redistributing dollars from the rich to the poor. An indirect utilitarian can argue that, because it maximizes total utility, equal weighting of everyone's utilities, together with the diminishing marginal utility of income, leads to an equal distribution.

For example, suppose that we have 4 candies to distribute between Ann and Bob. Both Ann and Bob get the same utility from each candy, and both of their utility schedules are the one in Table 6.2 and graphed in Figure 6.4. Suppose we distribute 3 candies to Ann and 1 candy to Bob. From Table 6.2, we can see that Ann will get 6 utiles from her 3 candies and Bob will get 3 utiles from his 1 candy. The aggregate utility for everyone in this simple model will be 6 + 3 = 9 utiles. This is the case in the second line of Table 6.3.

Ann's #	Bob's #	Ann's TU	Bob's TU	Aggregate utility
4	0	6	0	6 + 0 = 6
3	1	6	3	6 + 3 = 9
2	2	5	5	5 + 5 = 10
1	3	3	6	3 + 6 = 9
0	4	0	6	0 + 6 = 6

Table 6.3: When Bob and Ann get the same utility from each candy, an equal distribution of candies will maximize aggregate utility.

Looking through Table 6.3, we can see that an equal distribution of 2 candies to each of Ann and Bob maximizes the total aggregate utility. We could predict this from the declining marginal utility of resources and incomes. Anything but an equal distribution will give one person more candy than the other has. The person who has less candies will receive more utility through the return to an equal distribution than will the person who has more candies will lose in the process. For example, the utility that the poorer person gains from moving from 1 candy to 2 candies will be greater than the utility that the richer loses in moving from 3 candies to 2 candies.

The indirect utilitarian argument for equal distributive shares assumes that all parties get the same utility from resources. The argument breaks down if one party gets more utility from income or other resources than other parties do. Suppose in our model that Bob gets 3 times more utility from a candy than Ann does. For example, if 1 candy gives Ann 3 utiles, then 1 candy will give Bob 9 utiles. Table 6.4 shows what happens.

Ann's #	Bob's #	Ann's TU	Bob's TU	Aggregate utility
4	0	6	3 x 0 = 0	6 + 0 = 6
3	1	6	3 x 3 = 9	6 + 9 = 15
2	2	5	5 x 5 = 15	5 + 15 = 20
1	3	3	3 x 6 = 18	3+ 18 = 21
0	4	0	3 x 6 = 18	0 + 18 = 18

Table 6.4: When Bob gets 3 times more utility from a candy than Ann does, an equal distribution of candies no longer maximizes aggregate utility.

Utility is maximized in the model in Table 6.4 when Ann gets 1 candy and Bob gets 3 candies. We can maximize utility by giving more candies to Bob, who is more efficient at turning candies into pleasure. An equal distribution of candies no longer maximizes aggregate utility. An indirect utilitarian theory of distributive justice would imply the value of equality if everyone turned resources into welfare in the same way. Because this assumption is implausible, the indirect utilitarian theory of distributive justice is not a viable theory for those who think that equality is very important.

A utilitarian could defend high levels of executive compensation by trying to establish that high executive compensation leads to economic efficiency and thus higher happiness for all. Even if such an economic fact could be established, this utilitarian consideration would have to be balanced against distributive justice considerations.

EQUALITY OF WELFARE

Interpreting the equal consideration of interests in the indirect utilitarian way is unsatisfactory. Another way to consider everyone's welfare interests equally is to argue that everyone should get an equal level of happiness or preference satisfaction. **Equality of welfare** holds that a distribution of property rights in resources is just if, and only if, it results in everyone having the same level of welfare. Equality of welfare is different from indirect utilitarian justice because it says nothing about maximizing total welfare. It does not say just that we should weight everyone's welfare interests equally in a utilitarian calculation. Instead, it makes the stronger claim that we should satisfy everyone's welfare interests to the same degree. Equality of welfare would not supply any obvious ethical justification for high levels of executive compensation.

Equality of welfare is not an attractive theory either. It has not had many defenders, though we might read the communist slogan, "From each according to his abilities, to each according to his needs," as a call for equality of welfare. It is, however, interesting to survey the problems with equality of welfare, because plausible theories of distributive justice must avoid these problems.

One problem with equality of welfare as a theory of distributive justice is that amounts of welfare are very difficult to measure and compare between people. We looked at welfare measurement problems in our discussion of utilitarianism. One suggestion was to use willingness to pay, or how much income a person was willing to give up to buy some good or service, as a measure of the intensity of a person's preference for an economic resource. If we assume a person's welfare increase is proportional to the strength of the preference satisfied, then we get a measure of welfare. This suggests that we should distribute income equally to ensure equal welfare. The problem, as we just saw in our discussion of indirect utilitarian justice, is that people convert resources, such as increased income, into welfare at different rates. Therefore, we have no assurance that equality of income will lead to equality of welfare.

A second problem with equality of welfare as a distributional principle is the problem of expensive tastes. Some people acquire tastes for expensive items, such as champagne, and get no pleasure from inexpensive substitutes like beer. Other people enjoy inexpensive items like beer, and never acquire a taste for expensive substitutes such as fine wines. Does this mean that to equalize welfare we should devote extra resources to satisfying people's expensive tastes? It seems intuitively unjust that people should be entitled to more of society's resources because they have acquired expensive tastes. It seems more plausible to hold people responsible for their tastes and to ask them to moderate their consumption of champagne, even if this distribution gives champagne drinkers less welfare than it does to beer drinkers.

A third problem with equality of welfare is the problem of levelling down. In the face of a situation of inequality of welfare, there are two ways to proceed. The first is to raise the welfare level of the worse off, and the second is to lower the welfare level of the better off. From the point of view or equality of welfare, both situations are equally good. Equality of welfare appears to imply that we should reduce everyone to the same level of preference satisfaction if that is the only way to achieve equality of welfare.

#	Distribution	Ron	Sal	Tom
1	Equality of welfare (utiles)	60	60	60
2	Inequality of welfare (utiles)	65	70	75

Table 6.5: Levelling down of welfare.

In Table 6.5, equality of welfare appears to say that the first distribution is better than the second distribution because all three people receive the same welfare. However, if the only choice is between these two distributions, then most people's intuitions favour the unequal distribution, in which everyone is better off than in the equal distribution. The idea of levelling down people's welfare, just for the sake of equality, conflicts with the considered moral judgments of most people.

A fourth problem with equality of welfare is that it would tend to diminish personal responsibility. If people receive resources that would bring them happiness, or they waste or squander these resources, then the theory of equality of welfare requires that they should receive more resources in order to raise their welfare level back to equality. Equality of welfare fails to hold people accountable for using resources wisely. It also totally disconnects the activities of production and consumption. Since equality of resources guarantees a certain level of welfare, it provides no incentive for people to contribute to the production of the resources whose consumption create this level of welfare.

EQUALITY OF RESOURCES AND THE DIFFERENCE PRINCIPLE

A large problem with thinking of distributive justice as the equal consideration of welfare interests was that such theories could not properly take into account expensive tastes and unjust preferences that others have less. One way to avoid these problems is to think of distributive justice as assigning resources instead of welfare to people.

How people then use their fair share of resources would be up to them; if they want to buy champagne infrequently instead of buying beer frequently, then that is their business. The simplest version of equality of resources would just give everyone an equal share of income or an equal share of economic goods and services. **Strict equality of resources** holds that a distribution of property rights in resources is just if, and only if, it results in everyone having the same amount of resources.

Strict equality of resources solves measurement and comparison problem because it just assigns everyone the same income to buy whatever resources they wish to have. It solves the expensive tastes problem because people with champagne tastes cannot demand more than an equal share of resources to satisfy their expensive tastes. It holds people responsible for forming only preferences that are affordable with their fair share.

Unfortunately, simple or strict equality is still vulnerable to the problem of levelling down to achieve equality. Even if everyone would be better-off in a society with an unequal distribution of resources, strict equality of resources tells us that a distribution in which everyone gets the same share would be fairer, which is counterintuitive. Nor does it hold people responsible for contributing to the production of goods and services; even beach bums will still receive their equal share of income.

In what is perhaps the most influential modern account of distributive justice, the American philosopher, John Rawls (1921–2002), proposed a way to avoid some of these problems. He set out his general conception of justice in his 1971 book, *A Theory of Justice*.

> All social primary goods—liberty and opportunity, income and wealth,
> and the bases of self-respect—are to be distributed equally unless an
> unequal distribution of any or all of these goods is to the advantage of the
> least favored. (Rawls, 1971, p. 301)

He called his principle, in which an unequal distribution of resources is fair so long as it betters the position of the least well-off, the "difference principle." The **difference principle** says a distribution of rights and responsibilities is just if, and only if, everyone receives the same resources unless an unequal distribution results in the least well-off receiving more than in the strictly equal distribution. Plainly, an unequal distribution of liberties or of opportunities to compete fairly for positions does nothing to benefit the least favoured, so the difference principle will give everyone the same basic liberties and opportunities. However, it will not give everyone the same resources; there will be differences in how it distributes income and wealth.

#		Ron	Sal	Tom	Total
1	Utilitarian	$1100	$1100	$3000	$5200
2	Strict equality of resources	$1000	$1000	$1000	$3000
3	Difference Principle	$1200	$1300	$1500	$4000

Table 6.6: Utilitarianism, strict equality, and the difference principle.

Table 6.6 shows the differences between utilitarianism, strict equality, and the difference principle. Utilitarianism would require distribution #1 because it maximizes utility as measured by total financial resources of $5200. Strict equality of resources would require distribution #2 because it gives everyone the same share of resources, even though everyone would be better off in either of the other distributions. Rawls's difference principle would require distribution #3 because the least favoured person, Ron, would better off than in either of the other two distributions. Tom would do worse in #3 than he would in #1, but that does not matter to the difference principle, which focuses only on the position of the least favoured person.

Rawls's difference principle avoids many of the problems of other theories. It avoids the measurement and comparison problem by distributing easily measured resources like income and wealth. It avoids problems of expensive tastes and unjust preferences by distributing resources and not welfare. It avoids the levelling down objection because it permits inequalities of resources whenever doing so benefits the least favoured members of society. It partially avoids problems of diminished personal responsibility because it offers people incentives to contribute more to the production of goods and services. If someone's extra effort and productivity enlarges the total quantity of goods and services available for distribution, and if businesses must pay executives more than they do janitors to get executives to contribute more, then the difference principle will give them incentives in the form of larger shares. If offering people a production incentive leads to a larger economic pie, and thereby permits the least favoured to receive a larger slice, then the difference principle will endorse this. The difference principle will require a progressive tax system that permits only the level of income inequality necessary to help the least advantaged, and no more.

Some people object that Rawls's difference principle diminishes personal responsibility. It appears not to hold people responsible for their choices. For example, an able-bodied person could choose to become a beach bum, contribute nothing to the productive activities of society, and still receive the minimum income and wealth distributed by the difference principle. This goes against the considered moral judgment of many people who believe that people should have to take more personal responsibility for their lives than the difference principle requires.

A possible alternative is a starting-gate theory of equality of resources. Instead of continually transferring resources to those who squander them or who choose not to cooperate in productive activities, the theory of initial equality of resources would ensure only that people had the same starting point in life. **Initial equality of resources** says that a distribution of rights and responsibilities is just if, and only if, it is the result of people's free choices after everyone starts life with strictly equal distribution of resources. This suggestion would, for example, justify a heavy inheritance tax. The problem with this suggestion is that how a person's life turns out is only partly dependent on the choices they make with their initial resources. Sometimes how things go will also depend on brute luck. Recessions may cause investments to go bad, changing technology may make skills and training redundant, or poor health may lead to financial ruin. A theory of justice that holds people responsible under these conditions may be guilty of moral arbitrariness.

There are many different interpretations of what it means to treat people as moral equals, and thus many different considerations that weigh for and against levels of income inequality. Each interpretation has its strengths and weaknesses in facing problems of moral arbitrariness, measuring contributions, measuring welfare, dealing with expensive or unjust preferences, avoiding levelling down, and allocating personal responsibility. Decision-makers must bear in mind these sorts of considerations when they are struggling to make fair and just decisions.

SUMMARY

1. Decision-makers must treat people fairly, which means treating everyone as moral equals.
2. Treating people as moral equals does not mean treating them all the same. Justice permits treating people differently, as long as it is not for morally arbitrary reasons like their race or gender.
3. Decision-makers must pay attention to three types of justice: retributive, compensatory, and distributive. Issues of distributive justice can become very complex.
4. The moral equality of persons requires giving everyone an equal opportunity to compete for economic resources. Equality of opportunity, though, may mean more than just removing legal impediments based on race or gender. It may also mean compensating for skill deficiencies caused by factors beyond a person's control and for fixing structural barriers such as lack of childcare facilities.
5. Equality of opportunity to compete for positions leaves open the question of determining fair compensation for positions. Matching compensation to marginal contribution is difficult because of the complex way in which specialized positions divide labour in a firm.
6. The moral equality of persons requires equal respect for their self-ownership rights. Some people argue that self-ownership leads to unrestricted private property rights and to free exchange in a capitalist market system. However, it is difficult to account for the initial acquisition of idealized property rights, and the history of actual, present-day property rights includes conquest, theft, and unconscionable contracts.
7. The moral equality of persons requires equal consideration of their welfare interests. However, weighting everyone's interests equally in a utilitarian calculation creates an unattractive theory of distributive justice. It implies unfair distributions because people have very different ways of converting resources into welfare.
8. As a theory of justice, the equal satisfaction of welfare interests has difficulty with the interpersonal comparison of preferences, with discounting unfairly expensive tastes, and with avoiding the reduction of everyone's welfare to the lowest level in the name of equality.

9. Understanding distributive justice as equalizing resources rather than equalizing welfare avoids the problem of expensive, champagne tastes. However, strict equality of resources still cannot avoid the problems of levelling down for the sake of equality and of failing to require people to take personal responsibility for their productive contributions.

10. Rawls's difference principle calls for strict equality of resources unless an unequal distribution benefits the least well-off in society. The difference principle avoids the levelling down objection, and uses incentives to increase people's productive contributions.

11. However, the difference principle still gives a minimum income to beach bums who choose not to contribute to society, and gives no extra shares to people who, for reasons of brute bad luck, require more than a minimum share of resources to lead a comfortable life.

ONLINE LEARNING RESOURCES

You will find a collection of learning resources associated with this chapter on the book's website: http://sites.broadviewpress.com/businessethics/. Working through this material will help you understand and remember important concepts that we have discussed, and will help you apply them to issues in business ethics.

STUDY QUESTIONS

Answering the following questions will help you to understand the ethical theory in this chapter and will help you to create a set of review notes on the textbook.

1. Why does the moral equality of persons sometimes require that people be treated differently by just institutions?
2. Why does the same reasoning that leads to formal equality of opportunity apparently also lead to fair and to structural equality of opportunity?
3. Why is it difficult to determine the marginal contribution of each worker in Adam Smith's pin factory?
4. How does equal respect for self-ownership rights account for the initial acquisition of property rights in things?
5. What are the difficulties with the libertarian account of the initial acquisition of property rights in things?
6. How can utilitarianism claim to give equal consideration to everyone's welfare interests?
7. How can an indirect utilitarian theory of justice claim to entail an equal distribution of resources?
8. What goes wrong with the indirect utilitarian argument for an equal distribution of resources?

9. What are the problems with equality of welfare as a theory of distributive justice?

10. What are the problems of strict equality of resources as a theory of distributive justice?

11. How does Rawls's difference principle answer the problem of expensive tastes, the problem of levelling down for the sake of achieving equality, and the problem of taking personal responsibility?

12. What are the problems with Rawls's difference principle as a way of treating everyone as moral equals?

DECISION QUESTIONS

The whole point of learning ethical theory is to understand and ask questions like the following when you are analyzing an ethically problematic situation or case.

- Will the decision treat everyone with equal moral respect and consideration?
- Will the decision treat people differently for morally arbitrary reasons?
- Does anyone deserve praise or blame in the case?
- Should anyone receive reward or punishment?
- Does anyone deserve compensation for a harm, rights violation, or injustice?
- Will the decision distribute benefits and burdens fairly?
- Does the decision promote equality of opportunity?
- Does the decision respect property rights and contracts?
- Does the decision help the least advantaged?
- Would a decision to promote distributive justice lead to entitlement loss or to overall utility loss?

CASE STUDY

Analyze this case study using the ethical theory that you have learned so far. You will find a collection of learning materials applying to the case on the book's website: http://sites.broadviewpress.com/businessethics/. These materials will help you in your analysis.

How Should Faruq Vote on the Salary of the New CEO?

Faruq Habib is a board member of the Foundation for International Development in the Americas (FIDA). FIDA is a very large, international, non-profit, non-government organization that funds local development groups in Central and South America. It raises these funds by seeking donations in Europe and North America. In his day job, Faruq is a human resources professional employed by a large multinational in Toronto. He has always been committed to international development work. Seven years ago, when he had just graduated from university, he spent two years working in Honduras with a

Peace-Corps-like organization called Professional Service Overseas. When FIDA asked him to join its board last year, Faruq felt much honoured, since FIDA is a well-respected organization that could have its pick of senior professionals and public figures for its board. His employers were also pleased, and have been very accommodating regarding the time-commitments of his FIDA work.

FIDA does not work directly with people, but instead funds the work of local, Spanish-, and Portuguese-speaking groups that provide aid to and that do advocacy work on behalf of local people. Poor people in these countries often ask for very little because years of poverty have severely lowered their expectations. FIDA's work has been very successful raising local standards of living, which people much appreciate after the fact. Unfortunately, local government officials and local agri-businesses do not always approve of FIDA's activities.

FIDA is in the process of hiring a new chief executive officer. The search committee has recommended Joan Rockingham, who is an almost ideal candidate. Joan has a tremendous record of accomplishment in raising funds for international development organizations. She has told the search committee that she thinks she can raise donations to FIDA by $5,000,000.

Joan comes from a very well to do family, went to an expensive prep school, and then to Ivy League universities for her philosophy degree and for her MBA. Her study of political philosophy led her to reject living on her family's money, and to go into international development work. Nevertheless, she grew up with, and she still enjoys, all the finer things in life. Her family connections have always helped her with fund-raising.

The only problem with Joan's candidacy is that her asking salary is triple that of the outgoing executive director. FIDA is a global justice organization, and as such has a generally accepted, but unwritten, policy that the salary of the highest-paid member of the organization cannot be higher than three times the salary of the lowest paid members of the organization. Joan's asking salary is nine times the salary of the cleaning staff. The next best candidate, who is asking for the same salary as the previous CEO, is very competent and will be able to keep FIDA's work going at its current level.

Should Faruq vote to hire Joan?

VIRTUE ETHICS AND COMMUNITY MEMBERSHIP

Why is it important to avoid vices and cultivate virtues?

How do ethical obligations relate to community membership?

Why should the corporate character of business organizations be so significant?

Vices are stable character traits with negative moral significance, while **virtues** are stable character traits with positive moral significance. Virtues are forms of moral excellence.

Managers of businesses and other organizations aspire to excellence. The character traits of excellent managers include decisiveness, innovativeness, leadership, independence, openness, reliability, congeniality, charisma, reasonableness, shrewdness, resourcefulness, and persistence. A manager's excellence in these traits will help her flourish in her organization, and will help her organization flourish in its dealings with the rest of the world. These character traits are useful to the organization and to the manager herself, but they carry little moral significance.

Other character traits of excellent managers carry more moral significance. The moral excellences of good managers also include honesty, loyalty, trustworthiness, courage, fairness, temperance, generosity, tolerance, and sensitivity. A manager without these virtues will not flourish in her organization, and will not help her organization contribute to the flourishing of society as a whole. For example, those managers in the financial industry whose recklessness, greed, and dishonesty contributed to the financial crisis and recession of 2008 did not exhibit moral excellence. Neither their firms nor the world economy flourished as a result.

There is no sharp distinction between excellences with little moral significance and the excellences with more moral significance that are virtues. Fairness and honesty obviously carry high levels of positive moral significance whereas shrewdness and persistence carry less. Virtues tend to foster social cooperation in almost every interpersonal situation, whereas non-moral excellences and skills tend to be more self-centred and less universal.

Our excellences and virtues are part of who we are. They are character traits that help determine our identity. Acting virtuously, we prove what type of person we are. We confirm ourselves to be honest, trustworthy, and fair. Acting contrary to virtue, we demonstrate our vices. We confirm ourselves to be dishonest, untrustworthy, or unjust.

Virtues and vices are not conscious mental states like pain or pleasure, nor are they mental processes, such as rational calculations or applications of ethical principles. They are skills, traits, or dispositions. Because they are dispositions, we can talk meaningfully and non-metaphorically about the virtues of nation states, societies, communities, and corporations. A just society is disposed to respect the rights of its citizens and distribute benefits and burdens in a way that is fair. We can assess a business organization based on whether it is disposed to treat its customers honestly, its employees fairly, its owners with respect, and its suppliers with loyalty. Therefore, we can talk meaningfully about corporate character. A corporation can be just or unjust, for example, depending on how it is organized.

We can seek out the organizational features of a firm that affect its corporate character. Does it have a code of ethics, and are the actions of employees monitored for compliance with this code? Does it have properly implemented conflict of interest policies? Does it have an incentive system that discourages reckless behaviour? Does it provide ethics training for its employees? What is the ethical climate of the organization, and what is the example set by its leadership? Organizational features like these will determine the moral excellence of the firm. Decision-makers within the firm need to ensure the proper implementation and enforcement of policies that dispose the firm to treat stakeholders well and to cooperate and contribute to the wider society.

Our membership in a wider community affects our particular obligations. Our institutional roles and our community memberships give rise to prima facie moral obligations that we must balance with calculations of utility, respect for rights, and concern for distributive justice. Corporations, too, are members of communities. Decision-makers within corporations must take into account corporate obligations that arise through community membership. Virtue ethics gives us a picture of ethical decision-making in business that is richer than the legalistic framework of simply fulfilling contracts.

VIRTUE ETHICS AND HUMAN FLOURISHING

When we make an ethical decision, we consider three broad types of ethical reasoning. One, we consider the likely consequences of our decision and assess these consequences in terms of their contribution to total welfare. Two, we consider the motivation behind our decision, concentrating on the principles of justice and respect for rights that we are applying and following. Three, we consider what sort of person we become when we make such decisions. What would a person of good character, a virtuous person, a morally excellent businessperson, decide to do in this situation? Figure 7.1 shows how virtue ethics fits into a conceptual map of ethical theories.

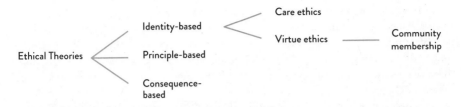

Figure 7.1: Conceptual map showing virtue ethics as an identity-based ethical theory.

The virtues appear in applied ethics in two different ways. One way understands the virtues as basic to ethical theory. Another way understands the virtues as serving the purposes of other principle- or consequence-based ethical theories. **Derivative virtues** are character traits that are justified because they help an agent fulfil the requirements of some other type of ethical theory. An obvious example of this is indirect utilitarianism. Direct utilitarianism requires us to perform a full cost-benefit analysis of the utilities of the consequences of each decision that we make. Indirect utilitarianism claims that this sort of calculation is beyond the finite intellectual capacities of decision-makers. Instead, it requires that people use rules of thumb, respect basic rights, and acquire virtues such as benevolence that will bring about the best consequences. Here, the requirement to be virtuous is derived from consequentialist ethical reasoning. Similarly rights-based ethical theories call for virtues of thoughtfulness, carefulness, and self-discipline and justice-based ethical theories call for a sense of fairness. Figure 7.2 shows these two different ways of using the virtues in ethics. In this chapter, we will consider the virtues as basic to ethics.

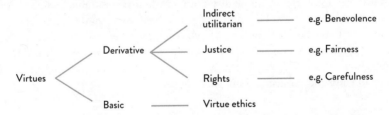

Figure 7.2: Virtues are basic to virtue theory, but can also be justified by other consequentialist and principle-based ethical theories.

A virtue is a stable character trait with positive moral significance. Virtues enable human beings and organizations to flourish in cooperation with others who have similar or complementary traits. Understanding virtue requires understanding the notions of character traits, human flourishing, and social cooperation that are important in virtue ethics.

Character traits are not mental states like a pleasurable experience or a desire for ice cream. Instead, they are enduring dispositions to behave in certain ways in appropriate circumstances. They are habits that we acquire through upbringing, education, self-discipline, and practice. To be virtuous, it is not enough to perform just one good action. One donation to charity is not enough to make a person generous. Nor is a strategy of acting well for personal gain an indication of virtue. Adopting honesty as the best policy does not make a person honest. Generous people are disposed to repeatedly share with the needy and honest people want to tell the truth, even when it is inconvenient or worse to do so.

People are **perfectly virtuous** if it is second nature for them do the right thing. Perfect virtue involves a form of moral perception; perfectly virtuous people "see" what they should do. They do the right thing intuitively. In this, they are like skilled drivers who naturally make the right decisions in dangerous circumstances, or skilled hockey players who instantly make the best play.

To follow a **virtue ethics rule of action** is to emulate how a virtuous person would act in a problematic situation. People who are not perfectly virtuous, which is most of us, can reason by imagining what someone whose moral excellence we admire—mothers, friends, bosses, business heroes, or religious leaders—would do in the situation that we face.

Virtue also requires practical wisdom. Moral perceptiveness, the ability to "see" the relevant ethical issues in a situation, and moral competence, the ability to "see" what to do in response to these ethical issues are forms of wisdom that are not readily reduced to calculations of consequences or applications of principle. Wisdom is also involved in the understanding of the various virtues and vices. A virtue is the mean between two vices, as courage is the mean between cowardice and recklessness. For example, it is generous for a business to make a reasonable donation to a charitable cause. However a disposition towards offering too little would be greedy, while a disposition towards offering too much might be imprudent. An honest business selling a product should be frank about the qualities of that product and its manufacturing. However to say too little would be dishonest, while to say too much might entail the disclosure of trade secrets. The boundaries between virtue and vice are not easy to determine, and may be different for different roles in society. We must learn a certain skill in applying virtue concepts. Doing so will give us a conceptual vocabulary for thinking about ethical decisions that is much richer than simple divisions into right and wrong, good and bad, or just and unjust.

Vice	Virtue	Vice
Dishonesty	Honesty	Over-disclosure
Timidity	Courage	Recklessness
Greed	Moderation	Self-sacrifice
Meanness	Generosity	Excessiveness
Unfairness	Justice	Rigidness

Table 7.1: A virtue is the mean between two vices: some examples of the rich conceptual vocabulary available within virtue ethics.

The notion of human flourishing as understood in virtue ethics is very different from the notion of happiness as understood by utilitarians. Virtue ethics understands flourishing as objective happiness, a form of happiness that an objective observer of a person's life could assess. Utilitarianism understands happiness as subjective happiness, as pleasurable experiences and satisfied desires that only the person who has them can assess. We can assess flourishing from the outside, but we can only assess subjective happiness from the inside. Only the person enjoying a beautiful sunset can judge how much pleasure seeing the sunset gives her. However, an external observer can judge the meaningfulness of a person's life and say whether the person is exhibiting good character, living his life well and flourishing or not. In the jargon of ethics, the theory of objective happiness in virtue ethics is *eudemonism*, and contrasts with the *hedonism* that is the theory of subjective happiness in utilitarian thinking.

Virtue ethics	Utilitarianism
Objective happiness	Subjective happiness
Human flourishing	Pleasurable experiences
Meaningful life	Satisfied preferences
Life well-lived	Financial resources
Eudemonism	Hedonism

Table 7.2: Concepts of happiness in virtue ethics and utilitarianism.

The virtues do not cause human flourishing; they partially constitute it. The relationship between virtue and objective happiness is NOT the relationship shown in Figure 7.3.

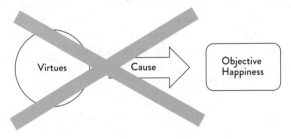

Figure 7.3: The virtues do not cause human flourishing.

Instead, we can better capture the relationship of virtue and flourishing in the enclosed circles of Figure 7.4. Having a good character is part of what it is to lead an objectively good life. Virtue ethics breaks down the opposition between ethics and self-interest by understanding a happy life as constituted by a combination of good character and good circumstances.

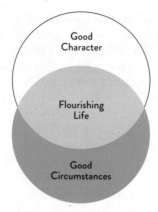

Figure 7.4: A combination of virtue and good circumstances creates a flourishing and objectively happy life.

The good circumstances required for a flourishing life include both natural and social circumstances. Virtues, which are character traits that enable people to cooperate for mutual advantage in society, are also required to create and sustain good social circumstances. A society where people are generally honest, trustworthy, and supportive will prosper and sustain the social conditions required for the flourishing of its members. The virtues have less effect on the natural conditions of a flourishing life. No amount of virtue or moral excellence will protect a person from cancer or heart disease. Good health is, in part, a matter of good luck. However, living in a well-developed society that can provide good health care to its members is a matter of social cooperation, which, in turn, depends on members of the society having the necessary cooperative virtues. In virtue ethics, a happy life is a good life, lived with virtues such as integrity, self-respect, and honesty. These virtues also contribute to the maintenance of happy social circumstances and to the flourishing of everyone in society.

VIRTUE AND SOCIAL COOPERATION

Some of the ancient virtue theorists, the Stoics, thought that all that is necessary for a life well lived is to be perfectly virtuous. Circumstances do not matter; even a life of extreme privation is a flourishing life so long as it exemplifies the virtues. Others of the ancient virtue theorists, the Aristotelians, thought that circumstances do matter and even a life that exemplified all the virtues could be a bad one in unfortunate circumstances. Here, we will follow the Aristotelians, and examine how the virtues contribute to creating and sustaining the circumstances in which people flourish. Two sorts of social circumstances are relevant to the flourishing. The first are social conditions: the preservation and development of the social practices, institutions, and communities that honour and reward people's virtues. The second are material conditions: the provision of those things, such as education, healthcare, insurance, and economic goods and services, which enable people's lives to flourish. We will examine some examples of the latter type of social circumstances.

People who live in a community that inculcates certain virtues will avoid the dilemmas of cooperation that afflict people motivated only by unenlightened self-interest. For example, in the Prisoner's Dilemma Game, two rational actors, motivated only by unenlightened self-interest, will each find that their best strategy is to cheat, no matter whether the other actor cheats or cooperates. The outcome of a prisoner's dilemma situation will be a less than optimal payoff for both players. However, people who live in communities that inculcate and sustain virtues of fidelity, trustworthiness, and reciprocity will achieve Pareto optimal outcomes. They can trust one another to keep their promises, and can rely on cooperative behaviour from each other. Virtues are permanent character traits; people do not suddenly behave out of character, so virtuous people can predict one another's behaviour accurately. As virtuous people who know each other to be virtuous, they will dare to take the cooperative strategy and flourish. Similarly, players of the Centipede Game who unthinkingly trust one another will make out better than will hyper-rational economists and chess grandmasters who reason by backwards induction to the least optimal payoff.

If Adam Smith's example of specialization and the division of labour in the pin factory generalizes to the productive capacity of society as a whole, then members of a society who can cooperate easily and cheaply will flourish. The material conditions of their lives will be much better than will the material conditions of a society whose members do not have the cooperative virtues—but that is not the ultimate aim that justifies things for the virtue theorists. Good material conditions are justified because they encourage virtue and allow flourishing. We can illustrate this with another sort of game, a co-ordination or assurance game called the Stag Hunt Game. Suppose that Jack and Jill can produce pins either individually or by cooperating. Jack and Jill have complementary excellences in producing pin parts. Jack has a talent for producing pinheads whereas Jill has a talent for producing pinpoints.

	Jack		Jill	
	Heads	Points	Heads	Points
Productivity per hour	9	1	1	9
Individual pin production in 10 hours	9		9	
Total individual pin production	18			
Cooperative part production in 10 hours	90	0	0	90
Total cooperative pin production	90			
Equal division of cooperative production	45		45	

Table 7.3: Abstract model of a pin factory showing the gains from cooperative production.

If Jack and Jill produce pins individually, then they can produce only 9 pins each per day. However, if they are able to coordinate their production by specializing in producing the pin parts that they produce most efficiently, then they can produce 90 pins per day. If they can then agree on a fair way of dividing the gains from cooperation, then they will each be better off. Cooperative production thus faces two problems. The first is the problem of coordinating specialized production. The second is the problem of dividing the gains from cooperation.

The problem of coordination arises because if Jack, say, specializes and produces 90 pinheads while Jill works individually and produces 9 complete pins, then Jack will be left with 90 useless pinheads. Jack will have nothing and Jill will have less than she could have had. Each producer has to have confidence that the other producer will specialize and produce jointly. Each producer faces the risk that the other producer will not cooperate, and that he or she will be worse off if he or she goes ahead and specializes. We can represent this situation as a Stag Hunt Game. [The original version of the game involved hunters choosing whether to hunt a large deer cooperatively or to hunt a small rabbit individually.]

Jill

	Specialize	Self-Sufficient
Specialize	45 / 45 UL	9 / 0 UR
Self-Sufficient	0 / 9 LL	9 / 9 LR

Figure 7.5: Social cooperation in the pin factory represented as a coordination game.

If Jack and Jill both accept the risk of specializing and divide the gains equally, then they can achieve the large payoffs in the upper left cell. If both refuse to take the risk of specializing, then they will get the small payoffs in the lower right cell. If one specializes and the other does not, then the one who specializes will get nothing, while the one who produces individually will get only a small payoff. Clearly both are better off if they both specialize, but if one specializes and the other does not, then they risk getting nothing. By producing individually, they can avoid the risk of getting nothing by accepting a small payoff. Both UL and LR are equilibriums in the game, since in UL or LR neither Jack nor Jill will have any incentive to change his or her strategy. The problem for Jack and Jill is to make sure that they settle in optimal equilibrium UL and not in sub-optimal equilibrium LR. If Jack and Jill can see one another and can easily verify that the other one is specializing, then they can easily solve this coordination problem. However, if they cannot easily verify and enforce cooperation, then they face a risk when they specialize.

Virtues are often character traits that enable human beings and organizations to flourish in cooperation with others who have similar or complementary traits. If both Jack and Jill possess the virtues of fidelity in keeping promises, trustworthiness in keeping agreements, courage in accepting the risks of cooperation, and honesty in their negotiations, and if they know one another to have these virtues, then they can much reduce the risks of specialization. A community that teaches and sustains cooperative virtues will flourish in a way that a mere collection of self-interested individuals will not.

Someone sceptical about virtue ethics might respond to this argument by pointing out another way of ensuring social cooperation in the face of defection and risk. Legal contracts can ensure cooperation. If Jack and Jill sign legal contracts with one another to supply complementary pin parts, contracts that specify adequate penalties for non-compliance, then they can reduce the risks of specialization and achieve the optimal equilibrium.

One problem with this way of achieving social cooperation is that it is costly. Negotiating a complex legal contract that endeavours to cover every eventuality is expensive. If anything goes wrong with the deal, then enforcing such a contract is also expensive. Lawyers charge very high fees. The fees involved in creating and enforcing agreements are transaction costs. These are the expenses of reaching and enforcing an agreement between negotiating parties. They include the costs of researching information about the situation, negotiating the agreement, and legally enforcing the agreement. Transaction costs introduce inefficiencies into economic cooperation.

A society that inculcates and sustains virtues of fidelity, trustworthiness, courage, and honesty in its members can have economic cooperation more efficiently than can a litigious society. Similarly, societies whose members do not steal, murder, or harm one another out of virtue is much less expensive to police than are societies whose members merely fear the law. A community whose members internalize and practice the character traits that sustain economic and social cooperation, is more efficient than a collection of atomistic individuals who are continually calculating the costs and benefits of non-cooperative or criminal activity.

Having overcome the risks of specialization and the division of labour, Jack and Jill still face the problem of dividing the gains from cooperation. Working alone, they make 9 pins each; working together, they jointly make 90 pins. How should they divide the 72 pins that are the gains from cooperation? If Jack gets 10 pins, and Jill gets 80 pins, both parties are better off than they would be working alone, but this division is patently unfair. Unfair divisions can lead to resentment and anger and to the breakdown of cooperation. To reach a fair division, Jack and Jill need a sense of justice, a disposition to propose and accept fair divisions of the gains of cooperation. The results of the behavioural economics experiment that we looked at earlier, the Ultimatum Game, suggest that people do have a sense of justice and believe others to have such a sense as well. Proposers in the Ultimatum Game will typically offer an equal division of rewards, and Deciders will typically punish what they see as an unfair division by refusing such an offer, even at some cost to themselves. The virtues of honesty, trustworthiness, and courage create social cooperation, and the virtue of justice sustains it.

Of course, villains can still free ride on the virtues of others. Widespread exercise of the virtues of moderation, truthfulness, fidelity, trustworthiness, and courage is required to realize the gains from social cooperation, but universal exercise of these virtues is not. One person without these traits may seize for himself an unfair share of the material gains from cooperation without compromising the general prevalence of cooperative behaviour. An important virtue in these circumstances is the widespread courage to call attention to and discourage, such greedy, dishonest, unfaithful, untrustworthy, and reckless behaviour.

SOCIAL PRACTICES AND COMMUNITY MEMBERSHIP

Virtue ethics differs from the other ethical theories that we have examined in its emphasis on the social context of an individual's life. Ethical egoism begins from the notion of isolated individuals whose rational pursuit of their own self-interest creates dilemmas with social cooperation. Utilitarianism also begins from the notion of individuals who make decisions that maximize the subjective, internal, mental experiences of other isolated individuals. Kantian rights theory, too, begins from the idea of the autonomous choices and crucial subjective interests of isolated individuals who need rights to protect them from the interference of others. Theories of distributive justice concern themselves with the distribution of goods and services that people consume in isolation. Virtue ethics, on the other hand, begins from the notions of individuals who are already cooperating in a society and of individuals whose flourishing depends on their ability to work well with other members of their community. The virtues are character traits that enable community members to work together effectively.

Not every society or community enables the flourishing of its members. We can imagine a nasty society, whose members are impoverished and oppressed, and in which people must be dishonest and untrustworthy in order to survive. Such a society encourages the vices. The virtues have their role in creating and maintaining a prosperous and just society that rewards and honours the virtues that sustain it.

Each social practice has its different skills, but all communities and social practices require virtues of honesty, fidelity, and so on for members and practitioners to flourish. The virtues relate intimately to communities and the social practices of their members. Virtues are skills in making ethical decisions that children learn within communities. Communities provide moral education in virtue. Adults may ultimately modify or reject the virtues that they learn as children, but childhood moral training provides the foundation for adult moral excellence. Communities sustain the virtues that they teach by honouring and sometimes rewarding virtue and by despising and punishing vice.

At the same time, the virtues inculcated by a community sustain the forms of social cooperation that make the community work. The relationship between virtue and community is reciprocal, as shown in Figure 7.6. The virtues enable social cooperation and therefore the existence of communities, while communities simultaneously inculcate, reward, and enable the practice of the various virtues.

Figure 7.6: A community teaches virtue to its members and enables them to exercise these virtues, while at the same time, the exercise of virtues of honesty, fidelity, and justice by community members sustains the social cooperation required for the existence of the community.

The gains from cooperation are twofold. In virtue ethics, a flourishing human life requires both economic goods and services and the exercise of the virtues. A good life requires a good set of social circumstances and the possession of a good character. Social cooperation provides community members with economic gains, as illustrated by Adam Smith's pin factory. This is one type of gain from social cooperation. Social cooperation also creates the type of community in which members can exercise the virtues whose possession is part of what it is to flourish and lead a good life. This is another type of gain from social cooperation, and is a gain that is internal to the cooperation itself.

Because of the intimate, mutually supportive relationship of virtue to community, virtuous people acquire obligations simply through their membership in a community. (Sandel, 2009) The influential contemporary virtue theorist Alasdair MacIntyre wrote:

> ... we all approach our own circumstances as bearers of a particular social
> identity. I am someone's son or daughter, someone else's cousin or uncle;
> I am a citizen of this or that city, a member of this or that guild of profes-
> sion; I belong to this clan, that tribe, this nation. Hence what is good for
> me has to be the good for one who inhabits these roles. As such, I inherit
> from the past of my family, my city, my tribe, my nation, a variety of debts,
> inheritances, rightful expectations and obligations. These constitute the
> given of my life, my moral starting point. This is in part what gives my life
> its own moral particularity. (MacIntyre, 1981, p. 220)

For example, we have particular, specific obligations to members of our families that we did not initially choose. We were born or adopted into these obligations. These are not general obligations, owed to everyone, that arise from utilitarian obligations to promote the general welfare, and they are not general duties to respect the rights of others. Nor are they the specific obligations that people take on by voluntarily signing contracts with one another. Instead, the obligations of community membership are non-voluntary, specific obligations that people have because of their membership in a mutually sustaining family, community, or society. Virtuous people acknowledge obligations of loyalty and solidarity to fellow community members, and virtuous communities acknowledge similar obligations to the larger communities of which they are a part.

	Obligations to all people	Obligations to specific people
Non-voluntary	Liberties and human rights	Community membership
Voluntary	N/A	Contractual rights

Table 7.4: The obligations of community membership, unlike contractual obligations, are not obligations that we ever agreed to, yet are still obligations that we owe to particular people.

The obligations of community membership are not always overriding obligations. For example, we should not promote a family member over a more deserving employee, to do so would be nepotism. Nevertheless, the fact that the relative is a family member is still an ethical consideration in our decision. It is just that other ethical considerations such as fairness and employee rights outweigh our ethical obligations of family membership. However, it is difficult to think of any business situations in which either community or family membership trumps justice and fairness. The special obligations of loyalty and solidarity to our "tribe" spoken of by MacIntyre above might prompt a white Scottish factory owner to hire fellow white Scots rather than black people. This is simple racism, and it should not be an ethical consideration in business at all.

CORPORATE CHARACTER

Virtues and vices are dispositions, not mental experiences like pains and pleasures, and so it makes sense for us to ascribe virtues and vices to organizations and business corporations. Societies, organizations, and corporations can have deep-seated dispositions to behave in certain ways. Societies can be fair or unfair, benevolent or malevolent, generous or stingy. Business corporations can also be fair to, honest with, respectful of, loyal to, trustworthy regarding employees, customers, and suppliers. Business firms have a corporate character that should exhibit these virtues.

Corporate character is determined by the way that individual corporations are organized. Many factors contribute to the implementation and maintenance of a good corporate character:

1. Competent ethical decision-making by management
2. Leadership setting a good example for all of the organization's members

3. An ethically meaningful Mission Statement
4. Corresponding good corporate governance
5. An explicit Code of Ethics
6. Effective monitoring of compliance with that Code of Ethics
7. Effective ethics training for decision-makers
8. Well-written and well-monitored Conflict of Interest policies
9. Individual accountability within the organization for decisions
10. The existence of a good ethical "climate" (implicit code of ethics) within the organization
11. The expectation and acceptance of only virtuous practices within the organization
12. Incentive structures for employees that encourage moral excellence in decision-making

The techniques of creating good corporate character are different from the techniques of educating virtuous children, but they are no less important.

Virtue ethics cares about corporate character for many reasons. Organizations inculcate character traits in their members. They reward certain character traits and inhibit others. People identify with their work, and thus with the organization that employs them. Their careers become part of their self-concept. Corporate character becomes, in part, their character. The nature of human flourishing within a corporation depends on the interpretation of virtue within that organization, which, in turn, depends on its corporate character.

We can now see the implication of this abstract discussion of virtue and community for business ethics. Businesses and other organizations have a dual role: On the one hand, business corporations, non-governmental organizations, and government departments are themselves communities. In the modern world, they are hugely important communities in many people's lives. Most people spend a large part of their adult lives working for organizations and corporations. For most people, their workplace is an essential venue for the exercise of their virtues. The exercise of virtue by employees simultaneously enables efficient cooperation in the workplace. As employees of a business corporation, and thus members of an economic community, workers acquire non-voluntary obligations of loyalty and trustworthiness that go beyond their employment contracts. Similarly, a virtuous business corporation acquires obligations of loyalty, honesty, and fairness to its employees that also go beyond their employment contracts.

On the other hand, business corporations and other organizations are themselves members of larger communities. Businesses must have virtuous character traits in order for social cooperation to take place efficiently in society as a whole. A market society in which business corporations generally deceive, manipulate, cheat, steal, and bully will not be a flourishing society, any more than a business corporation whose employees generally deceive, manipulate, cheat, steal, and bully will be a flourishing business. In the virtue ethics approach, businesses owe non-voluntary obligations of loyalty, fairness, generosity, and so on, to other members of their wider community, such as suppliers, customers, physical communities, and local governments.

For example, suppose a factory that has operated in a small American town for many years decides to lower production costs by moving its production to China. It is difficult to understand the ethical considerations against this decision without understanding the non-voluntary ethical obligations of a virtuous business to the wider community of which it is a member. From an economic utilitarian perspective, the business has raised global welfare by lowering costs in a free-market. From a principle-based perspective, the corporation has respected the human rights of all members of its community, and has fulfilled all its contracts with its local employees and suppliers. We can even interpret Rawls's difference principle of distributive justice as endorsing the decision because it will benefit Chinese workers, who are less advantaged than are American workers. Nevertheless, we still suspect that there are ethical considerations against this decision. The factory management has failed to consider unwritten obligations of loyalty and solidarity owed to other members of the small American community of which it is a member. A virtuous business would accept the existence of these obligations of reciprocity resulting from a shared history, and management would at least consider these obligations in making its decision. In the ethical pluralist decision-making framework, these obligations of community membership will not always outweigh other ethical reasons, such as utilitarian, rights-based, and justice-based ones. Nonetheless, they are legitimate ethical reasons and management ought to weigh them in its decision regarding the fate of the factory.

WEAKNESSES OF VIRTUE ETHICS

One problem with the virtue ethics approach is the great diversity of character traits that different communities have praised as virtues. Homer praised the ferocity, reckless courage, and exaggerated sense of personal honour of Bronze Age warriors in the siege of Troy. Aristotle praised the speeches and public service of those who contributed to Athenian democracy, while not just accepting, but justifying, the ownership of slaves and the oppression of women. The New Testament of the Christian bible stresses the virtues of faith, hope, charity, and meekness. The Victorians stressed the virtues of chastity, while condoning rampant hypocrisy. Virtues and vices are relative to community standards, and the standards of some communities are highly questionable.

This raises the question of whether virtue ethics is a form of cultural relativism. Different communities, with different cultures, teach, praise, and reward different virtues. Further, even when communities value the same virtues, they may have different interpretations of what it means to have that virtue. Therefore, it seems that virtue is relative to culture. Someone might defend virtue ethics against the charge of cultural relativism by pointing out that cultures teach virtues to foster social cooperation, and the circumstances in which people are trying to cooperate differ. For example, in the barbaric times of the Trojan War, a community needed to teach the warrior virtues to defend itself against outside aggression and so enable internal cooperation. Deciding whether all virtues have the same purpose—fostering social cooperation in society—in diverse historical circumstances would require extensive empirical investigation.

Some forms of virtue ethics may imply cultural conservatism as well as cultural relativism. Virtues are a character trait, which are dispositions to behave and not conscious decisions. Someone who is perfectly virtuous simply does the right thing automatically, without critical reflection. If virtues are merely unreflective dispositions to behave that a community inculcates and sustains, then it is difficult to see how community members can have the intellectual resources to take any sort of critical perspective on the virtues that they exercise automatically. If community standards are less than perfect, then how can community members reform their community from within? Reform of a community's standards from within is only possible if the community also inculcates the intellectual virtues required for critical reflection on those standards. A community needs to educate its members in the skills of critical thinking, the traits of scepticism, and the intellectual abilities of discussion and debate. Only a critical, sceptical community with an open forum for deliberation about the nature of virtue can develop and change from within.

The principal critics of virtue ethics and its communitarian background have been liberal philosophers such as Locke, Kant, Mill, and Rawls. They have worried that the creation of virtuous community members is incompatible with the values of liberty and autonomy. Locke's individuals in the state of nature were their own masters. They had self-ownership and pre-social rights to private property that allowed them to live their lives as they chose to do instead of as their community wished them to do. Kant conceived of people as fundamentally autonomous and able to live by principles that they reasoned out for themselves. Mill's harm principle forbade society to interfere with people for their own good or to make them into better, more virtuous citizens, and railed against the way social pressure made people conform to community standards. Rawls stressed people's basic rights to be free of interference from the wider society and the necessity of giving people a fair share of the resources that they would require to lead their lives according to their own conception of a good life, not the prevalent conception in their community. Liberals worry that communities of virtue will brainwash members into a common conception of the good life. Liberals also worry that communitarians will too readily sacrifice the rights of individuals for the good of the community. For example, Hitler's fascists in the 1930s and 1940s sacrificed the human rights of Jews and other minority groups in the cause of creating an ethnically pure German community. The idea that community membership can be a source of ethical obligations must be tempered with the idea that respect for rights and justice will frequently override community obligations.

Critics of virtue ethics worry, too, about the vagueness of character traits as guides to ethical action. Other approaches appear to give guidance that is more precise. Bentham offers the goal of the greatest happiness, Kant offers the categorical imperative, and Rawls offers the difference principle. Virtue ethics offers no such principles. The closest thing it can offer is the virtue ethics rule of action, which is to emulate the actions of a virtuous person, still imprecisely defined. On closer inspection, however, other ethical approaches are also vague in their implementation. For example, applying Bentham's greatest happiness principle requires sensitivity to the experiences of others and learned insight into what will happen to people's experiences in response to various courses of action. If utilitarianism requires people to develop the character traits of benevolence, sensitivity, and causal insight in order to work, then utilitarianism cannot be any more precise than are those virtues of benevolence, sensitivity, and insight. If the other ethical approaches each require their various derivative virtues in order to work, then none of them can be any more precise than is virtue ethics itself.

In virtue ethics, being virtuous is part of what it is to flourish. A critic of virtue ethics might suggest that virtue ethics thus leads to narcissism and self-indulgence. If people only do the right thing in pursuit of personal virtue and their own flourishing, then how can this be an admirable motivation? This criticism of virtue ethics misses its target. Virtuous people are not goal oriented; they do not think of how to achieve the goal of being virtuous, they are simply disposed to act automatically in a virtuous way. Nor, as we saw above, are virtuous people virtuous because being virtuous causes them to flourish. The relation between virtue and flourishing in virtue ethics is not casual but constitutive.

Finally, virtue ethics faces the problem of multiple community memberships. What virtues people should have depends on which communities they are members of. Different communities often require different interpretations of the virtues. People are simultaneously members of different communities. Therefore, people often face the problem of integrating incompatible character traits. For example, the type of honesty that a salesperson requires in her job may differ considerably from the type of honesty that is appropriate in her family life. As a salesperson, she may be disposed to disclose as much positive and as little negative information as she can legitimately get away with, whereas as a someone's life partner, she may be disposed to disclose as much information as possible, positive or negative. Balancing work and home life is a problem that everyone faces. Unless virtues, as acquired character traits, are responsive to situations, it would be impossible for people to acquire them. However, when they conflict, for example when New Testament virtues conflict with business virtues for a Christian executive, it may be difficult to integrate the two interpretations without considerable rationalization.

SUMMARY

1. Virtues are moral excellences, which are skills and character traits that enable human beings and organizations to flourish in cooperation with others having similar traits. Our virtues are parts of our identity as individuals. Virtues are usually the mean between two vices.
2. Virtues constitute, but do not cause, human flourishing. Flourishing individuals lead meaningful, well-lived lives that an objective observer would judge to be happy.
3. A flourishing human life requires both a good character (virtues) and good material circumstances.
4. Good material circumstances are largely the product of cooperative rather than individual production, as in Adam Smith's pin factory.
5. People with the virtues of moderation, honesty, fidelity, trustworthiness, and courage can finesse difficulties with cooperation

such as those illustrated by the Prisoner's Dilemma and the Stag Hunt Game. People with a sense of justice will be able to agree on the fair division of the gains from cooperation.

6. Furthermore, a virtuous community can avoid some transaction costs that arise in a society using only a network of contracts and property rights to organize itself.

7. People learn and exercise virtue in communities. By providing the opportunity for their members to exercise virtue, communities enable people to flourish and lead good lives. At the same time, the exercise of various virtues by community members enables the social cooperation that sustains the community.

8. As members of families and communities, virtuous people acquire obligations to specific others that are not voluntary in the way that contractual obligations are voluntary. These include obligations of loyalty and solidarity to other family and community members, and obligations to the community as a whole.

9. Because virtues are traits and dispositions to behaviour, and not mental states, we can meaningfully ascribe virtues and vices to business corporations and other organizations. Managers can implement good corporate character through how they govern and organize their organization.

10. Ethical reasoning based on virtue ethics must be careful to avoid cultural relativism, cultural conservatism, the maintenance of unhealthy community standards, paternalism, the suppression of autonomous thought, and too great a split between the demands of the multiple communities of which one person may be a member.

ONLINE LEARNING RESOURCES

You will find a collection of learning resources associated with this chapter on the book's website: http://sites.broadviewpress.com/businessethics/. Working through this material will help you understand and remember important concepts that we have discussed, and will help you apply them to issues in business ethics.

STUDY QUESTIONS

Answering the following questions will help you to understand the ethical theory in this chapter and will help you to create a set of review notes on the textbook.

1. Write down a list of vices that are common in the workplace.
2. Explain the difference between happiness in utilitarianism and happiness in virtue ethics.
3. Explain the importance of social cooperation in human life.

4. How can a community that inculcates virtue in its members avoid the dilemmas of cooperation?
5. Why is cooperation less costly in a community that fosters virtue than in a group of people who rely on contracts and property rights?
6. Describe the circular relationship whereby virtue sustains community and community sustains virtue.
7. How do virtuous people and organizations acquire non-contractual obligations to specific others simply through belonging to a community?
8. Describe an example of an obligation of community membership that is not based on a contract, respect for a right, or maximizing overall welfare.
9. Explain the notion of corporate character.
10. Why does a community that teaches and maintains virtue run the risk of not protecting rights to liberty and autonomous choice.

DECISION QUESTIONS

The whole point of learning ethical theory is to understand and ask questions like the following when you are analyzing an ethically problematic situation or case.

- What character traits should the decision-maker strive to exhibit in the decision?
- Should the decision-maker exhibit certain virtues, such as honesty, courage, etc.?
- Should the decision-maker avoid vices, such as sleaziness, timidity, etc.?
- How can the decision contribute to making the community or organization flourish?
- Does the character of the organization help cooperation in a market society?
- Does the organization have traits that prevent any parties from flourishing?
- Does the organization need to change its structure?
- Would a decision to promote virtue lead to rights violations or utility reductions?

CASE STUDY

Analyze this case study using the ethical theory that you have learned so far. You will find a collection of learning materials applying to the case on the book's website: http://sites.broadviewpress.com/businessethics/. These materials will help you in your analysis.

Should Gillian Trade on Her Inside Knowledge?

Gillian Lee is the senior administrative assistant to Jerry Adams, the vice-president of operations for Global Potash Enterprises. GPE is staking its future on its purchase of a mineral concession in northern Saskatchewan. The GPE stock price has been very volatile recently as investors await the publication of a geologist's report on the size of a potash deposit on GPE's concession. Right now investor opinion is optimistic, and GPE stock price is at a 52-week high. The geology report is due out in two days, but Jerry has already received a preliminary copy, and Gillian saw it on his desk. Not only did she see the report, she took a moment to glance inside it. The report is very bad news. There is not enough potash in the ground to make mining worthwhile, and GPE is in trouble. Its stock price is likely to collapse when investors see the report. Also GPE will have to make significant staff layoffs. Gillian is happy at GPE and Jerry has been a great boss, but she sees that she will be let go or asked to work for a secretary's salary.

Ever since GPE gambled on this potash concession, Gillian has been fantasizing about what she might do. One of her tentative plans involves betting against the stock price of GPE by secretly buying put options on GPE stock. She knows the penalties for insider trading are severe, that securities regulators are very diligent at discovering perpetrators, and that suspicion will fall on Jerry and those around him because of Jerry's position as VP. However, she has a second cousin, Patrick Lee, in Hong Kong who buys and sells securities. She thinks that if she goes to an Internet cafe, sets up a new webmail account, emails her cousin Sally Wong, and asks Sally to ask Patrick verbally to buy her 50,000 put options on GPE stock, then securities regulators will never know what she did. Her credit is good with Patrick, and she can trust Sally and him as family members. Exercising those put options will not make her hugely wealthy, but it will enable her to fund an MBA and get a new and better job.

Though she has dreamed up this plan, and she does not think that regulators will notice, she is still worried. She is an administrative assistant, not an officer of the firm. Yet, she feels an obligation to her firm's stockholders to further their interests, and an obligation to Jerry not to take advantage of his trust. She has always been loyal and honest at work. She has many friends at GPE, and enjoys being a member of the GPE community. She does not feel much obligation to the speculators who will be selling her the put options, even though she will perhaps be deceiving them. Because she is not an officer, insider activity reports would not reveal her trades to the market. Her relatively small transaction will have little effect on GPE's final share price, or put any stockholder at an unfair disadvantage. GPE has paid both for the concession and for the geology report.

Should Gillian put her plan into action?

Chapter 8

FEMINISM, EQUALITY, AND CARE ETHICS

Are there considerations of justice that apply especially to women?

Is there a distinctly feminist ethics of care?

What special responsibilities does a care ethic create?

We have seen how important specialization and the division of labour are to business prosperity. A market society can cost-effectively implement these forms of social cooperation by educating its citizens in such character traits as honesty and trustworthiness. These traits enable human beings to flourish in cooperation with other people who have similar or complementary character traits. However, specialization and the division of labour occur not only in business life, but also in family life. Men and women divide the labour of raising children. In market societies, up until the 1970s, men specialized in the business of providing economic resources for the family, while women specialized in the care of children. Men and women often developed different skills and character traits, traits that were necessary to their different roles in the family. Until recently, most market societies taught men the character traits of assertiveness, competitiveness, and strategic rationality that brought success in the public world of business, and taught women the character traits of caring, nurturing, and taking responsibility for the health of relationships that brought success in the domestic world of raising children.

This scheme of specialization and division of labour within the family may have been efficient, but it was frequently not fair. We can see this unfairness in the following caricature of a 1950's family. Ron and Sally are married with children. Ron is a hard-driving executive. He is hard working, honest, and trustworthy, but also ambitious, competitive, and tough. He plays by the rules of the game, but he plays only to win, and consequently has no friends at work. Sally married Ron straight out of high school. She is a wonderful stay-at-home mother, caring and nurturing, yet firm when necessary. She has lots of friends, and by sharing them with Ron, she provides him with a pleasant social life. Because Ron earns a lot of money, he controls the family finances and decides what they can afford. When Sally looked into finding part-time work, she found that she had no marketable skills, and that the available low-skill jobs offered only hours that conflicted with the needs of her children. Outside of the family circle, such as at the bank or at the car dealer, she finds that her social status depends on her role as Mrs. Ron, and not on her own domestic accomplishments. Ron and Sally are both very happy with their lives.

Creating the division of domestic labour without continuous coercive interventions required training men and women in different, gendered character traits. Men such as Ron were educated in the public virtues that are useful in the world of business, whereas women were educated in the domestic virtues that are useful in the world of the family. Training and preserving domestic virtues frequently involved keeping women out of the public world. Societies often denied young women, such as Sally, the opportunity to work in the public sphere. Sometimes this denial was enforced by law, sometimes by social opinion, sometimes by failing to provide women the necessary education, and sometimes by structuring the world of work to be hostile to those caring for dependent children. Society frequently denied equality of opportunity to women.

In this chapter, we will examine issues of gender equality and justice in the business world, and consider how best to resolve obstacles that hinder those goals. We will then consider another ethical theory, Care Ethics, which has emerged from the work of contemporary feminist philosophers.

EQUALITY OF OPPORTUNITY FOR WOMEN

Equality of opportunity says that a distribution is just only if it assigns positions in the workplace according to morally relevant criteria such as skill, and not according to morally arbitrary criteria such as race, gender, or sexual orientation. As we have seen, there are several interpretations of equality of opportunity.

Formal equality of opportunity requires men and women to have equal legal rights, so that that there are no legal impediments to any person competing for positions or promotions. The only issue should be whether applicants have the requisite skills. On this view, competition for positions should be gender neutral, and there should be equal pay for work of equal value.

Fair equality of opportunity goes further. It requires both that there be formal equality of opportunity, and that society give everyone a fair chance to acquire the skills needed to compete for positions and promotions in the workplace. A society that offered equal educational resources to both men and women would satisfy this principle.

There may be cases where affirmative action and positive discrimination in favour of women is acceptable within formal and fair equality of opportunity. Sometimes being a woman is a necessary part of a job specification. Nursing homes for elderly women might hire only female attendants because of the modesty requirements of their patients. Business schools with largely male faculties might discriminate in favour of hiring new female professors because they believe that female professors provide role models for female business students.

Achieving full equality of opportunity for women may, however, require more than better resources or preferential hiring. Let us suppose that, in a society that educates everyone equally, a firm that practices equality of opportunity ends up with an

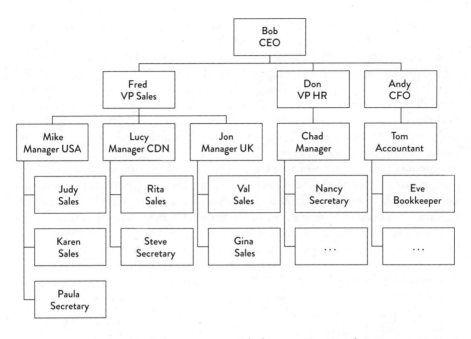

Figure 8.1: What is wrong with this organization chart?

organization chart such as the one in Figure 8.1. What could have gone wrong? The nine women in the chart have most of the subordinate, lower paid jobs as sales and administrative staff, whereas the nine men have most of the higher paid, managerial jobs. Perhaps there is a structural reason for this situation.

It may be that the implicit specifications for the various positions systematically impede women. The managerial positions may require long hours and frequent travel, so that an implicit requirement of the positions is that the manager be free of responsibility for the care of young children. Traditionally, most of the responsibility for the care of children has fallen on women, and this is still often the case. So many women do not meet this implicit requirement, and do not apply for the positions. The design of the managerial jobs is, by itself, a barrier to the participation of women. Because of the structure of the workplace, women do not have an equal opportunity to become managers.

Structural equality of opportunity requires that organizations design positions in such a way that women can fill those positions. In this example, businesses can implement structural equality of opportunity through the design of jobs and in the provision of services such as daycare. Other examples of structural inequalities of opportunity arise because of the different physiques of men and women. Typically, women are shorter and lighter than men are. Therefore, a job that specifies a minimum height or weight may create a barrier to the participation of women, even though it does not specifically require that all applicants be male. Such specifications are often not intentionally sexist; they may arise because of the size of the equipment used on the job.

For example, firefighting equipment is quite heavy and requires that firefighters have a certain size and strength, which excludes most women from becoming firefighters. However, the nature of firefighting may not have determined the weight of firefighting equipment. The people who, in the past, designed firefighting equipment may have expected men to be using it, and designed it to suit typical male physical capabilities. Lighter equipment might be equally efficient at fighting fires and more suitable to the capabilities of both men and women.

Structural barriers to equal opportunities for women were not necessarily the product of intentional sexism, or of an explicit patriarchal plot to keep women in subordinate positions. Instead, the historical construction of job specifications often reflected traditional expectations about the roles of men and women. Historically, job specifications arose within a cultural framework that saw it as natural and normal for men to perform managerial and firefighting jobs and for women to work in the home.

Job specifications and job circumstances reflect a social reality, not a natural reality. Therefore, human intervention can change them. Justice requires that firms perceive the existence of morally arbitrary barriers to the participation of women and act to remove those barriers. They can do so by redesigning equipment, providing daycare, creating flexible work hours, and so on. Structural equality of opportunity for women requires attention to these details.

DOMESTIC JUSTICE

In the past, the division of family labour has required that men and women have different dispositions, attitudes, and character traits. Typically, they began to learn these traits when they were children, taught by their family. Boys learned the competitive team-sport traits that enabled them to thrive in the world of business, whereas girls learned the nurturing traits that enabled them to care for the next generation of children. Stereotypically, boys have learned to compete with one another while obeying the rules of a game, and girls have learned to play with dolls in imitation of childcare.

As well, both boys and girls learned a sense of justice. The sense of justice learned by boys and girls inside an old-fashioned family was not necessarily in accord with the moral equality of persons. Among subsistence farmers, in an economy without money, the amount of labour performed by men and women was approximately equal. Since neither men nor women received any remuneration, their work had an equal financial value of zero for both. In a developed market economy, however, the business of men traditionally created financial resources for men, whereas the domestic duties of women went unpaid. Men, like Ron, were paid, and this gave them control over the financial resources of the family. Furthermore, in the conceptual framework of a market economy, people understood the value of work to be how much others were willing to pay for it. Consequently, a market economy placed a high value on the traditional work of men and no value on the traditional work of women, like Sally.

Therefore, the sense of justice that children acquired within an old-fashioned family was liable to be incorrect in at least two ways. Children learned, first, that men should control financial resources, and, second, that women's domestic work was of less value than was men's public work. Women often learned to adapt their preferences to what they received under this conventional distribution of financial resources and to be content with their domestic lives. Women also learned that their domestic skills of caring and nurturing others were of less value than the competitive skills of men, and that their intuitive ethical reasoning and emotional partiality had no place in the public world. Moral education within the traditional family severely failed the cause of women's equality.

Democratic societies, even ones with an egalitarian bent, have been loath to attempt reform of moral education within the family. Democratic societies are committed to the moral equality of persons, and this means they are committed to a right to privacy that permits people to lead their own lives very largely without interference from the government. Democratic societies have taken this right to privacy to imply that the government should not interfere in family life, unless doing so is necessary to prevent harm to others. The right to privacy appears to imply that the state should not interfere in the moral education of children within the family.

Democratic societies do have a vital interest, however, in the moral education of children. We have seen that state coercion is an inefficient way of enforcing commercial cooperation; it is much more efficient if citizens learn and internalize the character traits of honesty, trustworthiness, and so on, that make business transactions work without state intrusion. A similar point holds for state enforcement of the basic tenet of a democratic society, the moral equality of persons. A democratic society should distribute rights, liberties, and economic resources equally. It should not discriminate based on morally arbitrary factors such as sex, race, and sexual orientation. A democratic society will be much more efficient and far less intrusive if its citizens have a basic sense of justice that respects this moral equality. Citizens acquire their basic sense of justice as children within their family. If children, such as those of Ron and Sally, learn that, contrary to the principle of moral equality, gender is an appropriate way to distribute resources, family labour, and the value of work, then they will not learn the sense of justice required to support a democratic society.

This distinction between private and public life has created a dilemma for democratic societies. On the one hand, their commitment to a right to privacy and the harm principle commits them to staying out of moral education within the family. On the other hand, they require that children learn within their families that discrimination based on gender is unjust in order for a democratic society to function effectively. Democratic societies cannot both respect the privacy of the family and inculcate a sense of justice if the predominant conceptual framework of the society normalizes the subordination of women.

THE OPPRESSION OF WOMEN

We have found democratic societies caught in a dilemma regarding the equal moral status of women. To resolve this dilemma, feminist ethics emphasizes the role everyone should play in understanding and contesting the patriarchal cultural framework that makes the subordination of women's interests seem natural and legitimate.

Understanding this cultural framework requires that we understand the nature and sources of power and oppression.

Following the economist, J.K. Galbraith, we can distinguish three forms of power. (Galbraith, 1983, pp. 5–6) **Coercive power** is the ability to dominate through force or the threat of force. A thief who robs at gunpoint exercises illegitimate coercive power over a shopkeeper. A police officer who arrests the thief exercises legitimate coercive power over the thief. **Economic power** is the ability to dominate through economic incentive or economic threat. A wealthy North American business owner who bribes a poorly paid Asian official exercises economic power over the official. **Conditioned power** is the ability to dominate through internalized beliefs and attitudes. Subordinates see their unquestioned submission as natural, and the dominant understand their dominance as ordinary and normal. Galbraith describes the conditioned power exercised by men over women as follows.

> However, it will be evident on brief thought that male power and female submission have relied much more completely on the belief since ancient times that such submission is the natural order of things.... But only a part of the subordination of women was achieved by explicit instruction—explicit conditioning. Much and almost certainly more was (and is) achieved by the simple acceptance of what the community and culture have long thought right and virtuous.... This is implicit conditioning, a powerful force. Overall, this conditioned submission proceeded from belief, belief that masculine will was preferable to undue assertion of their own and the counterpart belief by men that they were entitled by their sex or associated physical and mental qualities to dominate..... There is proof of this power of belief in the nature of the modern effort at emancipation—the women's movement.... a major part of the effort has been the challenge to belief—the belief that submission and subservience are normal, virtuous, and otherwise appropriate. (Galbraith, 1983, pp. 25–26)

This sort of power enables Ron to subordinate Sally's interests to his own. In their old-fashioned family relationship, both Ron and Sally see an objectively unjust distribution of resources as subjectively fair and natural.

Collective cultural oppression underpins the individual exercise of ideological power. In the case of coercive power, an individual feature of a thief, his possession of a gun, causes the thief's coercive power over the shopkeeper. No individual feature of Ron causes his ideological power over Sally. Rather, Ron's dominance has the same cause as Sally's submission. They both share an oppressive cultural framework that legitimizes Ron's domination and Sally's subordination. **Oppression** is the exercise of power by means of the structure of a group, a community, or a society as a whole. Oppression has an accumulative structure. One instance of whatever it is that creates oppression is not enough by itself to oppress anyone; oppression requires the general prevalence of that which creates it. For example, structural inequality of opportunity becomes oppressive to women only when it becomes general. By itself, one fire department in a large city that uses overly large firefighting equipment may not oppress women. However, if all fire departments, police departments, and ambulance departments employ equipment designed for the physiques of men, then this society oppresses women by excluding them from whole classes of employment.

Marilyn Frye suggested that oppression is metaphorically like a cage. (Frye, 1983, pp. 4–5) Each instance of discrimination is like a bar of the cage. Though it may be an obstacle to someone, each bar is not itself oppressive. Oppression is like the cage itself, a framework of obstacles that collectively exercises power over women's lives by making certain activities almost impossible for them. The framework of obstacles that creates oppression can be intellectual as well as physical. Societies and cultures have conceptual frameworks that they construct through the shared beliefs of all members of the society. A **conceptual framework** is a mutually supporting, seldom questioned, and resilient set of fundamental assumptions about the world, about human nature, and about ethical values, that affects how people think and act in the world. People employ the assumptions of their conceptual framework in their reasoning without reflecting on or even noticing these assumptions. It is difficult for us to see the conceptual framework of our own culture because we live our lives inside it. It is easier to see how conceptual structures change over time. The best known example of a changing conceptual structure is the scientific revolution in which Copernicus' view of the solar system orbiting around the Sun replaced the ancient Ptolemaic view of the Sun, Moon, and planets rotating around the Earth.

It is possible for a society's conceptual framework to be oppressive. An **oppressive conceptual framework** is a conceptual framework that makes relationships of domination and subordination seem normal, natural, and unquestionable. Again, it is easier for us to see the oppressive nature of the conceptual frameworks of other, distant people than it is for us to see our own. Consider the conceptual structure of Ancient Greece as Aristotle described it in the fourth century BCE.

> And it is clear that the rule of the soul over the body, and of the mind and the rational element over the passionate, is natural and expedient; whereas the equality of the two or the rule of the inferior is always hurtful. The same holds good of animals in relation to men; for tame animals have a better nature than wild, and all tame animals are better off when they are ruled by man; for then they are preserved. Again, the male is by nature superior, and the female inferior; and the one rules, and the other is ruled; this principle, of necessity, extends to all mankind. Where then there is such a difference as that between soul and body, or between men and animals ... the lower sort are by nature slaves, and it is better for them as for all inferiors that they should be under the rule of a master. (Aristotle, 350 BCE, *Politics*, Book I, Part V)

Athens of the fourth century BCE was a patriarchal, slave-owning society that was also humanity's first attempt at democracy. It was a democracy, however, that recognized the moral equality of male citizens while accepting the moral inferiority of women and foreign slaves. The Athenian conceptual framework contained a logic of domination that made for unthinking acceptance of the moral inferiority of women seem natural and normal.

A **logic of domination** is a structure of argumentation that justifies relationships of domination and subordination within an oppressive conceptual framework. (Warren, 1990, pp. 127–28) We can see this logic of domination at work in the passage from Aristotle. Aristotle represents men as having minds with a predominately rational rather than a passionate element, and animals, slaves, and women as lacking this rational element. It seems natural and expedient to Aristotle that those lacking the rational element are not morally equal to those who possess it, and that the latter should rule the former. We can reconstruct Aristotle's thinking in the following structure of argumentation:

1. Men have the characteristic of rationality and women do not.
2. Whoever is rational is morally superior to whoever is not.
3. Therefore, men are morally superior to women.
4. Whoever is morally superior is justified in dominating whoever is morally inferior.
5. Therefore, men are justified in dominating women.

Fortunately, people seldom explicitly defend a patriarchal logic of domination such as Aristotle's. Yet people often implicitly assume that women are more intuitive, emotional, and partial in their decision-making than men are, and that men are more calculating, principled, dispassionate, and impartial in their decision-making than women are. This can have a tendency to make people think that men are therefore better decision-makers, and that men should generally hold positions of power. Such thinking can seem natural and normal within the conceptual structure of our society. However, when we see where such thinking can lead, then we should guard against uncritically accepting or promoting it.

CARE ETHICS

To what extent gender-associated differences are genetically based is often a matter of debate. Nevertheless, it's clear that the efficient raising of the next generation of children historically brought about a gender-based specialization and division of labour within the family. Men specialized in the skills, character traits, and attitudes required in the workplace (the public virtues) while women specialized in the complementary skills, character traits, and attitudes required in the home (the domestic virtues). Their families, their schools, their colleges, and the expectations of their society as a whole educated and conditioned boys and girls in these different virtues. In recent times, feminists have contested this conditioning, and families, schools, colleges, and social expectations. The result is the beginnings of a society with a fairer division of labour.

Still, an oppressive conceptual framework may remain. It contains a logic that is reminiscent of the logic of domination that Aristotle assumed. The logic runs like this:

1. Men's ethical reasoning tends to be principled, dispassionate, and impartial.
2. Women's ethical reasoning tends to be intuitive, emotional, and partial.
3. Ethical decision-making should be principled, dispassionate, and impartial.
4. Therefore, there is no place for women's style of ethical reasoning in ethical-decision making.

As we have seen, the cost-benefit calculations of utilitarianism, the emphasis on respecting rights and principles of justice in deontology, and even the emphasis on virtues of fairness, courage, and honesty in virtue ethics suggest that ethical decision-making is principled, dispassionate, and impartial.

However, there is considerable evidence that women's moral development and women's decision-making in matters of morality is different from that of men and from that of traditional ethical theory. In her ground-breaking study of women's moral development, *In a Different Voice*, Carol Gilligan argued that women have a different conception of moral decision-making.

> In this conception, the moral problem arises from conflicting responsibilities rather than from competing rights and requires for its resolution a mode of thinking that is contextual and narrative rather than formal and abstract. This conception of morality as concerned with the activity of care centres moral development around the understanding of responsibility and relationships, just as the conception of morality as fairness ties moral development to the understanding of rights and rules. (Gilligan, 1982, p. 19)

Some critics have objected that this position enshrines the "female essence" that feminism so often has seen as the basis of oppression, exclusion, and inequality. But some feminists have embraced this difference, and have argued instead that a female-associated ethics of care ought to be encouraged. A care ethic incorporates caring for less powerful others and nurturing important relationships into ethical decision-making. There is some controversy whether care ethics should replace traditional, rule-governed ethics or whether it should supplement it. In keeping with our ethically pluralist approach, we shall adopt the latter approach and investigate how considerations drawn from care ethics can help us make better decisions in ethical matters.

In recent times, feminist thought and political action have changed the conceptual framework of contemporary culture. The deeply held assumptions behind the old-fashioned family no longer seem natural and normal to everyone. It is now more common for fathers to be involved in the lives of their children, and for mothers to work outside the home in important, well-paid public positions. Consequently, the domestic style of ethical reasoning, traditionally associated with women but increasingly learned by men, is spreading from the home to the workplace. Employing the reasoning of care ethics in public life is becoming increasingly both common and acceptable.

Care ethics is an ethics based in the special relationships, like that of mother and child, which people have to one another and in the relationship skills and emotional traits that make such attachments possible. It is an identity-based feminism, which affirms that historically there have been differences between men and women's ethical reasoning, and argues that these create an alternative feminist standpoint in ethics. Childbearing, motherhood, and care for dependents give women a special perspective on ethical decision-making. Care ethics recognizes that these relationships are relationships of unequal power, but insists that they should not give rise to subordination. Care ethics makes a more radical claim than liberal feminism makes. Liberal feminism is justice-based. It claims that the interests and rights of women should receive the same consideration as the interests and rights of men. Gender is usually morally irrelevant, and justice should be mostly gender neutral. The exceptions involve ensuring structural equality of opportunity to enable motherhood and the care for dependents. Care ethics, however, suggests that the justice-based approach to ethical reasoning requires supplementation by ethical reasoning based on relationships and responsibilities.

We cannot formulate care ethics in simple principles such as, "Act always to produce the maximum human happiness," or "Act only according to a maxim that you can will to be a universal law." In this respect, care ethics is like virtue ethics. It emphasizes the teaching and learning of ethical skills, traits of character, and emotional responses that are required to nurture human relationships. Relationship to others is vital to a human life. Human beings can neither grow nor thrive in the absence of relationships to others. Creating and sustaining such relationships requires skill, attention, and the appropriate attitudes and dispositions. A care ethics that brings these traits into the workplace will include at least three components:

1. An emphasis on moral perception
2. An emphasis on relationships and responsibilities
3. An emphasis on partial and particularistic moral reasoning

We can illustrate these components of the ethics of care with an extended example.

Tina and Vera are sales staff in a toy store. Managers have caught both of them stealing merchandise. Tina is newly hired. She lives with her well-off partner and has no children. She has had many sales jobs in the past. She does not get along well with her fellow employees and is often grumpy with customers. She has stolen a toy to sell at a weekend flea market in order to supplement her pay, which she feels is very poor. Vera is a long-term employee, who is helpful to all. She is a single mother living in low-income housing. Short of money because of a temporary crisis, she has stolen a toy for her child's birthday present. She intends to pay for the toy with her next paycheque.

First, the care ethics emphasis on moral perception suggests that decision-makers should learn and cultivate sensitivity to the needs of others and to the nature of the relationships between people. This means developing a nuanced sensitivity to the individual particularity of real people, not just an abstract understanding of the common humanity of human beings. The practitioner of care ethics will perceive the emotional needs and hurts of the persons he is considering and not simply treat them as autonomous, rational, utility maximizers. He will examine the whole context of the ethical situation and not create only a simple model of the situation that abstracts from its details so that it readily falls under some principle or other. He will discern the contextual differences between ethical situations rather than look only for the similarities that will enable him to apply abstract ethical principles to the case. The practitioner of care ethics will cultivate the virtues of moral sensitivity and discernment.

At our hypothetical toy store, a stereotypical Fair-Minded Manager will abstract from the details of the lives of Tina and Vera and from her relationship to the two clerks. She will see both women as competent adults who have made the bad choice to steal from the store. She will thus be disposed to punish them equally. On the other hand, a Caring Manager will attend to the different characters of Tina and Vera. Tina's character is problematic whereas, except in this particular situation, Vera is loyal, cooperative, and dependable. A Caring Manager will pay attention to the different contexts of the two women's lives. He will notice that Vera has a tough time financially and has big responsibilities at home, whereas he will see that Tina is much better off financially and has few domestic responsibilities. He will also pay attention to the different relationships that the two women have to the business and to himself. He will thus be disposed to see their cases differently. This does not mean that he will automatically fire Tina and let Vera off with a warning. His reasoning must also take into account considerations such as fairness, respect for rights, and his particular duties to the toy store's owners. The difference is that the Caring Manager, but not the Fair-Minded Manager, will perceive and thus be able to take into account the significant differences between Tina and Vera.

Second, the care ethics emphasis on relationships and responsibilities will incorporate an ethical concern for responsibilities to particular others and a concern for the quality of relationships with others. Practitioners of care ethics will be disposed to care for the quality of their relationships to others and to care for the relationships between others. They will see life is about cooperation and reciprocity, not about conflict and competition, therefore they will focus on strengthening that sustains social cooperation rather than on respecting rights, applying principles of justice, or calculating how to maximize happiness.

In the toy-store case, the Fair-Minded Manager will take Tina and Vera to be fully responsible for their own decisions. She will take no responsibility for either of them. She will regard her long-term relationship to Vera as a source of partiality that is an impediment to her ethical reasoning. The Caring Manager will recognize his different relationships to Tina and Vera, and of each of their relationships to the firm. He will consider the long-term relationship of reciprocity and cooperation that he and the firm have had with Vera. He will take some, though not full, responsibility for Vera's life and the quality of Vera's relationship to the firm and its customers. He will take the firm to have more responsibilities to its long-term employees such as Vera than to its newly hired employees such as Tina. He will incorporate his different responsibilities to the two clerks into his ethical reasoning along with his other ethical concerns regarding fairness, theft, and happiness. Again, this does not mean that he will automatically fire Tina and merely warn Vera, but it does mean that he will be disposed to consider his differing responsibilities to the two women in his ethical judgment.

Third, the care ethics emphasis on particularistic moral reasoning means that practitioners of the ethics of care will not mechanically dismiss their perception of, and care for, different relationships to different people because such relationships detract from the impartiality of their ethical reasoning. The act of promising gives promisors special obligations to their promisees. Shared community membership gives virtuous people special obligations to fellow community members. These ethical obligations exist, even though they do not override all other considerations in ethical reasoning. Similarly, caring relationships give practitioners of the ethics of care special obligations to particular others. This results in partiality of concern, which caring people must balance against other ethical considerations. Care ethics requires the cultivation and application of the virtues of both caring and wisdom. Balancing care for special relationships against other ethical reasons requires ethical judgment that is more than just the application of principles, the calculation of utilities, or even the cultivation of virtues of fairness and impartiality.

Standard ethics	Care ethics
abstract principles	context & partiality
common humanity	particular individuals
competition & conflict	cooperation & reciprocity
atomistic individuals	relationships
justice	caring
rights and duties	responsibilities
calculation of consequences	wisdom

Table 8.1: Comparison of the different emphases of conventional ethics and the ethics of care.

In the toy store case, the Fair-Minded Manager sees Tina and Vera only as people who have made wrong choices. She believes in treating like cases alike and in applying principles of impartial justice. She understands stealing as an infringement of the firm's property rights, no matter who does it. The Caring Manager sees the cases of Tina and Vera differently. They have different characters, their stealing arises in different contexts, and he and his firm have different relationships to the two women. He is more concerned about his and his firm's strong relationship to Vera than he is about their weak relationship to Tina. He takes on some responsibility for Vera, and is less worried about impartiality and property rights than is the Fair-Minded Manager. Rather than trying to be impartial and fair, he tries to be wise and caring in his decision about how to treat the two women, and to seek solutions to the ethical problem that accommodate his responsibility to care.

CONCERNS REGARDING CARE ETHICS

We have several reasons for being worried about justifying care ethics. If we understand care ethics as an intended replacement for all other forms of ethics, then these constitute strong objections to a care ethic. If we understand a care ethic, however, as giving us important ethical reasons that we must weigh along with reasons drawn from other ethical perspectives, then these considerations tell us that care ethics has limitations, and not that care ethics is false.

Firstly, standard ethical theories make a virtue of their impartiality. Standard theories are universal in scope and apply their recommendations to everyone equally. It is the very essence of justice that just decisions treat everyone the same unless there are morally relevant grounds for treating them differently. Yet, as we have seen, the ethics of care abandons total impartiality. Consider, for example, Tina's moral outrage at having been punished more severely than Vera, given that both of them were guilty of exactly the same stealing. She would say that it's unjust, and so would her union, and they would both be right.

Care ethics reminds us that special relationships sometimes provide morally relevant grounds for being partial in our decisions. Consider a case where a woman sees two children drowning in a pool. She does not have time to save them both. One of them is her son and the other is unknown to her. She decides to save her son. Her special relationship to her son and her special responsibilities for her son give her morally relevant reasons for deciding to save him rather than the unknown child. The ethics of care calls our attention to important and morally relevant considerations. On the other hand, it is important for a care ethic to avoid nepotism. In the business world, special relationships based on family and friendship can conflict with treating others as moral equals in the distribution of positions and rewards. Balancing care against justice is a difficult task requiring experience and wisdom.

Secondly, it is difficult to see how to extend an ethic of care to poor people in distant countries (or to people in future generations) with whom we have no relationships. It is easier for ethical theories based on universal and impartial moral consideration to look after the interests of distant or future people than it is for ethical theories based on special relationships to particular people. This objection applies most strongly to the idea that a feminist ethic of care should replace standard ethics. The objection applies only weakly to the idea that a care ethics provides us with reasons to care for special people, reasons that we must balance against other impartial reasons of fairness and respect for human rights generally. As well, a defender of care ethics can point to the lack of success of impartial moral theory in actually promoting the interests of distant and future others. Abstract principles of justice seem unable to guide the actions of real people, whose motivations tend to be concrete and specific. Perhaps the task of global ethics is to create special relationships between nearby people and faraway people in need. For example, the non-governmental organization, Plan International (Foster Parent Plan), raises aid for international development projects through a system of child sponsorship. Though Plan International actually spends aid money on global justice and community development, this system allows donors to correspond with a particular sponsored child in a community that Plan is aiding, and to form a relationship with him or her. People, who would not give development aid for abstract reasons of justice, do give aid because of these particular relationships.

Thirdly, it is difficult for an ethic of care to define just how much care we should give to others. A caretaker must care both for others and for herself. How much care is appropriate for others and how much for her? The justice-based approach offers a ready solution; a caregiver is entitled to a fair share, just as others are. An alternative is to interpret an ethic of care as parallel to a virtue ethic. A virtue is often a mean between two vices. For example, courage is the mean between cowardice and recklessness.

Figure 8.2: Courage is the mean between cowardice and recklessness.

In virtue ethics, we require practical wisdom to determine when courage becomes foolish recklessness on one side, and when courage becomes weak fearfulness on the other. Similarly, care is the mean between selfishness and self-sacrifice.

Figure 8.3: Care is the mean between selfishness and self-sacrifice.

The practitioner of care ethics requires practical wisdom as well as a sense of justice to determine the boundaries between care and selfishness and between care and self-sacrifice.

SUMMARY

1. Historically, families involved specialization and the division of family labour between men, who acquired the public virtues of business life, and women, who acquired the domestic virtues of family life.
2. One consequence of this division of family labour was structural inequality of opportunity in the workplace. When women joined the workforce, they often found that implicit job specifications included having men's physiques or having men's traditional freedom from responsibility for the care of dependent others.
3. In old-fashioned families, men worked for pay outside the home, and women worked for no pay inside the home. This division of labour created a situation in which men controlled the family's financial resources and in which society valued men's public work more highly than it did women's domestic work. Children learned that this was a natural and normal state of affairs, and, as a result, traditional families did not teach a gender-neutral sense of justice.

4. Democratic states, which need their citizens to learn to treat each other as moral equals, did not try to change this situation because they respected a right to family privacy.

5. Conditioned power, which is the ability to dominate through internalized beliefs and attitudes, enabled the subordination of women to men. Historically, both men and women accepted an oppressive conceptual framework whose unquestioned assumptions legitimized male domination. Feminists have effectively criticized the naturalness and normalness of these assumptions, and the patriarchal conceptual framework is losing its hold on people.

6. Whether through upbringing or biology, women appear to have a different way of approaching ethical decisions than do men. A feminist ethics of care seeks to bring the different ethical perspective of women out of the domestic sphere and into the public sphere of paid work.

7. Care ethics emphasizes perceiving the needs of people involved in a problematic business situation. It emphasizes the decision-maker's responsibilities to the people involved and to the relationships between them. It emphasizes the importance of attending to particular people and to special relationships in our ethical reasoning.

8. A care ethics that seeks to replace conventional morality will have difficulties with using impartial reasoning when it is called for, with responsibilities to distant others or to unborn generations, and with balancing caring for others against self-sacrifice.

9. An ethic of care that adds to, rather than replaces, conventional ethical approaches to problematic business situations can work around these difficulties.

ONLINE LEARNING RESOURCES

You will find a collection of learning resources associated with this chapter on the book's website: http://sites.broadviewpress.com/businessethics/. Working through this material will help you understand and remember important concepts that we have discussed, and will help you apply them to issues in business ethics.

STUDY QUESTIONS

Answering the following questions will help you to understand the ethical theory in this chapter and will help you to create a set of review notes on the textbook.

1. Why did men and women historically acquire different skills and character traits?

2. Why, even when laws became gender-neutral and women became well educated, did women still face structural inequality of opportunity in the workplace?
3. Why did women in old-fashioned families face inequality in financial resources and in the value put on their work?
4. Why does the traditional family pose a dilemma for a democratic state?
5. Describe a patriarchal conceptual framework and explain why it is oppressive to women.
6. How does the feminist ethic of care differ from a liberal feminist emphasis on equal rights for women in solving problems in the workplace?
7. Describe three important components of applying care ethics to the world of business.
8. Why would a care ethic that sought totally to replace standard, universalizing, and impartial ethics have difficulty accounting for our responsibilities to future generations?

DECISION QUESTIONS

The whole point of learning ethical theory is to understand and ask questions like the following when you are analyzing an ethically problematic situation or case.

- Is sexual or racial harassment involved?
- Are there institutional barriers to women, or parents of small children, etc.?
- Is affirmative action permitted or obligatory?
- For which individuals should the decision-maker show special care?
- Should the decision-maker pay particular attention to anyone's emotional needs?
- Which relationships should the decision-maker help to flourish?
- Would enhancing these relationships give the decision-maker special responsibilities?
- Would a decision to care for special relationships lead to partiality and unfairness?

CASE STUDY

Analyze this case study using the ethical theory that you have learned so far. You will find a collection of learning materials applying to the case on the book's website: http://sites.broadviewpress.com/businessethics/. These materials will help you in your analysis.

Harry and Preferential Hiring

Professor Harold (Harry) Jenkins has just become Dean of the Faculty of Management at Eastern University. At just 35 years of age, Harry is the youngest Dean in EU history. EU has approximately 2,000 students majoring in management studies and another 200 doing their MBAS. The EU management faculty has 50 professors and 20 support staff, with the following gender breakdown.

	Men	Women
Professors	45	5
Support staff	2	18
Students	1,000	1,200

The EU teaching faculty is a good one. Its members are very competitive and do a lot of excellent research. University support for instructional development and a system of student and peer evaluation help ensure that faculty members are committed to teaching excellence. The faculty, staff, and students are on a first name basis.

The EU management faculty has received permission from the EU Board of Governors to hire a new assistant professor of finance. The search committee has recommended two names to Harry. One is a young woman, Dr. Anna Orsini, who received her PhD five years ago and has since been teaching part-time while she raised two small children. The other is a young man, Dr. Jon Schmidt, who spent five years working on Wall St. before recently completing his PhD. Both appear to be good teachers, but Jon has significant work-experience, and several publications, whereas Anna has published just one article based on the research in her thesis, and no relevant work-experience. As the Dean, Harry must make the final decision regarding whom to hire.

Harry thought that Jon would fit right in to the culture of the management faculty. He would make a fine colleague, would engage with other faculty members on their research, and provide a model to students of how to manage a busy and successful career. Harry thought that Anna would not fit so readily into the present culture of the department, but would instead challenge it. She would contribute to changing the department into a more caring, more cooperative, and less competitive workplace. She would also provide a good role model for the many female students in the department, and would be a supportive colleague for the five other female professors. Hiring Anna would show a commitment by EU Management Studies to nurturing the potential excellence of women as well as men.

Would it be ethical for Harry to hire Anna?

Chapter 9

MORAL ACCOUNTABILITY

How can we determine causal responsibility for the outcome of a decision?

Whom should we hold morally accountable for their motivations or characters?

Can a whole organization be morally accountable for a decision?

When we analyze a business decision from an ethical point of view, often the most difficult problem is determining who or what is morally accountable for the decision and its consequences. This chapter will give a sense of just how difficult this question is, and will survey some of the ethical considerations that go into answering it.

Let us recall the imaginary case of Amy from Chapter 1. Amy works for a company where the stockholders are dissatisfied with the company's returns. The Board of Directors tells the CEO that profits must improve. The CEO tells the VP in charge of production to cut costs, but does not say how. The VP convenes a cost-cutting committee to make a recommendation. Amy proposes to the cost-cutting committee that her firm outsource the production of a popular clothing item to an offshore contractor operating in a lower wage environment. The committee recommends this to the VP. The company signs a contract with an offshore firm.

Suppose, first, that this arrangement becomes very profitable for Amy's company. At the end of the year, the board of directors decides to give handsome bonuses to the executives who are responsible for the new arrangement. The CEO has to decide how to distribute this bonus fund. Should he give it all to Amy? Should he give some to the VP who convened the cost-cutting committee? Should he reward the whole committee for its decision? Should he include the members of the committee who voted against the idea? Should he pay a bonus to the contractor, or to the overseas workers, or even to himself for leading such a great team? This is both an economic and an ethical decision. The CEO will be concerned to create incentives for good management decisions, to build team cooperation, and to make everyone feel properly rewarded. However, the correct decision is not obvious, and it will require skill and good judgment on the part of the CEO.

Now suppose disaster happens. To cope with the increased production, the overseas contractor adds a shoddily built extra floor to the factory building. The building collapses while people are working inside, and hundreds of garment workers die in the rubble. Who is morally accountable for the factory workers' injuries? Is it the factory owner, who built the unsafe factory? Is it the CEO, who ordered the cost cutting? Is it the committee, which recommended moving production offshore? Is it Amy, who suggested employing an overseas contractor? Is everyone in this diffuse chain of causation fully morally accountable? Is everyone partially accountable and many people must share accountability? Is the chain so diffuse that no one is morally accountable? Does it make sense to say that Amy's company, a legal fiction and a nexus of legal contracts, can be morally accountable? An agent is **morally accountable** for an action and its consequences if we should praise or blame her for her freely made decision and for its results. Who is morally accountable in this case?

We are going to find that different ethical theories give different sorts of answers to these questions. Like moral judgments generally, judgments about moral accountability are complex and difficult. Luckily, we can use the same sorts of ethical considerations that we use in decision-making to help us look at the ethical reasoning involved in assigning moral responsibility for the outcomes of decisions. We do not have to study new ethical theories; we just have to apply the ones we already know to these new sets of questions.

THE "IS/OUGHT" GAP

Chapter 2 showed that we should not base our ethical judgments solely on factual judgments because ethical judgments have action-guiding force and factual judgments do not. There is a logical gap between statements about how the world is and statements about how the world should be. Philosophers refer to this important conclusion as the "is/ought" gap or as the fact/value distinction. The existence of the "is/ought" gap means that we cannot derive an ethical conclusion from an argument consisting of purely factual premises.

To say that someone is morally accountable for the outcome of her decision is to make a value judgment. It is a value judgment because it says that we should either praise or blame her for her decision, that we should either admire or scorn her for her character, or that we should either reward or punish her for the result of her decision. These are not factual judgments; they are ethical judgments.

To say, however, that someone is causally responsible for an outcome is to make a factual judgment. It is a factual judgment because it says that some action that he intended to perform and then did perform caused the outcome to happen. It is a factual judgment because to see if it is true, we need to investigate his mental state, his physical behaviour, and the existence of a causal connection between his action and the outcome.

Because of the "is/ought" gap, to say of someone that he is causally responsible for an outcome is not to say that he is morally accountable for the outcome. His causal responsibility is a factual judgment, whereas his moral accountability is a value judgment. To move from causal responsibility to moral accountability, we require an additional premise taken from ethical theory. One ethical theory that connects causal responsibility and moral accountability is the theory of retributive justice. According to principles of retributive justice, society ought to punish a person for an action if he intended his action to cause a particular harm to others and his action actually did cause this harm. The criminal law mirrors the moral theory of retributive justice. In most legal systems, there are two requirements for a person to be guilty of certain crimes: he was the cause of the harm (in legal Latin, *actus reus*—the "guilty act") and if he understood that he was causing harm and that this was wrong (*mens rea*—the "guilty mind"). To secure a conviction and get the defendant punished, the prosecution must prove that both of these conditions were present in the alleged crime.

The retributive-justice-plus-causal-responsibility model of moral responsibility is prevalent in our culture. People often defend their actions by arguing either that they did not intend a bad result or that we cannot prove that their actions caused the bad result, and then consider it unfair if we blame them for their actions. For example, Amy might easily argue that she has no responsibility for the factory collapse because she only intended to increase company profits, or because her role in the decision was so small that it did not cause the unsafe building to collapse.

Nevertheless, retributive justice is not the only approach to ethics or to moral accountability. Virtue ethics would hold Amy accountable for the character traits that she displayed in her actions. Was she either stupid or willfully ignorant in not knowing of the safety risks in overseas factories? Knowing these risks, was she careless or reckless in advising offshore production? Ethical theories that appraise the motives of decision-makers might also hold Amy accountable. Was she thinking only of her yearly bonus, and did greed motivate her in her recommendation? Did she disregard principles of respect for human rights or of the fair distribution of risk? There are reasons for holding people morally accountable other than the combination of retributive justice and causal responsibility.

As well, the notion of causal responsibility is not as precise as we might initially assume. The determination of causality is a scientific operation; science is precise and objective, and so we might expect determination of causal responsibility to be precise and objective also. Yet, when we examine the determination of causal responsibility in more detail, we find that the notion of one condition being the cause of another is not as simple as we would wish. In the next section we will look at the scientific notion of causal responsibility in some detail in order to show the difficulties that arise in determining causal responsibility in business contexts.

CAUSAL RESPONSIBILITY

The determination of causal responsibility is important to the determination of moral accountability for two reasons. The first reason is prediction. In advance of a decision, a moral agent needs knowledge of cause and effect in order to predict the results of her decision. The decision maker needs to know something about what will happen when she chooses this course of action or that one. For example, she has to know the effect of deciding to ship a product at one time rather than another in order to know whether the shipment will fulfil her contractual obligations (promises) or not. The second reason is retrospective. Some ethical considerations, particularly considerations of retributive and compensatory justice, require that, after the decision, we know the cause in order to assign moral accountability (praise and blame) to the correct agent.

There are several main theories of what it is to be the causal condition of an outcome. The first is a theory that the cause of an outcome is a necessary condition for the outcome. One condition is a **necessary condition** for a second if the first state of affairs is required for the production of the second one. For example, the presence of oxygen is necessary for fire. However, a necessary condition may not be enough to produce the second condition, because the presence of further conditions may also be required. Oxygen alone is not enough to produce fire. To say that X is necessary for Y is to say that whenever Y occurs, X had to have been present. In legal reasoning, this is called the "but for" test for causation. To test whether X is a necessary condition for Y, we ask: but for X (that is, without X), would Y have occurred? If the answer is yes, then X is not a necessary condition for Y. If the answer is no, then X is a necessary condition for Y. Oxygen is necessary for fire: but for (without) the presence of oxygen, the fire would not have occurred.

The view that a causally responsible condition for an effect is a necessary condition for the effect has several weaknesses. One problem with the necessary condition test is the existence of causal chains. We often can see a chain of conditions all of which are necessary for the effect to happen. Members of the chain are all causal conditions of the outcome, and we need a reason for picking one of them. Amy's situation is like this: One, investors are unhappy. Two, the board directs the CEO. Three, the CEO instructs the VP. Four, Amy makes her suggestion to the committee. Five, a contact is signed. Six, the owner orders a new factory floor. Seven, the work is shoddy. Finally, a disaster happens. All seven of these conditions are necessary for that disaster. But for any of them, there would have been no disaster.

Legal reasoning would probably focus on the role of the overseas factory owner because he is the last person in the causal chain whose decision could have prevented the disaster. However, legal reasoning might also pass legal responsibility further up the chain if someone else had made their decision while foreseeing that the overseas factory would have significant safety issues. A similar issue would arise in assigning moral accountability. If we could reasonably expect Amy, or other decision-makers in Amy's company, to have investigated the risk of such safety issues, then we should hold her or them accountable for the disaster, at least in some part.

Another problem with relying solely on a necessary condition analysis of causal responsibility is the frequent existence of other factors that would have brought about the consequence anyway. Suppose, in our original example of overseas production, that if Amy had not suggested outsourcing, then her colleague, Ben would have immediately done so. It would no longer be the case that, but for Amy's suggestion, the disaster would not have occurred. So in this case, Amy's suggestion is not a necessary condition for the disaster. But she may be considered morally accountable for it anyway.

A second theory of causal responsibility is the view that a cause is a sufficient condition for an effect. A **sufficient condition** is a condition that is enough to bring about the effect even if it is not required to bring about the effect. Whenever the sufficient condition is present, the causal outcome is also present. We can show that X is not sufficient for Y by producing a case where the X is present and Y is absent. This notion of causal responsibility works for the situation described in the last paragraph. Either Amy or Ben's action would be sufficient, by itself, to cause the committee to consider an outsourcing strategy.

The main problem with assigning responsibility by the action that is a sufficient condition is that it is very rare that one person's action is sufficient all by itself. Actions are sufficient to bring about a result only given the proper combination of other background conditions. So, for example, throwing a switch is sufficient for lighting a light bulb assuming that the light bulb is not burned out, that the power is on, that the circuit connecting the switch and the bulb is not interrupted, and so on. When we count doing X as sufficient for Y, and thus that the person who did X is responsible for Y, it is almost always the case that doing X is sufficient for Y given a large number of other actions by other people. And that makes it hard to sort out who is really morally responsible. In our example, Amy's action is sufficient to cause the committee to consider outsourcing, but that's true only because of the background conditions: the committee has already decided to follow Amy's recommendation; the CEO has established the corporate structure to make this chain of decisions possible, and so on.

More particularly, the theory that causal conditions are sufficient conditions does not work in cases of joint production involving specialization and the division of labour. Suppose that, instead of producing pins, Jack and Jill are in the business of cooperatively producing a useful and valuable chemical, C. The formula for production of chemical C is this:

1 litre of chemical A + 1 litre of chemical B → 1 litre of product C + 1 litre of pollutant D

	Jack		Jill	
	A	B	A	B
Productivity per hour (litres)	9	1	1	9
Assume Jack and Jill each work a 10-hour day.				
Self-sufficient production of pollutant D	9		9	
Total self-sufficient production of pollutant D	18			
Specialized production of chemicals A and B	90	0	0	90
Total joint production of pollutant D	90			

Table 9.1: Model of a chemical factory producing pollutant D.

Jack is better at producing chemical A and so he specializes in producing A, whereas Jill is more efficient at producing chemical B and specializes in producing B. Together they produce valuable chemical C by reacting together chemicals A and B.

Unfortunately, chemical D is produced as a by-product of this chemical reaction, and chemical D makes people sick. In low doses, chemical D is harmless, but when production of chemical D passes a threshold of 20 litres per day, it becomes a harmful pollutant. Table 9.1 shows a model of the chemical factory. Working independently and self-sufficiently, Jack and Jill will produce 18 litres per day of chemical D, which is not a harmful amount. Working together, in a joint production model where they specialize and divide their labour, they will produce 90 litres of pollutant D per day, which is a harmful amount.

We can see that neither the work of Jack nor the work of Jill is enough to produce a harmful amount of pollutant D. The work of neither Jack nor Jill is a sufficient condition for the pollution, so neither Jack nor Jill is causally responsible for the pollution. If causal accountability grounds our appraisal of moral accountability, and we interpret causal conditions as sufficient conditions, then we can hold morally accountable neither Jack nor Jill for the harms of pollution. In a sufficient-condition model of causal responsibility, members of most organizations that employ specialization, the division of labour, and joint production (which includes most business firms) would evade accountability for their contributions to harmful corporate behaviour.

A third suggestion for the nature of causal responsibility is that a causal condition is a **NESS condition**, a Necessary Element in a Set of Sufficient conditions. The NESS condition theory will assign causal responsibility to both Jack and Jill. Jack's specialized work and Jill's specialized work will together form a set of jointly sufficient conditions for the production of 90 litres per day of pollutant D, an amount that is over the threshold of harm. The work of each of them is a necessary element in this set of sufficient condition. Without Jack's contribution, the factory would not produce 90 litres of pollutant D, and without Jill's contribution, the factory would not produce 90 litres of pollutant D. Therefore, the work of both is a necessary element in a set of sufficient conditions.

Unfortunately, we can find a typical business situation where the NESS theory does not properly account for causal responsibility. The NESS theory breaks down for committee decisions. Suppose the cost-cutting committee in our extended example has 7 members, and that all of whose members must vote. The motion that Amy puts forward to recommend overseas production passes by 5 votes to 2 votes. Amy, of course votes in favour of the motion. The 5 votes in favour of the motion are jointly sufficient for the motion to pass. If Amy were to have voted differently, or if she later changed her vote, the motion would still have passed by 4 votes to 3 votes. Amy's vote is not a necessary element in the set of votes sufficient for passing the motion. Therefore, Amy is not causally responsible for the motion's passing. Amy's vote is not a necessary condition of the motion passing, because passage of the motion is over-determined; the motion would pass anyway, no matter how she voted. Amy's vote is not sufficient for passage of the motion because her vote would not be enough by itself to pass it. Had the vote been 4 to 3, Amy's vote would have been a NESS condition of passing the motion because her vote would have been necessary, along with 3 other votes, to its passage. However, Amy's vote is not a NESS condition because the motion passes 5 votes to 2. Apparently, in a case where the motion passes by two or more votes, causal responsibility for disasters can evaporate in a committee meeting.

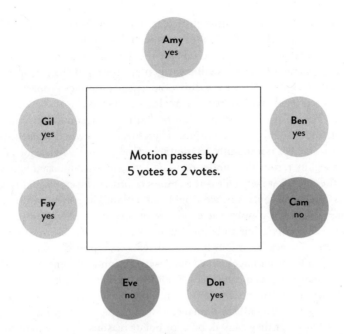

Figure 9.1: Committee passes motion by a 5 to 2 vote:
Amy's vote makes no difference to the outcome.

To further complicate these issues, we should notice that omissions can also be causal factors. A person can decide to actively do something, and this can obviously become a causal factor. Importantly, though, a person can passively decide to do nothing, and this too can become a causal factor. For example, in the Amy example, perhaps the factory owner did not actively decide to order shoddy construction, but simply omitted to get the advice of competent engineers before building another floor. The factory owner's omission is still a potential causal factor in the building collapse.

There are two lessons to draw from this catalogue of problems for theories of causal responsibility. The first lesson is that, though the notion of causation is a scientific notion, it is not clearly defined and easy to apply. The second lesson is that there is no clear connection between causal responsibility and moral accountability. Thinking about the causal responsibility of decision-makers for outcomes is often useful in thinking about moral accountability, but moral accountability is an ethical notion, not a scientific one.

LEGAL RESPONSIBILITY

Legal systems have developed most of the theories of causal responsibility that we have surveyed in their search for ways to determine legal responsibility. Criminal law attempts to stop, deter, and penalize rights violations by justly punishing violators for their crimes. As a form of retributive justice, it aims to punish those who, with a guilty mind, cause harm to others. The law of torts in civil law aims to ensure that the reckless or careless compensate their victims for the damages that they cause to them or their property. Generally, judges will award compensation if the plaintiff shows that the defendant had a duty of care regarding the defendant or her property, and that the defendant caused the damage to the victim or her property.

Though notions of legal responsibility and moral accountability influence one another, they are not the same notion. There are cases where someone might be legally responsible but not morally accountable. One example is vicarious liability. An employer is legally responsible under tort law for wrongs committed by an employee who is on the job. However, unless the employer orders the employee to commit the wrong or is careless in some way, we would neither hold the employer morally accountable for the wrong, nor absolve the employee of accountability. Vicarious liability is a policy that enables victims to recover damages from someone who is likely more able to pay the damages. Vicarious liability also makes it possible to hold corporations legally responsible for damages, since corporations can only act vicariously through their officers, managers, and employees. Another example is the legal concept of "deep pockets." When several agents are causally responsible for damages, the law may order the wealthier agent to pay all the damages. All of the agents may be morally accountable for the harms that they caused, but, for policy reasons, the law may hold only the wealthy individual legally responsible for compensating the victim.

Even though legal responsibility and moral accountability are not the same concept, the concept of legal responsibility has influenced the concept of moral accountability in two misleading ways.

First, the idea from criminal law and retributive justice that we must prove that someone's guilty mind caused the harm sometimes misleads us into thinking that we are only morally accountable for the harm if we both intended and were successful in causing it. We have seen some of the difficulties involved in assigning causal responsibility. In the next section, we shall see that it is not always necessary to prove causal responsibility in order to hold someone morally accountable.

Second, the law of torts aims to make the victim whole again, which means that once the victim is fully compensated nothing more is owed by the perpetrators to the victim. For example, if the total damages were $10,000, then once the victim receives the $10,000, then the perpetrator has fulfilled his legal responsibility and no one is liable to pay any more money. This idea from tort law may mislead us into thinking that there is only so much moral accountability to go around, and once we show someone to be blameworthy, then we have finished. Moral accountability, however, is not a conserved quantity in the way that damages are. For example, just because we find that the owner of the collapsed factory is morally accountable for his decision to build unsafely, it may still be the case that Amy's company is also morally accountable for not anticipating the disastrous consequences, or that Amy is herself blameworthy for not considering the risks of the strategy that she promoted. We will discuss below how holding a corporation morally accountable for the result of its actions does not preclude also holding its officers and employees accountable for their decisions.

ETHICAL APPROACHES TO MORAL ACCOUNTABILITY

We have seen that it is very difficult to determine causal responsibility for an outcome. As well, we have seen that determining moral accountability involves a value judgment, and thus, implicitly, reasons drawn from an ethical theory. Rather than search for an elusive determination of causal responsibility, we can instead examine decision-makers and their decisions from the perspective of each of the ethical theories that we have studied. Different theories will often conflict in their assignment of moral account-ability. Consequently, we must weigh these various reasons to arrive at one overall judgment of moral accountability. If we cannot come to an overall judgment of moral accountability, then we must content ourselves with irreducibly plural judgments.

An example of an irreducibly plural judgment of moral accountability might have occurred if the offshore production strategy had ended in success rather than disas-ter. In that case, the CEO might have judged to herself, "I should blame Amy for her self-interested motives, and despise her for the greedy character she has shown, but I should reward her for her plan because her initiative has caused greater profits for the company." Here the CEO has a motive-based reason for blaming Amy, a character-based reason for despising her, and a consequence-based reason for rewarding her. Even if we fail to come to an overall judgment of moral accountability, this should not prevent us from paying attention to our partial judgments.

Figure 9.2 reviews the main types of ethical theories and ethical reasoning that philosophers have identified. Identity-based reasoning holds moral agents accountable for the sort of person that they are. It recommends that we morally praise those who are virtuous in their behaviour or caring and wise in their relationships. If we are virtuous in our own behaviour, we are entitled to be proud of ourselves. It recommends that we morally blame those who show themselves to have vices such as envy, greed, sloth, and so on, or who are uncaring in their relationships with others. If we are ourselves vicious or uncaring, then we should feel ashamed. Virtue ethics claims that we are morally praiseworthy if we exhibit good character, and blameworthy if we exhibit bad character.

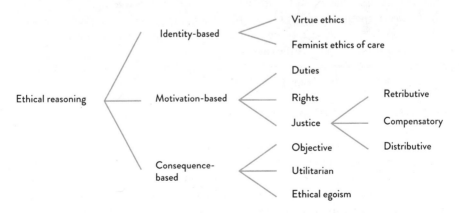

Figure 9.2: Review of the main forms of ethical reasoning.

Motivation-based reasoning looks first to a moral agent's personal reasons for her decisions. If she thinks only of her own gain and is reckless of the rights of others, then we should blame her for her behaviour. If her reasoning is based on principles, if she tries her best to respect the rights of others and to fulfil her duties to them, then we should praise her for her efforts, even if she is unsuccessful. If we ourselves make decision with the wrong motives, then we should feel guilty about what we have done.

In order to assign moral accountability in retributive justice, we must find that an agent caused the outcome and intended or planned to cause that outcome. This gives us an ethical reason to punish the agent for a negative outcome or to reward him for a positive one. Similarly, in order to require that one agent pay compensation to another, we must find that the first agent is causally responsible for the harm to the second, and that the first agent failed to fulfil a duty that the first agent had to respect the property rights of the second. Retributive justice and compensatory justice reasoning look to considerations similar to those in legal reasoning.

As we have seen in the chapter on justice, historical theories of distributive justice, such as libertarian theories or contribution-based merit theories, require a determination of causal responsibility to determine fair shares. In business contexts, however, determinations of causal responsibility are not always possible. Consider again the example of the pin factory. The work of neither Jack nor Jill is sufficient for the increased output after specialization and the division of labour. On this account, neither is causally responsible for the gains from cooperation. The work of both Jack and Jill is necessary to achieve the gains from cooperation. In addition, the work of each is a necessary element in a set of sufficient conditions for the gains from cooperation. On the latter of these two accounts, both Jack and Jill are causally responsible for all of the gain. Therefore, none of these disputed causal facts is useful in telling us how to distribute the gains from cooperation in a fair and just manner.

Non-historical theories of distributive justice, however, do not require assessments of causal responsibility. These theories will use other, non-causal moral principles, such as Rawls's difference principle, to determine legitimate expectations and fair shares. These theories are impervious to difficulties in assigning causal responsibility.

Causal responsibility plays a role in consequence-based reasoning about moral accountability. When an agent is making a decision, utilitarian ethical theory requires the decision-maker to predict the causal consequences of her decision. Amy, for example, should consider everyone's welfare, including offshore workers, in her decision to promote out-sourcing the company's clothing line.

CORPORATE ACCOUNTABILITY

Business firms are often large organizations with complex ownership structures and complex decision-making procedures. Should we hold business corporations morally accountable for their actions? Joint stock corporations are certainly legally accountable for the consequences of their actions; for example, people can sue them for compensation for damages that they cause. If we think that moral accountability requires causal responsibility, and that causal responsibility requires that an agent's psychological state, the agent's intention, must cause the outcome, then we will be inclined to say, "No." Business corporations have a legal personality, but not a psychological personality. Unlike people, business corporations do not literally have intentions or other psychological states. Reductionism regarding corporate moral accountability is the theory that only individuals within a corporation can be morally accountable but the corporation as a whole cannot be morally accountable.

However, if we use a committee as a simple model of corporate decision-making, then we can see that reducing a committee decision to the decisions of individual committee members can be hugely difficult. When motions pass by more than two votes, then no member's vote is causally responsible for the committee decision on any of the views of causal responsibility that we have discussed. In the above example of a 5 to 2 vote, Ben's yes-vote and Cam's no-vote are neither necessary nor sufficient for the motion to pass, nor are their votes a NESS condition of the motion passing. Each is in no way causally responsible for the motion's passage. The same is true of all members of the committee. Individual moral accountability appears simply to evaporate in committee decision-making. We cannot reduce accountability for the committee decision to the causal responsibility of its members.

The opposing view to reductionism about corporate moral accountability is holism. Holism regarding corporate moral accountability is the theory that the corporation as a whole is morally accountable for its decisions and for actions of its agents and employees. The holistic view would be false if all ethical reasoning was purely motive-based. Motives are psychological states such as intentions, corporations do not have psychological states, and thus it would make no sense for corporations to be morally accountable. However, there are other forms of ethical reasoning.

In the chapter on virtue ethics, we looked at the notion of corporate character. **Corporate character** presumes that a corporation has non-mental dispositions to behave, which can be judged as virtuous or vicious, and which are determined by its ethical code, its compliance mechanisms, its ethical climate, its governance, and its incentive structures. From a utilitarian point of view, we can hold corporations accountable for whether their behaviour promotes overall human welfare. From a rights-based point of view, we can notice that corporations enter into legal contracts with employees, suppliers, and consumers. Legal contacts are composed of promises of offer and acceptance. If we think that we are morally accountable for keeping our promises to corporations, then we should equally think that corporations are morally accountable for keeping their promises to us. For example, if we are morally accountable for our promises to pay our mobile phone bills to telecommunications companies, then, presumably, telecommunications companies are morally accountable for keeping their promises to provide us with services.

As we have seen, there are many forms of ethical reasoning. Some forms of ethical reasoning give us good reasons to hold business corporations morally accountable, and some give us reason not to do so. If we weigh these reasons and decide that a business corporation is morally accountable for its decision and the outcome, then does that mean that board members, managers, and employees of the corporation are not morally accountable? Does moral accountability stop at the corporate level, or can we also hold individual members of the corporation morally accountable too?

Legal principles of tort law and vicarious responsibility can mislead us on this question. If someone sues a corporation for damages and the court orders the corporation to pay compensation of one million dollars, then the corporation is responsible for paying the one million dollars, and its personnel are not. The corporation is vicariously liable for the actions of its employees doing corporation business. Board members, managers, and employees are not legally responsible for coming up with additional compensation. The one million dollars is full compensation for the damages, and if the company is liable to pay it all, then others are not required to pay more.

Even if a corporation is legally responsible and pays all the required compensation, individuals within the corporation may still be morally accountable. The analogy between legal responsibility for paying compensation for damages and moral accountability does not hold. Just because a corporation as a whole is morally accountable, it does not follow that individuals within the corporation are not morally accountable. All individuals within the decision-making structure are still responsible for their motives and character, and how they express these in the decision-making process. Perhaps we can hold none of the individuals causally responsible for the outcome of the corporate decision, just as we can hold none of the committee members in the example above causally responsible for the committee's decision. Nevertheless, all individuals in the firm are potentially complicit in the corporate decision. All must consider their role in the decision and the sort of character and motivations that they display. In our ethical reasoning, we should hold agents inside organizations morally accountable for their characters and motivations even if we cannot hold them causally responsible for corporate decisions and their outcomes.

In complicated organizations such as business firms, it is often difficult either to determine causal responsibility or to assign moral accountability. We have seen examined a plurality of theories of moral accountability that corresponds to the plurality of theories of ethics generally. Additionally, in some cases where we would normally hold people morally accountability, we may decide to excuse them because they could not have done otherwise. In the next chapter, we will examine such excusing conditions, and then suggest a rough flow chart that will help us navigate the complicated issue of moral accountability in business organizations.

SUMMARY

1. An agent is morally accountable for a decision if we should praise or blame the agent for the decision and its results.
2. Value judgments about moral accountability are more than just facts about causal responsibility. Sometimes moral accountability requires causal responsibility, as in retributive justice, and sometimes it does not, as in judgments about character or motive.
3. Facts about causal responsibility are not as precise as most facts of science. Some people think causal conditions are necessary conditions, but these "but for" conditions have difficulty with over-determination. Some think they are sufficient conditions, but these have difficulties

with situations of joint production that are analogous to Adam Smith's pin factory. Some think they are NESS conditions, but these have difficulty attributing causal responsibility for committee decisions.

4. The analogy between moral accountability and legal responsibility breaks down in case of vicarious responsibility and deep pockets. Unlike compensation, accountability is not limited in size.

5. Different forms of ethical reasoning give different reasons for holding agents morally accountable. These reasons include the decision-maker's character, motives, duties, special responsibilities, causal role, and the welfare consequences of possible assignments of accountability.

6. Some philosophers think that business organizations, such as joint-stock companies, cannot be morally accountable because they do not have mental lives. Corporate accountability reduces without remainder to the accountability of individuals within the organization.

7. Other philosophers think that there are good ethical reasons for holding corporations morally as well as legally responsible for the results of their decisions. For example, we can talk meaningfully of corporate character. Just because the corporation is morally accountable, it does not mean that individuals within the corporation are not also morally accountable for their decisions and actions.

ONLINE LEARNING RESOURCES

You will find a collection of learning resources associated with this chapter on the book's website: http://sites.broadviewpress.com/businessethics/. Working through this material will help you understand and remember important concepts that we have discussed, and will help you apply them to issues in business ethics.

STUDY QUESTIONS

Answering the following questions will help you to understand the ethical theory in this chapter and will help you to create a set of review notes on the textbook.

1. Explain why retributive justice requires determining causal responsibility for an outcome whereas judging that someone is dishonest does not.

2. Explain why the possible existence of other factors that would have brought about the consequence anyway creates a difficulty for the theory that causal conditions are necessary conditions.

3. Explain why the possibility of joint production creates a difficulty for the theory that causal conditions are sufficient conditions.

4. Explain why the possibility that a committee decision may pass by 2 votes creates a difficulty for the theory that causal conditions are Necessary Elements of a Set of Sufficient conditions.

5. Why can we hold a decision-maker accountable for her motives even if we cannot show her to be causally responsible for a bad outcome?

6. Can we hold both corporations and their managers to be morally accountable for the same morally wrong action? Why, or why not?

DECISION QUESTIONS

The whole point of learning ethical theory is to understand and ask questions like the following when you are analyzing an ethically problematic situation or case.

- What are the likely causal consequences of the decision-maker's alternative decisions?
- Is the decision a necessary condition for the outcome?
- Is the decision a sufficient condition for the outcome?
- Is the decision a necessary element in a set of sufficient conditions for the outcome?
- Does a committee structure block the assignment of causal responsibility to individuals?
- What do the various ethical theories say about the decision-maker's accountability?
- Should we hold the decision-maker accountable for the character traits she displays?
- Should we hold the decision-maker accountable for the motivation behind his decision?
- Does anyone share moral accountability with the decision-maker?
- Is an organization solely or partially morally accountable for the outcome?
- Should we hold individuals morally accountable as well as the organization?

CASE STUDY

Analyze this case study using the ethical theory that you have learned so far. You will find a collection of learning materials applying to the case on the book's website: http://sites.broadviewpress.com/businessethics/. These materials will help you in your analysis.

Should Isabella Encourage Deception?

Isabella Lopez is the northern area sales manager for Kudos Kitchen and Recreation, a large retailer of household appliances and consumer electronics with stores across North America. Kudos is losing market share to online retailers, such as Nile, and needs to extract more profit from the sales that it does make. One advantage that Kudos has over Nile is the personal contact between Kudos' sales staff and Kudos' costumers. Personal contact allows the Kudos sales staff to sell more extended warranties than Nile is able to sell online. Extended warranties are an important profit centre for Kudos, as they are for other appliance and electronics retailers.

Yesterday, Isabella's boss and Kudos VP of sales, Roger MacDonald, circulated an email to his five area managers asking their opinions on a new sales policy regarding extended warranties. The new policy would aim to increase extended warranty sales by allowing store managers to raise the commission on extended warranty sales for high performing salespeople. The standard is 15%. The new policy would allow store managers to raise the rate to 20% for any warranty sales over $2,000 per month. Kudos would also allow store managers to reveal each salesperson's warranty sales at monthly sales meetings and to terminate any sales staff who failed to sell at least $1,000 worth of extended warranties for two months in succession. Roger's hope is that this new policy will increase the incentives for sales staff to sell extended warranties and thereby help Kudos' bottom line.

Isabella worries about the effect of this policy on the interaction between sales staff and customers. Three-year extended warranties are highly profitable because appliances and electronics are most likely either to break down from manufacturing defects soon after purchase, or to break down from wear and tear toward the ends of their designed life. The probability of a payout on a three-year extended warranty is low because the manufacturer's warranty covers the first year, and most products are designed to last longer than three years. In order to sell extended warranties, sales staff must avoid telling customers the return rate for the second and third year of a product's life, and must get customers to focus on horror stories regarding the very few products that customers actually do return. Isabella's worry is that Kudos' store managers may use the new policy to increase their staff's usage of hard-sell practices.

Roger has asked for opinions from his area managers, and their views often sway his decision. Isabella is almost certain that West, Central, and South will get behind the policy suggestion, but that East will criticize it. She is worried about the consequences of the new sales policy, but she also wants Kudos to be profitable and for Roger to see her as a team player.

What should Isabella say to Roger?

Chapter 10

RESPECTING AUTONOMY AND PRIVACY

Should we consider business corporations to be moral agents?

What are the main threats to autonomous decision-making?

Why is respecting privacy important?

We have seen that a person, or perhaps a business corporation, is morally accountable if we should praise or blame the agent for the outcome of the agent's freely made decision. In the last chapter, we saw some problems with determining causal responsibility for outcomes. In this chapter, we will consider some problems with concluding that an agent's decision is a freely made decision.

Suppose that her boss orders Nancy, the firm's IT specialist, to spy on the other employees' use of social media outside of work. Nancy does not think this is right, but does it because she fears being replaced. Is Nancy morally accountable for her decision to spy? The answer will depend on whether we think her decision was morally autonomous. **Moral autonomy** is the capacity to govern oneself according to one's own ethical reasoning. Agents' decisions are morally autonomous when they apply to themselves ("*auto*" in Latin) the moral law ("*nomos*"). We shall start from the default position that agents' decisions are usually morally autonomous, and then ask what sorts of conditions interfere with their autonomy. In a more extreme example, suppose that one person puts a gun to a second person's head, and coerces him into making a particular decision. Here it is obvious that the second person's decision is not morally autonomous, and that we should not hold him morally accountable for his decision. Should we similarly excuse Nancy from moral accountability?

Now consider the effects of Nancy and her boss' spying on the other employees. Suddenly there are repercussions at work for their activities outside of work. Realizing that their boss is spying on them, many employees change their private behaviour and become less open with their friends on social media. Does the firm's spying wrongfully interfere with their personal lives? This brings up an ethical concept similar to, but not the same as, moral autonomy: personal autonomy. **Personal autonomy** is the capacity to make authentic decisions about one's own life. It is the ability to choose freely one's conception of the good life, to pursue this conception, and to either endorse or change one's choices. Modern societies hold the values of personal autonomy and personal freedom in high esteem, but this is a new historical development. Pre-modern communities stressed the values of following tradition and obedience to authority. Pre-modern conceptual frameworks provided few intellectual resources for community members to reflect critically on how to lead their own lives. Here we shall look at a plurality of ethical reasons both for and against the importance of the personal autonomy that our modern culture so values.

The firm's spying also raises another important value of modern society, one that is under threat from the increasing power of computer technology. This value is privacy. **Informational privacy** is the condition of being able to control access by others to information about oneself. Governments and internet technology firms are becoming increasingly adept at finding out information about individuals, and increasingly willing to use this power for security or commercial purposes. Most of us dislike others infringing our personal privacy. However, it is not obvious why others should have an ethical obligation not to seek out personal information about us. Once again, we will apply our ethically pluralist methodology to look at the various ethical reasons both in favour of and against informational privacy. Given that everyone knows that information on social media is public, do Nancy and her firm violate the informational privacy rights of the other employees?

CORPORATE MORAL AGENCY

We may be able to hold Nancy and her boss accountable for their spying because they are moral agents, but can we hold their firm accountable in any way? What sort of entities can have moral autonomy and be held morally accountable for their decisions? We know that most adult human beings can be morally autonomous, but what about business corporations? Are business corporations moral agents? Being a moral agent is a precondition for being held morally accountable. As we defined it earlier, a moral agent is an entity to which we are prepared to assign praise or blame, which can respond to moral reasons, and which we are prepared to hold morally accountable. To possess moral agency, an entity ideally should have certain capacities. These include moral sensitivity, responsiveness to ethical reasons, and decision-making abilities. An interference with people's moral autonomy can be an interference with their moral agency because it interferes with their capacity to respond to ethical reasons and to make ethical decisions based on those reasons.

To be sensitive to the existence of moral issues, an ideal moral agent requires a range of emotional capacities. The agent needs empathy, the ability to understand the feelings of a whole range of other people. The agent also needs sympathy for other people, which is the capacity to have an interest in reducing their pain and suffering or promoting their well-being. The agent must be disposed to feel guilt or shame at her own moral transgressions, and to feel anger or indignation at the transgressions of others. She must be sensitive to praise and blame, so that she can feel morally accountable for her actions.

To be responsive to ethical reasons, an ideal moral agent must have a range of intellectual and emotional capacities that vary with the type of ethical reasoning involved. To apply consequentialist reasoning, an agent must be able to make rough calculations of the aggregate net welfare benefits of different decisions. To apply principle-based reasoning, such as respect for rights and a regard for justice, an agent must be able to apply abstract principles to particular cases. To apply character-based reasoning, an agent must be able to cultivate virtues, avoid vices, and become sensitive to and take responsibility for her relationships with others.

To make competent ethical decisions, an ideal moral agent needs an understanding of ethical concepts, an understanding of cause and effect relationships, an ability to make plans, and an ability to form and carry out intentions.

Most adult human beings possess, or should possess, the capacities required for moral agency. Most children have the emotional repertoire necessary for moral sensitivity, but lack the reasoning and decision-making abilities required for full moral agency. Infants and comatose human beings have none of these capacities. Some very complex animals may have rudimentary capacities for moral sensitivity, but no animals have ethical reasoning and decision-making abilities.

Many important decisions in the world of business are made, not by individual adult humans, but by business firms, corporations, non-government organizations, municipalities, and state governments. Such organizations are not individual human beings with mental lives, but are the creations of a legal system. They do not literally have the psychological capacities, such as the emotions of guilt and shame or the ability to reason ethically, that moral agency requires. Yet we are inclined to praise or blame them for their decisions, and to hold them morally accountable. How is this possible?

One way to understand corporate agency is through the notion of vicarious psychological capacities. A business corporation is a legal "personality," a nexus of legal contracts and property interests, not a brick-and-mortar factory or office building. As such, it can act in the world only through its employees and its legal agents who are human beings. The business corporation, as principal, signs contracts only through its appointed agents. In law, it is vicariously responsible for the actions of its employees on company business. It can only delegate; it cannot act directly.

By analogy, we can understand the moral sensitivity of a company as vicarious sensitivity. The directors, managers, and employees of the corporation all have psychological responses, such as shame or empathy, to situations requiring ethical decisions, and they can bring this sensitivity to the decision-making process within the company. Similarly, we can understand the responsiveness to ethical reasons of the company as vicarious rationality. The officers and employees of the company have the intellectual capacities to understand the necessary ethical reasoning. If we understand the output of corporate decision-making as vicarious action through the officers and employees of the company, then we should also understand the input to corporate decision-making as the vicarious moral sensitivity and vicarious ethical rationality of its officers and employees as well.

The final decision-making in a large organization may be a collective and holistic process rather than a simple individual decision. In a small sole proprietorship, where the owner is the operator, the decision-making process may involve only that person's psychological deliberations. However, in a large joint-stock company, the decision-making process may be a highly organized and regulated process that is more analogous to a committee decision. The role of deliberation and decision by individuals may be much harder to define. Just as it was difficult to pick out the causal role of individual members in motions passed in committee, it will be difficult to determine the causal role of officers, managers, and employees in corporate decisions. Table 10.1 summarizes the role of the psychological, vicarious, and holistic capacities of moral agents in several types of organizations.

Governance	Moral sensitivity	Responsiveness to ethical reasons	Decision-making ability
Owner/operator	✓ (Psychological)	✓ (Psychological)	✓ (Psychological)
Committee	✓ (Vicarious)	✓ (Vicarious)	✓ (Holistic)
Corporation	✓ (Vicarious)	✓ (Vicarious)	✓ (Holistic)

Table 10.1: The moral agency of organizations.

Even if we conclude that organizations such as business corporations are capable of a form of moral agency, we should not forget that a determination of corporate moral accountability does not block a determination of the moral accountability of individual directors, officers, and employees. Legal responsibility, in terms of full compensation to the plaintiffs in a tort action, may stop when the corporation pays the full amount, but moral accountability does not. Even if the causal role of individuals in a corporate decision is unclear, individuals within the corporation are still morally accountable for their motives and for the moral character that they have displayed in the decision process.

INTERFERENCES WITH AUTONOMY

Philosophers have worried extensively over whether a freely made decision is even possible. This is the metaphysical problem of free will. Science tells us that every event in the world is causally determined. All decisions made by agents are events in the world. Therefore, all decisions are causally determined. If a decision is causally determined, then it is not a freely made decision. Therefore, no decision is a freely made decision. Solving this metaphysical problem is beyond the scope of our interests in business ethics. We will assume for the purposes of this chapter that, in the absence of external interference, most of our decisions are made freely. We are normally autonomous, both personally and morally. This leaves the problem of what constitutes an interference with an agent's personal or moral autonomy.

Moral autonomy is the capacity to govern oneself according one's own ethical reasoning. An interference with people's moral autonomy is an interference with their moral agency because it interferes with their capacity to respond to ethical reasons and to make ethical decisions based on those reasons. Because "ought" implies "can," when her boss interferes with Nancy's moral autonomy such that the boss's interference prevents Nancy from making the morally correct decision, then Nancy is not morally accountable for her decision and its outcome. Interferences with moral autonomy can reduce or excuse someone's moral accountability. Some threats to moral autonomy potentially excuse agents from moral accountability.

Personal autonomy is the capacity to make authentic decisions about one's own life. It is the ability to choose freely how one lives one's life. The very same sorts of conditions that can undermine moral autonomy also undermine personal autonomy. In what follows, we will consider some of the factors that can interfere with autonomy, both moral and personal.

A first potential interference with autonomy is the threat of coercion. If a coercive threat is severe enough, then it overwhelms the victim's moral sensitivity, responsiveness to ethical reasons, and decision-making capacity. For example, if a gangster threatens the family of an office administrator unless she steals the petty cash for him, then we should not hold the administrator morally accountable for her decision to hand over the cash. A **coercive threat** that interferes with autonomy is a perpetrator's morally unjustified declaration of the intent to cause harm to the victim. For example, if a supervisor says to an employee, "Mow my lawn at home, or I will fire you at work," then this would be a morally unjustified threat that would interfere with the employee's ability to make a decision. Coercive threats are only potential excusing conditions because we still must decide whether the threat is severe enough, relative to the importance of the decision, to say that it excuses the victim from moral accountability.

A second threat to autonomy is lying or deception. A **lie** is a linguistic communication which the perpetrator believes to be untrue and with which the perpetrator intends to deceive his victim. **Deception** is a non-linguistic action or omission that the perpetrator intentionally uses to cause her victim to believe something false. Both lying and deception interfere with their victim's capacity to make authentic, informed decisions. They interfere with their victim's ability to reason properly. Perpetrators use both to defraud victims. **Fraud** is obtaining a benefit from a victim by lying or deception. Lying, deception, and fraud can sometimes occur in marketing, where a salesperson may be tempted to give false information to a customer in order to make a sale. Deception can undermine personal autonomy. For example, suppose a salesperson deceitfully implies to a customer that an insurance policy will cover all medical expenses, when, in fact, many exclusionary clauses are buried in the fine print. Based on this false information, the customer purchases the insurance and the customer's life may go badly. Deception can also undermine moral autonomy. For example, suppose a salesperson deceitfully tells a customer that some product creates no pollution, when in fact it does. Based on this false information, the customer may decide to purchase the device. If the customer thinks that contributing to pollution is wrong, then the salesperson has interfered with the customer's moral autonomy.

A third threat to autonomous decision-making involves failure to disclose information. Proper reasoning requires possession of all the information that is relevant to the decision. If a perpetrator intentionally fails to disclose information to which the decision-maker is entitled, then the perpetrator compromises the victim's ability to perform sound ethical reasoning and to make good decisions. Lack of information, or possession of false information, interferes with decision-making. Morally unjustified non-disclosure of information by others also interferes with autonomous decision-making. However, we are not always entitled to information. Potential perpetrators should weigh their obligation to disclose information to others against their own right to informational privacy. For example, salespeople may be obligated to disclose fully the specifications of their products to potential customers, but they may not be obligated to disclose private information about their firms' costs of production. In such cases, people must make difficult judgments. Is a salesperson ethically required to disclose to a potential customer that another cheaper product the company sells is just as good?

A fourth threat to autonomous decision-making is a situation involving conflict of interest. Conflicts of interest occur when the self-interest of professionals, managers, agents, and board members differ from the interests of their clients, customers, principals, or organizations. Conflicts of interest occur even if members of the first group actually fulfil their obligations to the members of the second. For example, a financial adviser, who also sells mutual funds on commission, has a conflict of interest with her client even if the mutual fund that she recommends to her client, and for which she receives a commission, is in fact the best fund for that client. She is still in a conflict of interest situation, even when she gives the correct advice. She can mitigate this conflict of interest by disclosing her own interest in selling the fund to her client. One problem with this situation is that her personal interests in having the client buy a certain fund may distort her financial judgment. A second problem is that non-disclosure of her personal interest violates the trust required in the relationship of financial adviser to client. A third problem is that conflicts of interest can undermine the autonomy of decision-makers. Why is this?

Conflicts of interest usually arise because of asymmetric information. Because our society is so complex, specialization and the division of labour is the norm with regard to information as well as with regard to production. By cooperating in the discovery and management of information, we can process much more information together that we can alone. Hence, people characteristically depend on others for information in their decision-making process. For example, a CEO cannot know everything relevant to a management decision, such as choosing an ethical supplier, and so must depend on information and advice from the company lawyer, the financial officer, the sales manager, etc. Lawyers, accountants, and sales managers are all authorities in their specialized areas. Nevertheless, the CEO must still determine how much credence to give to the advice of each of them. To make an autonomous judgment, the CEO must assess their expertise and their judgment. In assessing their advice, the CEO also needs to be certain of their motivations. Is their advice sound or is it shaded by self-interest? It is relevant to the CEO's reliance on the advice of the financial officer for the CEO to know that the financial officer is a large shareholder in one of the suppliers under consideration. For the CEO to make a truly autonomous decision, the CEO needs both to know the information provided by the financial officer and to know that the financial officer's information is reliable. To know that the financial officer's information is reliable, the CEO needs to know either that it is free of conflict of interest or, at least, to know that a conflict of interest exists so that the CEO can critically scrutinize the financial officer's advice. Conflict of interest situations like this one undermine the autonomy of the CEO, not by affecting the truth of the information on which the CEO makes the decision, but by affecting the reliability of the information on which the CEO makes the decision.

A fifth threat to someone's autonomy is lack of competence in decision-making. Cognitive impairments and emotional disorders compromise people's decision-making abilities. For example, people with severe ADHD often make impulsive decisions that they later regret. We often condemn certain types of advertising to children because children's decision-making skills have not yet developed well enough for them to make autonomous choices. Lack of competence can also come from lack of training. People sometimes say that everything that they have ever learned about right and wrong, they learned at their mothers' knees. A morally problematic childhood or adolescence can also compromise peoples' decision-making competence.

A sixth threat to autonomous decision-making is someone's immersion in an oppressive conceptual framework. As we have seen, an **oppressive conceptual framework** is a widely shared set of strongly held and resilient beliefs about the world, values, and human nature that makes relationships of domination and subordination seem normal, natural, and unquestionable. Because unjust relationships seem so normal, natural, and unquestionable, an oppressive conceptual framework makes if difficult, if not impossible, for people to understand that certain options are unjust or otherwise immoral. Contesting an oppressive conceptual framework involves a collective, ideological, and political process such as the activities of the civil rights movement, the feminist movement, the LGBT movement, and the animal rights movement.

A seventh threat to autonomy is emotional manipulation. Just as lies, deception, non-disclosure, and conflicts of interest can affect the cognitive component of peoples' decision-making, so too can manipulation affect the emotional component. By inducing the emotion of fear, a credible, though unenforceable, coercive threat, for example, can manipulate and even overwhelm a person's decision-making. Emotional manipulators can influence other emotions such as their victims' feelings of pride, shame, guilt, solidarity, trust, lust. Influencing these emotions will also influence their victims' decisions because emotions have cognitive consequences. Emotions focus a decision-maker's attention on a particular stimulus, and make it difficult for the decision-maker to attend to other aspects of the situation. As one familiar saying goes, "Love is blind." Only with time and the help of friends or psychotherapists, are people in the grip of strong emotions, such as lust or romantic love, able to see other options. As another familiar saying goes, "Marry in haste, and repent at leisure." Emotional manipulation, such as sexual manipulation, can greatly influence decision-making.

Not all attempts to influence emotion, however, are threats to autonomy; many such efforts are legitimate attempts to persuade a people that, by making them aware of emotional consequences, actually increase their autonomy. For example, an anti-smoking ad including a vivid emotionally affecting picture of a dreadful smoking-related disease may increase people's understanding and appreciation of the consequences of their continuing to smoke, and thus increase their ability to make an informed choice. We must make a difficult distinction between emotional manipulation and legitimate persuasion. For example, advertising sometimes conveys facts about a product, but is often an attempt to influence potential customers' feelings for a product. False advertising is obviously unethical, but the distinction between emotionally persuasive and emotionally manipulative advertising is difficult to draw. For example, we might think about how far insurance advertising may go in playing on people's fears about unlikely dangers before we would think that it begins to overwhelm the judgment of average and reasonable people in its audience.

MORAL AUTONOMY AND MORAL ACCOUNTABILITY

In considering threats to autonomy as potential excusing conditions for moral accountability, we will face making difficult distinctions. Some threats are so severe that they obviously excuse their victims from being morally accountable for their decision. Some attempts at emotional manipulation are so mild that they excuse no one. Making this distinction will always be a contestable judgment. If Lily threatens to splash Max with a drop of water, this threat will not excuse Max from accountability. Nor if Lily threatens to splash Max with a second drop of water, will this threat be an excuse for Max. Yet if Lily credibly threatens Max with a week of water-boarding torture, then this will excuse Max from accountability. Just because there is a slippery slope between an innocuous threat and a coercive threat, this does imply that there is no distinction between innocuous and coercive threats. There is no well-defined point between a full head of hair and baldness, but that does not imply that no one is ever bald. A contestable judgment is always required.

Figure 10.1 shows a simple flow chart of the factors that go into assessing a moral person's moral accountability. After determining that the person or corporation is a moral agent, we next have to ask if the agent's decision was autonomous. We do this by assessing whether there are any conditions present that interfere severely enough with the agent's decision-making to constitute excuses for making the decision. For example, we might ask if the agent was so misled by someone else that the agent could not be reasonably expected to decide correctly what to do. Then we proceed, as in the last chapter to ask about the agent's causal responsibility, motivation, and character. As we saw before, determining the causal responsibility of particular individuals within organizations can often be impossible because of division of labour and decision-making by committees. Nevertheless, we can still hold individuals morally accountable for their motivations and their characters.

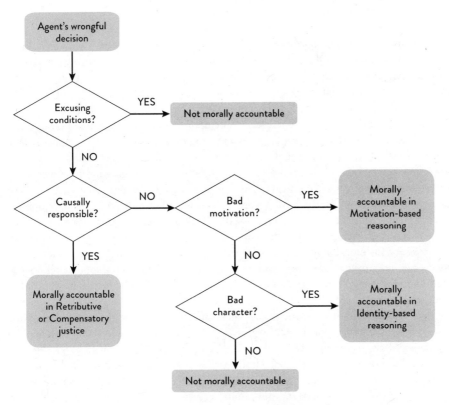

Figure 10.1: Simplified flow chart for assessing an agent's moral accountability.

Figure 10.1 summarizes our discussion of moral accountability and moral autonomy. Starting at the top left of the flow chart in Figure 10.1, we should check if the agent, who has made a wrongful decision, faces any threats to her autonomy that are severe enough to excuse her from accountability for her decision. For example, if she faces a credible, severe, and morally unjustified threat that forces her to make the wrongful decision, then we will not hold her morally accountable. Next, we should determine whether the agent is causally responsible for the outcome of her freely made decision. If so, then we should hold her accountable for making amends for her decision as a matter of compensatory or retributive justice. If not, then we should look to her motivation for her decision, and to the sort of character that she displays in making her decision. If necessary, we should blame her for the principles she is violating or the vices that she is demonstrating.

PERSONAL AUTONOMY

The threats to autonomy that we have just discussed are also threats to both moral and personal autonomy. Moral autonomy is the capacity to govern oneself according to one's own ethical reasoning. Personal autonomy, on the other hand, is the capacity to make authentic decisions about one's own life. It is the ability to choose freely one's conception of the good life, to pursue one's conception of the good life, and to change this conception if one no longer endorses it. Contemporary societies with free-market economies place a high value on personal autonomy and on the rights of individuals to make choices freely. Traditional societies usually place less value on personal autonomy. Even those market economies that now place a high value on personal autonomy generally placed a much lower value on it earlier in their histories. Is the high value that we place on personal autonomy merely a cultural construct that arose to buttress the development of capitalism? Alternatively, are there any ethical justifications for our valuation?

We should first observe that the capacity for personal autonomy is very similar to the capacity for moral autonomy, except that its focus is different. Personal autonomy focuses on how to lead one's personal life, whereas moral autonomy focuses on how to lead one's life where it intersects with the lives of others. The capacities for reasoning and decision-making are very similar, only the sensitivity is different. Moral sensitivity involves interpersonal emotions such as sympathy for others, guilt at harming others, and anger at others for their transgressions. The sensitivity involved in the capacity for personal autonomy involves interpersonal emotions such as love and lust, but also purely personal emotions such as joy and sorrow or enjoyment and suffering. Because personal autonomy and moral autonomy are so similar, all the threats to moral autonomy are also threats to personal autonomy. For example, having adequate truthful information is a requirement of personal autonomy and lying, deception, and unjustified non-disclosure are threats to personal autonomy as well as moral autonomy.

This similarity between personal and moral autonomy provides one indirect reason that personal autonomy is ethically important. Moral accountability requires moral autonomy, and moral autonomy requires the absence of the same threats, such as coercion and deception, as personal autonomy does. Thus, we cannot protect moral autonomy without, at the same time, protecting personal autonomy.

In this text, we have adopted a pluralist approach to applied ethics. Instead of adopting one ethical theory and trying to show how it can explain all moral values, we have examined proposed moral values from a variety of ethical perspectives. Different ethical approaches give us different insights into moral value. Our task is then to assess these various ethical considerations and try to reach a decision of what is best overall. We can illustrate this process by examining different ethical approaches to the ethical value of personal autonomy.

We can find reasons for the importance of personal autonomy by surveying the various forms of ethical reasoning that we have been employing. The character traits of leading a life that is authentically one's own and of taking personal responsibility for one's life are each personal virtues. Authenticity and personal responsibility both require personal autonomy. We would hardly call a woman's life authentic if she lives it under the control of an abusive partner who continually threatens her. Nor, in such a situation, would we say that she is able to take personal responsibility for her life. Freedom from the threat of coercion, and personal autonomy generally, are necessary for people to exhibit the personal virtues of authenticity and personal responsibility. On the other side of the argument, however, virtue ethics stresses the importance of community membership and the moral virtues that enable people to cooperate in communities. Moral virtues such as loyalty and dependability require that people make commitments to their communities that they do not lightly revise. Personal autonomy requires that people can always revise their commitments, whereas virtues that enable people to cooperate in communities require that people be steadfast in their commitments. Therefore, the fact that cooperation is required in order to live well in communities may give us a reason to limit the extent of personal autonomy.

Feminist ethical considerations also point in two directions regarding the value of personal autonomy. On the one hand, justice-based feminist concerns about the domination of women by men, normalized by a patriarchal conceptual framework, are reasons for promoting personal autonomy. On the other hand, an ethics of care emphasizes the importance of personal relationships in people's lives. The strong commitments that people make to one another in order to create these relationships are not commitments that people should easily revise. It is possible, for example, for a son to repudiate his mother, but it does not happen easily, and it carries a great ethical cost to both mother and son. The commitments involved in relationships impose limitations on the value of being able to revise a plan of life freely.

Ethical approach	Reasons for importance of personal autonomy
Identity-based	
Virtue ethics	PRO: Authenticity and personal responsibility are virtues that require personal autonomy CON: ignores community commitments
Feminist ethics	PRO: Counter to ideological oppression CON: ignores relationships
Motivation-based	
Kantian duties	Respect for persons implies respect for their autonomy
Rights	Kantian theory of rights: Autonomous, informed consent is foundational Special rights: Contracts require autonomous consent
Consequence-based	
Experience-based utilitarianism	None
Preference-based utilitarianism	Preference for autonomy Anti-paternalism—people make own best choices
Economic utilitarianism	Model of rational maximizing agent includes autonomy
Informed-preference	Rational deliberation requires good information

Table 10.2: Ethical pluralism and personal autonomy.

In the Kantian tradition, the fact that people are autonomous is an ethical reason for us to respect them. Kant's notion of autonomy may have been what we are calling moral autonomy, the capacity to apply universal principles to one's decisions. Nevertheless, Kant's writings also began an ethical approach that saw both moral and personal autonomy as foundational values that give us reason to respect autonomous agents. The Kantian theory of natural rights depends on the power of the right-holder either to insist that others follow their correlative duties, or not to insist that they do, according to the right-holder's choice on the matter. This theory, however, only makes sense if we presume that the right-holder's choice is informed and is not subject to coercion. People can have moral rights over personal matters only if their choices on these matters are autonomous. For example, patients undergoing surgical interventions, which outside the hospital would be grievous bodily harms, must give informed consent to these medical procedures. Procedures on human beings without the capacity for personal autonomy, such as children, require the informed consent of their guardians. The Kantian theory of moral rights requires that others may infringe our rights only with our autonomous consent. The special rights that people acquire in the formation of contracts do require personal autonomy. Contracts formed under the threat of coercion are void, and contracts formed through deception are fraudulent. The formation of contracts presumes that no one compromises the personal autonomy of the parties.

Experience-based utilitarianism provides no direct reason for valuing personal autonomy. The obligation of a utilitarian of this type is to maximize the balance of pleasurable experience over painful experience. If maximizing net pleasure requires giving people happy-syrup in their drinking water without their knowledge or consent, then so be it. Pleasure, with or without autonomous choice, is what is ethically valuable.

Preference-based utilitarianism, on the other hand, does give an indirect reason in favour of personal autonomy. This reason stems from the empirical claim that people generally have the best information about their wishes and desires. People are therefore in the best position to make choices about which outcomes they will most enjoy. As we have seen, people are fallible and do not always prefer the outcomes that they will enjoy most. Yet, people are more likely to be correct in their choices about how to lead their own lives than a paternalistic government, for example, would be. Consequently, powerful actors, such as the government, should not try to exert undue influence over the choices that people make as they form their preferences and conceptions of the good life. Maximizing preference satisfaction requires personal autonomy and the absence of paternalistic interventions.

Economic utilitarianism depends on a model of economic actors as rational decision-makers who are concerned to maximize their own interests. According to this model, by maximizing their self-interest within the rules of the market, economic actors will maximize the total economic welfare created by the market economy. This model presupposes the autonomy of economic actors. The system must prevent firms from coercing, deceiving, or manipulating information to economic actors as they make their self-interested decisions. If a market manipulator gives consumers false information, then they will often make decisions that do not lead to maximum aggregate economic welfare.

Weighing these ethical considerations, we get a case for the overall ethical value of personal autonomy. The caveats are the necessity of allowing for the responsibilities created by community membership and personal relationships. These considerations count against the easy revision of certain community and relationship commitments, though they still support their revision under oppressive or abusive circumstances. Experience-based utilitarian considerations support a disregard for personal autonomy, but we have seen in an earlier chapter that this form of utilitarianism is not a hugely plausible ethical theory. The interest theory of rights is compatible with the value of autonomy provided we can find support for a crucial interest in personal autonomy in other ethical theories. As the survey above shows, we can find considerable support for the ethical importance of personal autonomy.

One way to protect and promote a crucial interest in personal autonomy is to say that people have a moral right to personal autonomy. A moral right is a morally justified claim on others that imposes a correlative duty on them. A negative right is a general moral right that others not interfere with the right-holder. One type of right is a liberty right, or a liberty to do the actions that a person wishes to do. Someone's negative liberty is the right that others not interfere with her actions. Personal autonomy is concerned, not with actions, but with the decision-making, that precedes action. Correspondingly, someone's **negative autonomy right** is the right that others not interfere with his decision-making. Just as there can be positive moral rights to assistance as well as negative moral rights to non-interference, someone can have a **positive autonomy right**, which is the right that others assist her with her decision-making.

PRIVACY

Physical privacy is a person's condition when she is free from intrusion by other people. It is the condition of being let alone to do one's "own thing." In general, peoples' private property rights and their political liberties protect their physical privacy. For example, people can exclude others from their homes, and people's homes are not subject to unreasonable searching by the police.

It is important to interpret physical privacy as referring to the privacy of individuals rather than of families. Feminist thinkers have criticized the notion of family or domestic privacy because, in the past, it has served to prevent the state from intruding into family life to protect women and children. If the state is supposed to let families alone in their domestic life, then the state is not justified in intruding into family life to stop abusive relationships. However, if the state is supposed to enforce the rights of each individual to be let alone in how she lives her life, then the state is justified in making intrusions into family life to protect individuals from abuse. At the same time, however, feminists tend to trust mothers' caring relationships to their family more than they trust the ministrations of the patriarchal state.

Informational privacy is a person's condition of being able to control access by others to information about himself. Traditional threats to informational privacy include factors such as the nosiness and scrutiny of family, neighbours, businesses and the police. Contemporary threats to informational privacy include the collection of information on the Internet, which facilitates selective advertising and creates the potential for fraud. The Internet also facilitates the illicit sharing of financial records, trade secrets, and health records, leading to diminished control over who accesses these records and increased potential for fraud. Modern technology is also beginning to enable the collection and sharing of a person's genetic information. Disclosure of a person's genetic information, for example, would change the balance of bargaining power when he went to purchase affordable health insurance.

Informational privacy has connections to personal autonomy. On the one hand, the informational privacy of other people is in tension with the full information about them that we require for autonomous choice. As we have seen, one way to interfere with someone else's autonomy of choice is to fail to disclose to her information that she requires to make an informed choice. Sometimes the information that one person requires for a decision is also information that another person legitimately believes is a trade secret.

On the other hand, privacy regarding a person's own information is a requirement for autonomy. When he formulated his Harm Principle of 1859, John Stuart Mill proposed that the only legitimate reason for the government to intrude on the liberties and private actions of its citizens is to prevent harm to other people. At the same time, Mill also warned against the power of social pressure.

> Protection, therefore against the tyranny of the magistrate is not enough: there needs protection also against the tyranny of society to impose, by other means than civil penalties, its own ideas and practices as rules of conduct on those who dissent from them; to fetter the development, and if possible, prevent the formation, of any individuality not in harmony with its ways, and compel all characters to fashion themselves upon the model of its own. (Mill, 1859, p. 8)

According to Mill, social pressure can "enslave the soul" of an individual and bring her attitudes into conformity with the norms of the surrounding culture. This sort of social pressure is a threat to personal autonomy because it "compels all characters to fashion themselves upon the model of its own."

Informational privacy is an efficient defence against the sort of cultural oppression that Mill saw in Victorian English society. If people are able to control the access of other members of society to information about themselves, then they can reduce the social pressure on them to conform. If, because of the strong enforcement of individuals' informational privacy, society collectively is unable to access information about its members, then society will not be able to scorn or ostracize them. If others do not know that an individual thinks in ways not in conformity with social norms, then others will be much less likely to pressure them into conformity. Freedom from the scrutiny of others is required for personal autonomy and full freedom of conscience.

Care ethics is concerned with the ethical value of various types of relationships. We control the types of relationships that we have through our behaviour toward each other, our feelings about each other, and the intimacy of the knowledge that we reveal to each other. We have professional feelings toward our bosses, behave toward them in business-like ways, and reveal only a defined amount of information to them. We have affectionate feelings toward our spouses, behave toward them in loving ways, and reveal much more information to them than we do to our bosses. Control over what we reveal to other people is an important part of our ability to determine the nature of our relationships with them. (Rachels, 1975) A good example of controlling relationships through control of information is the use of privacy settings on social media sites. If we are unable to keep information about ourselves private, then we will be unable to control the types of relationships that we have with people. Employers who use the Internet to discover information about employees that is not appropriate to the employer/employee relationship unilaterally change the employment relationship, and thereby damage their healthy relationships with employees.

Self-ownership rights imply control of personal information that is not common knowledge. Self-ownership rights include control of access to personal and commercial information. People can have property rights in valuable commercial information such as production techniques, financial records, intellectual property, and trade secrets.

Economic utilitarianism, however, suggests a consideration against consumer and commercial privacy. The economic utilitarian argument in favour of a market economy is that, under conditions of perfect competition, a free market will maximize the aggregate financial value of the goods and services available to all participants in the economy. The requirements of perfect competition include conditions such as the absence of monopoly. The requirements also include all economic actors having full information since, without full information, actors will make inefficient choices. Consequently, the conditions that make markets efficient are in tension with the value of informational privacy. For example, the phenomenon of insider trading involves managers appropriating private commercial information belonging to the owners of a company and using this information to trade on the stock market for their own gain. On the one hand, this seems like the theft of information. On the other hand, however, traders pay close attention to the buying and selling of stocks by officers of companies, which quickly gives them fuller information about the company. This violation of informational privacy thus leads to a quick dissemination of information about the company that the stock traders need to make accurate pricing decisions. Not protecting private commercial information can make the market more efficient.

We must weigh the reasons for and against protecting informational privacy in each particular context. Only then can we decide on an appropriate degree of privacy to protect.

SUMMARY

1. Moral agency is the capacity for moral accountability. It requires sensitivity to moral situations, responsiveness to moral reasons, and the ability to make decisions.
2. Most adult human beings are moral agents. Through their officers and employees, complex business corporations possess vicarious moral

sensitivity and responsiveness. Corporations employ highly organized holistic decision-making.

3. Even though business corporations have a form of moral agency and are morally accountable for their decisions, this does not block us from also holding their shareholders, directors, officers, and managers accountable for their character flaws, motivations, and inputs to corporate decisions.

4. Moral autonomy is the capacity to govern oneself according one's own ethical reasoning.

5. Personal autonomy is the capacity to decide how to live one's own life and to revise one's life choices when one chooses to do so. Personal autonomy is subject to the same potential interferences as is moral autonomy.

6. Coercive threats, deception, failure to disclose information, conflicts of interest, decision-making incompetence, oppressive conceptual frameworks, and emotional manipulation can diminish people's capacity for autonomy. Severe cases of any of these conditions will excuse people from moral accountability for their decisions.

7. Modern market economies place a high value on personal autonomy because their economic justification presupposes that individual economic actors always make decisions that are in their own rational self-interest. Liberal democracies value personal autonomy because people are less likely to make mistakes about how to lead their lives than is a paternalistic government.

8. Sustaining community membership and personal relationships requires that people do not readily revise their commitments, and both can be at odds with an overvaluation of personal autonomy.

9. Informational privacy requires that people be able to control access by others to information about themselves. Informational privacy is an efficient defence against social pressure to conform. People need to control intimate information about themselves in order to have different types of personal relationships.

10. Self-ownership requires informational privacy because information is a financially valuable asset. However, market efficiency requires perfect competition, and perfect competition requires that consumers and producers always have full information.

ONLINE LEARNING RESOURCES

You will find a collection of learning resources associated with this chapter on the book's website: http://sites.broadviewpress.com/businessethics/. Working through this material will help you understand and remember important concepts that we have discussed, and will help you apply them to issues in business ethics.

STUDY QUESTIONS

Answering the following questions will help you to understand the ethical theory in this chapter and will help you to create a set of review notes on the textbook.

1. How could someone argue that we should hold business corporations morally accountable for their decisions?
2. If we hold a corporation morally accountable for its decisions, then why can we also hold its managers morally accountable?
3. When one person threatens a second person, how can this excuse the second person from moral accountability? Give an example.
4. When one person deceives a second person, how can this excuse the second person from moral accountability? Give an example.
5. When one person fails to disclose information to a second person, how can this diminish the personal autonomy of the second person?
6. What is the importance of personal autonomy to modern market societies, in comparison to traditional societies?
7. Why will a care ethics be suspicious regarding the over-valuation of personal autonomy?
8. Why is the potential effect of social pressure on personal autonomy an ethical consideration in favour of the ethical value of informational privacy?
9. Describe an economic utilitarian consideration against the ethical value of complete informational privacy.
10. Why are rights to informational privacy, which are based on self-ownership considerations, in tension with the conditions of perfect competition and market efficiency?

DECISION QUESTIONS

The whole point of learning ethical theory is to understand and ask questions like the following when you are analyzing an ethically problematic situation or case.

- Can the decision-maker freely decide what to do?
- Is the decision-maker an autonomous moral agent?
- Is an organization involved as a moral agent?
- Are there any conditions present that excuse the decision-maker from morally accountability?
- Is anyone coercing the decision-maker?
- Is anyone lying to or deceiving the decision-maker?
- Is anyone manipulating the decision-maker?
- Is anyone in a conflict of interest?
- Is anyone withholding information from the decision-maker?

- Does the decision-maker have all the information that we can reasonably expect her to obtain?
- Will the decision interfere with anyone's personal autonomy?
- Does the decision properly respect everyone's privacy?

CASE STUDY

Analyze this case study using the ethical theory that you have learned so far. You will find a collection of learning materials applying to the case on the book's website: http://sites.broadviewpress.com/businessethics/. These materials will help you in your analysis.

Should Jake Embed the Spyware?

Jake Markos is a very clever young man. He graduated summa cum laude in computer science from a prestigious west coast institute of technology, and has never encountered a computer-programming task that he could not handle easily. Jake's problem is that he is unbearably shy. He does not like meeting new people or even looking people in the eye. Though he is attracted to women, he has never felt comfortable talking to them or trying to get to know them better. After graduation, many companies courted him. He accepted a job as the programmer at ALAC Marketing where he could work mostly on his own. He likes his job because it is challenging enough to be absorbing, and he dreads ever going through the process of finding another one.

Jake's boss is Nathan Brook. Nathan well understands Jake's skills and vulnerabilities. One day, the Diabetes Foundation asks ALAC to construct a tool for its website that would survey Diabetes Foundation donors on the directions that the Foundation should take in its support for new research. As part of its corporate social responsibility mandate, ALAC does work for the Diabetes Foundation at cost. ALAC also has a highly profitable contract to market an expensive new drug, Circulex, for a large pharmaceuticals company. Circulex aids blood circulation in the legs, and will be useful to diabetics who have circulation problems in their extremities. Nathan realizes that the Diabetes Foundation donor list includes many well-off people with diabetes, just the sort of potential customers to whom the pharmaceutical company wishes to market Circulex.

The next day, Nathan visits Jake's workroom in the basement of the ALAC building. He suggests to Jake, purely orally of course, that Jake embed a bit of extra code in the survey tool that Jake is constructing for the Foundation. This code would transfer the email addresses, though not the passwords, of Foundation donors to Jake's computer. Nathan's intent is to use these email addresses to market Circulex. Nathan justifies this idea by pointing out that ALAC's work for the Diabetes Foundation is non-profit and that the survey tool does not explicitly promise anonymity to the donors who take it. He further suggests that unless Jake complies, Jake will have to look for work elsewhere. Jake is visibly reluctant and upset.

The following day, Nathan sends his assistant manager, Maia Harrick, to see Jake. Maia is about Jake's age and is both very attractive and very ambitious. After reminding Maia that her performance review is coming up soon, Nathan indicates to Maia that she should get Jake to add the spyware to the survey tool by any means possible. Maia knows very well how to use her good looks to get what she wants. She pays a lot of attention to Jake, pretends interest in the intricacies of hiding spyware in otherwise legitimate software, and acts as if she is impressed at his skill. On leaving, Maia implies that she will visit Jake often to see how the project is going.

What should Jake do? Will Jake be morally accountable for his decision?

Chapter 11

FREE ENTERPRISE AND GLOBAL JUSTICE

Is the capitalist system ethically defensible?

In a perfectly competitive market, is self-interest our only obligation?

Will international free trade lead to global development or to global injustice?

Is the free-enterprise system a good thing? All business activity takes place in the wider context of a market economy. In this chapter we will examine the ethical justifications for a market economy and the capitalist system. We will be concerned mostly with the tension between the efficiency of the free-enterprise system and the requirements of fairness and distributive justice. We will consider this tension first in our domestic economy and then in the global economy.

To begin with, we will examine four intellectual foundations for capitalism and the world of business. The first claims that the free-enterprise system is a set of rules that will allow self-interested agents to avoid Pareto-inefficient outcomes. The second claims that the free-enterprise system respects human rights to private property and freedom of exchange. The third claims that the free-enterprise system, under certain conditions, maximizes human welfare. The fourth claims that, when combined with redistributive taxation, the free-enterprise system can be a fair system that maximizes the welfare of the least well off. We have already surveyed these justifications in the chapter on justice.

A market economy is a system of laws, enforced by the state, that constitute the rules of doing business. These rules include criminal and property laws, which define and defend economic assets. The rules include tort laws, which make people liable to compensate others for infringements of property rights. As well, the rules include contract law, which is concerned with the formation and enforcement of contracts between market participants.

Adam Smith suggested that we should encourage butchers, brewers, and bakers to pursue their own interests according to the rules of cooperation embodied in the market because an "invisible hand" would lead them to promote the interest of society.

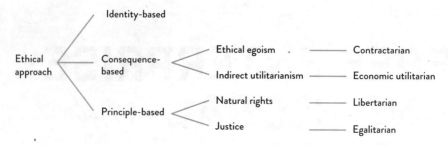

Figure 11.1: A conceptual map of ethical justifications for the free-enterprise system.

Suppose that we understand the interest of society as being the sum of the welfare of all members of society, and suppose that we understand human welfare as something that economists can compare between people and measure in dollar terms. If we make these assumptions, then Smith appears to have anticipated the fundamental theorem of welfare economics, which says that a free-market economy, under conditions of perfect competition, will maximize the welfare of its members.

Many people believe that the only obligation of people in the world of business is to obey its legal rules. If Adam Smith is correct, then economic utilitarian reasoning justifies this belief. A corollary is that the spread of the free-market through free trade around the globe is also a good thing. It is important, therefore, to understand the limitations of the economic utilitarian argument. We will critically examine this argument's financial theory of value, important situations—market failures—where the argument's assumptions break down, and its implications for domestic and global justice.

CONTRACTARIAN JUSTIFICATION

Before turning to the economic utilitarian justification for a market economy, we will review the contractarian and libertarian justifications. A contractarian ethic is the view that ethics is an enforced contract among ethical egoists designed to prevent dilemmas of cooperation such as prisoner's dilemma situations. This view suggests that the free-enterprise system is a set of laws that will allow self-interested agents to achieve Pareto-efficient outcomes. An outcome is Pareto-efficient if no other outcome is possible that makes at least one person better off and no person worse off.

We can see how this works if we imagine a state of nature before market rules are established. Two hunters must decide whether to trade or fight over their catch. Suppose that Gog has caught a deer, but that he would rather have a wild boar. Gog would get twice as much satisfaction from consuming a wild boar than from consuming a deer, but would get the most satisfaction from consuming both. Conversely, Magog has caught a wild boar, but he prefers to have a deer. Magog would get 1 unit of satisfaction from a wild boar, 2 from a deer, or 3 from having both.

Gog and Magog meet in the woods, and each must decide whether to trade with the other hunter or to fight and steal the other's catch. The best outcome for each is a surprise attack and a successful theft. However, if the other hunter is ready to attack back, then each will leave with what he caught. The payoff matrix for units of satisfaction is as in Figure 11.2. If Gog thinks that Magog expects to trade, then his best strategy is a surprise attack to steal Magog's wild boar, gaining him 3 utiles instead of 2. If Gog thinks that Magog plans to attack him, then his best strategy is to fight back because 1 utile is better than 0. By similar reasoning, Magog has a dominant strategy, which is also to fight. Therefore, the two hunters will both fight, and they will end up in the lower right cell. This is a Pareto inefficient outcome because the top left, trade-trade, outcome is better for both. They face a prisoner's dilemma.

		Gog	
		Trade	Fight
Magog	Trade	2 2	0 √3
	Fight	3 √ 0	1 √ √1

Figure 11.2: Unregulated choices between trading and fighting.

Now suppose that a local chieftain, who understands the prisoner's dilemma, allows Gog and Magog to join her tribe if they wish. This chieftain has established the rules of a market by enforcing property rights and contracts in her tribe. She does this by penalizing any hunter who fights or steals with a fine. The new situation is shown in Figure 11.3 where any payoff that involves fighting is penalized by 2 units of satisfaction.

		Gog	
		Trade	Fight
Magog	Trade	2 √ √2	0 √ 3-2=1
	Fight	3-2=1 √0	1-2=-1 1-2=-1

Figure 11.3: Regulated exchange that imposes a fine of 2 units for stealing or fighting.

We can now see that Gog will trade no matter what he thinks Magog will do because 2 > (3 - 2) and 0 > (1 - 2). Similarly, Magog will also trade no matter what he thinks Gog will do, and the two hunters will reach equilibrium in the top left cell with 2 units of satisfaction each. Trade-trade is a Pareto-optimal solution because no other outcome is possible that makes either one of the hunters better off without making the other worse off. In fact, all the other cells of the table involve both hunters being worse off. Within the rules of the market, self-interest will lead the hunters to a Pareto-efficient outcome.

Calling economic markets "free enterprise" or "the free market" can be somewhat misleading. In the state of nature, Gog and Magog are completely free of any regulation. When Gog and Magog join the tribe, the chieftain starts to regulate their behaviour by market rules, which are a form of government regulation. The dispute between defenders of free enterprise and their egalitarian critics is a dispute over what type of regulation is legitimate, not over the existence of government regulation *per se*. From the premise that Pareto efficient outcomes are the best outcomes, defenders argue that the state should only impose those laws that make the market function. From the premise that Pareto efficient outcomes should be tempered by fairness, egalitarian critics argue for more extensive government regulation and redistribution.

RIGHTS-BASED LIBERTARIAN JUSTIFICATION

As we saw in the chapter on justice, a libertarian justification of a minimally regulated, free enterprise economic system follows the history of contract and property rights back to the negative rights of self-ownership. Self-ownership is the opposite of slavery because self-owners have the right to manage and sell their own labour. John Locke argued that, in the state of nature, anyone who has "mixed his labour with" an un-owned thing comes to own that thing fairly, as long as he or she leaves "enough, and as good" for others. He concludes that initial appropriators have a natural right to property that they fairly acquire in this way. Their property rights include the right to give, sell, or trade this property with others. Therefore, later people have a natural right to any property that they have acquired through a history of fair exchanges that began with fair initial acquisition.

Libertarians such as Robert Nozick have modified Locke's argument to justify unbridled capital accumulation beyond the point at which there is as much and as good left for everyone. By her labour, the initial appropriator adds value to natural objects and thus Nozick claims that she comes to own these modified natural objects. His argument then assumes that, because of the productive efficiency of free-market systems, some of this value will accrue to those who missed the initial appropriation, leaving them better off than they would have been in a state of un-owned nature. Therefore, capitalism satisfies the requirement that enough, and as good, be left in common when we understand "enough, and as good" in this value-added approach. In the chapter on justice, we looked at some problems with the libertarian justification for a free-market economy, so we will not review them here.

INDIRECT ECONOMIC UTILITARIAN JUSTIFICATION

In the chapter on consequentialism, we saw that there are two types of utilitarianism. Direct utilitarianism treats utilitarianism as a moral decision procedure that we must employ for each action that we undertake. It advocates evaluating each possible action that we might perform according to a calculation of the utilities of its outcomes. Indirect utilitarianism treats utilitarianism not as a decision procedure for actions, but as a moral standard for the application of the tools of non-utilitarian ethical theories. It advocates obedience to rules, respect for rights, inculcation of virtues, or even self-interested behaviour if that is what is required to produce maximum aggregate utility.

An indirect utilitarian justification argues that the free-market system, a system within which everyone pursues his or her own self-interest, will produce the maximum aggregate preference-satisfaction for everyone. This is an indirect utilitarian justification because it asks everyone to use an ethical-egoist decision procedure, rather than a direct utilitarian decision procedure. This is Adam Smith's point about the self-interested butchers, brewers, and bakers creating a market economy that makes everyone maximally well off, even though maximizing the overall welfare did not guide their decisions.

Because this ethical justification is an economic utilitarian one, we will quickly review what this means. Economic utilitarianism is a form of preference-satisfaction utilitarianism where we measure the utility of a good or service to someone according to her willingness to pay for it. Willingness to pay is the maximum amount of money that someone would be willing to exchange for an economic good or service. Someone's willingness to pay (WTP) is always her marginal WTP. Marginal WTP is what she would pay for one more unit of the commodity. Marginal WTP is seldom equal to the market price. Production costs affect the market price of a commodity, so demand and supply together determine market price. Market prices are relatively easy for economists to measure. The marginal WTP for a commodity is actually the consumer's reservation price. A reservation price is the maximum amount of money that a consumer would be willing to exchange for one more unit of the commodity in the absence of a defined market price for that commodity. Reservation prices will vary depending on how many units of the commodity the consumer has already consumed. Reservation prices are very difficult for economists to measure.

To understand the indirect economic utilitarian justification of the free-market system, we must review some elementary economics. In our earlier discussion of justice, we distinguished between total and marginal utility. The total utility of a group of economic goods or services is the sum of all the benefits produced by the consumption of those goods or services. The marginal utility (or marginal benefit) of an economic good or service is the marginal benefit gained through the consumption of one additional unit of that good or service.

Microeconomics makes an important empirical assumption about marginal utility. The **law of diminishing marginal utility** states that as the consumption of a given economic good increases, the marginal utility produced by the consumption of one additional unit of the good tends to decrease. People tend to get satiated with consumer goods. For example, as people consume more and more cookies, they will receive less and less benefit from each additional cookie and will thus be willing to pay less for it.

Microeconomics makes another important empirical assumption about the marginal costs of producing goods. The **law of increasing marginal cost** states that, in the short-run, the marginal cost of producing each additional item will tend to increase. This tendency arises because a rational producer will use her cheapest alternative to produce the first item, then use her next cheapest alternative to produce the second item, and so on. For example, a producer will tend to pick the low-hanging fruit on a tree first, before deciding to incur the additional cost of ladders and mobile cranes. Notice, however, that the average cost of each additional item may decrease as the fixed costs of production are spread over more and more items.

We can sketch the indirect economic utilitarian argument by considering the supply and demand curves in Figure 11.4. First, we will see how self-interested decisions by market participants will lead to the production and consumption of 2,000 items. Second, we will show that the production and consumption of this number of items (2,000) maximizes overall total net benefits for all market participants. We will conclude that self-interested behaviour within the rules of the market causes maximum total net benefits.

For every possible price of an item available for sale, the demand curve for a market tells us the quantity of items for which one or more consumers would be willing to pay that price. This price measures the marginal benefit that each of these willing consumers would receive if they consumed that item. It is at least one consumer's reservation price for buying that item. The demand curve slopes downward to the right to reflect the law of declining marginal benefits (MB).

For every possible price of an item available for sale, the supply curve tells us the quantity of items for which one or more producers would be willing to accept that price. This price measures the marginal cost that each of those willing producers would incur if they produced one of these items, and is the least amount that these producers would be willing to accept for that item. The supply curve slopes upward to the right to reflect the law of increasing marginal costs (MC).

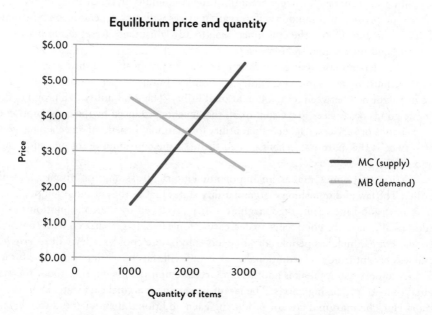

Figure 11.4: Supply (MC) and demand (MB) curves for a large market.

The market modelled in Figure 11.4 will be in equilibrium when participants produce and consume 2,000 items at a price of $3.50. This is the point where supply equals demand, and the marginal benefit to someone of consuming the last item equals the cost to someone else of producing it.

This quantity of 2,000 items will be the equilibrium quantity of items that self-interested participants will produce and consume. If any producer tried to sell a higher number of items, then this producer's marginal cost of producing such items would be higher than any self-interested consumer would be willing to pay for them. Therefore, it would not be in any producer's self-interest to produce more items. However, if the quantity available were less than 2,000, then self-interested consumers would be willing to pay more for additional items than their marginal cost of production. Therefore, some self-interested producers would be motivated to supply this demand. The self-interested behaviour of producers and consumers will result in an equilibrium quantity of 2,000 items at a price of $3.50.

We can also see this equilibrium quantity of 2,000 items will maximize total net benefits to all market participants. If the quantity were less than 2,000, the marginal benefit to some consumer of consuming additional items would be more than the marginal cost to some producer of producing those items, and so producing and consuming additional items would increase the total net benefit. If the quantity were greater than 2,000, then the marginal cost to any producer of producing additional items would be higher than the marginal benefit of consuming them to any consumer, and so producing and consuming fewer items would increase the total net benefit. When supply equals demand, the marginal benefit (MB) to some consumer of consuming one more item equals the marginal cost (MC) to some producer of producing that item. The point where MB = MC, and demand equals supply, will maximize total aggregate net benefits at a price of $3.50 with a quantity of 2,000 items produced and consumed.

Therefore, an "invisible hand" will lead market participants, acting purely from motives of self-interest, to maximize their aggregate utility.

The indirect economic utilitarian justification for the market claims that the self-interested actions of individual market participants will maximize aggregate net benefits for all market participants. The claim is utilitarian because it justifies the claims that the right thing to do is to maximize overall welfare. Utilitarianism is indifferent regarding who receives the benefits. It is economic utilitarian because it measures the marginal benefits of commodities by what people are willing to pay to consume them, and it measures marginal costs by what people are willing to accept for producing them. It is an indirect utilitarian justification because it does not tell people to be utilitarian in their decision-making, but instead to be egoists who maximize their own self-interest within the rules of the game.

ASSUMPTIONS OF THE ECONOMIC UTILITARIAN JUSTIFICATION

Economists can show generally that, under conditions of perfect competition, self-interested market participants will maximize their overall welfare as measured in financial terms. The assumption of perfect competition in economics is like the assumption of a frictionless plane in physics. Both models make calculations easier, and both make false assumptions about the real world. The standard economic assumptions of perfect competition include the following: There are many buyers and sellers. Market participants face no barriers to entry and can freely move in and out of the market. No firm is a monopoly (single seller), or is a monopsony (single buyer), or participates in an oligopoly (few sellers). Producers receive constant returns to scale (no economies of scale). Consumers have full information about the market prices of all alternative goods, and producers have full information about production techniques.

Students of economics tend to regard these deviations from the conditions of perfect competition as market imperfections rather than market failures. They tend to think that even if we cannot achieve conditions of perfect competition, the closer we can bring the market to perfect competition, the closer it will come to maximizing overall economic welfare. The usual solution to the problem of external benefits illustrates this reasoning. An **external benefit** or positive externality is a benefit arising from the economic activity of an agent for which the market price of the product does not compensate the agent. For instance, in the absence of patent laws, no one would compensate inventors for technological discoveries, and the lack of incentives for inventors would impede overall technological progress. Granting patents to their inventions creates incentives for inventors, though it also creates monopoly conditions in the marketplace. Despite the associated monopolies, patent laws plausibly create a second-best scenario that will come close to maximizing economic welfare.

Nevertheless, tiny market imperfections can also lead to huge market failures that do not maximize overall financial welfare. The problem of external costs illustrates this reasoning. An **external cost** or negative externality is a cost arising from the economic activity of an agent that is born by others because the market price of the product does not incorporate this cost. Environmental pollution is a good example; factories sometimes pollute rivers so that they can avoid paying the costs of the proper disposal of their effluent. The emission of greenhouse gasses is an example of an apparently tiny market imperfection that may lead to a catastrophic market failure. Because of our dependence on fossil fuels, almost all production results in small emissions of carbon dioxide. Producers externalize the cost of these emissions because there is no market mechanism for charging them. Each tiny emission is apparently harmless, yet billions of such emissions can accumulate into atmospheric carbon dioxide levels that will cause dangerous climate change. Dangerous climate change would be a giant market failure created by the accumulation of tiny market imperfections.

We will say that conditions, where the assumptions of perfect condition do not hold and markets are not efficient, are **market failures**. Another assumption that often fails to apply is that there are no open-access resources. An **open-access resource** (a commons good or a non-excludable good) is a resource from which it is difficult to exclude other individuals. Examples of open-access resources include fishing and whaling in international waters and the use of the atmosphere and the oceans as dumping grounds for pollution. Open-access resources often become over-used. An example is the cod fishery on the Grand Banks off Newfoundland where unrestricted over-fishing led to the collapse of the cod stock. We will return to the problems of open-access resources in the next chapter on sustainability.

Assumptions	Failures of these assumptions
Perfect competition	Few buyers and sellers Barriers to entry and exit Monopsony, monopoly, or oligopoly Increasing returns to scale
No lack of information	Prices of alternatives unknown Informational barriers to market entry
No external benefits	Technological discoveries without intellectual property
No external costs	Environmental pollution
No public goods	Police and legal system required for market Solutions to environmental problems
No open-access goods	Open access to natural resources Tragedy of the commons (Chapter 12)
No transaction costs	Weaknesses of the Coase Theorem (Chapter 12)
Willingness to pay measures welfare	Problems with Cost-Benefit Analysis

Table 11.1: The assumptions of the indirect economic utilitarian justification of markets.

A further assumption of the indirect economic utilitarian justification of free markets is that there are no public goods. **Public goods** are open-access goods whose use by one person does not diminish their availability to others. The police, legal system, and national defense, which enforce the rules of the market, are all examples of public goods. It is difficult to exclude any citizens who do not pay their share from access to the benefits of these systems. A few free-riding citizens will not substantially affect the availability of these public goods. Consequently, the market will not itself provide police, law courts, and armed forces, and a market economy will require a coercive taxation system. We will return to this problem in the next chapter on the environment because solutions for many environmental problems involve the provision of public goods.

In addition, perfect competition assumes that the market exchanges have no transaction costs. **Transaction costs** are the costs of reaching and enforcing an agreement between negotiating parties. They include the costs of researching information about the situation, negotiating the agreement, and legally enforcing the agreement. In the real world, market participants do face many transaction costs, and the assumptions of perfect competition will fail. One reason the invention of the Internet may have caused economic growth is that it reduced transaction costs in the market by making it easier and less costly for willing buyers and willing sellers to find one another. In the next chapter, we will see how the existence of transaction costs undermines an important argument for a free-market approach to protecting the environment.

Perhaps the biggest assumption of the indirect economic utilitarian justification for the market is that willingness to pay (WTP) can be used to measure preference-satisfaction. The economic utilitarian approach assumes that WTP measures the intensity of preferences and that everything valuable is a commodity that people buy and sell. In our discussion of WTP in the chapter on utilitarianism, we saw that WTP is not a very good measure of the intensity of preferences for the following reasons:

1. Because of the law of diminishing marginal utility, a person's WTP for a commodity will change depending on her prior consumption of the commodity.
2. When the market price is known to her and she knows that she can obtain the commodity from someone at a certain price, then she will not be willing to pay more than that market price. She will usually be reluctant to reveal her reservation prices, and may not even be aware of what they are. In the presence of market prices, WTP is very difficult for economists to measure.
3. Her WTP is relative to a certain level of income and wealth (ability to pay). Ability to pay affects willingness to pay. If she were a billionaire then she would be willing to pay more that she would if she were a pauper.
4. Her WTP is relative to a certain level of information. Her WTP measures her actual, uninformed preferences, not the preferences that she would have if she had full information. For example, not knowing that the pizza is poisoned, the amount she is willing to pay does not correspond to the amount this slice will turn out to contribute to her happiness.
5. Her WTP is not invariant, but relative to the prices of other commodities. Her WTP for one commodity will depend on what else she could get for her money. If substitutes or alternatives become available more cheaply, then she may be less willing to pay as much for the commodity in question. Relative prices vary between different national markets, and vary over time within any given market.
6. Finally, she is unlikely to have a defined WTP for everything that she wants. She is unlikely to place a dollar value on her life, integrity, honesty, or on selling herself into slavery. The biggest problem for the economic utilitarian approach is the assumption that there is a common financial measure for what people value.

LIBERAL EGALITARIAN JUSTICE

As we have seen in the previous section, there are flaws in the economic utilitarian justification for the free market. That justification unrealistically assumes the existence of perfect competition, and inaccurately treats the achievement of an efficient market equilibrium as the maximization of utility. However, there are also non-utilitarian objections to this justification, including concerns of justice.

One general problem with any sort of utilitarian ethical justification is that, because utilitarianism is concerned only with aggregating and maximizing utility, it pays no attention to whether the distribution of that utility is fair. For example, the argument from declining marginal utility to an equal distribution proved to be very weak because people cannot be assumed to convert economic resources into utility at the same rate.

In the nineteenth and twentieth centuries, socialist and communist egalitarians advocated centrally planned economies with strict equality of welfare. Their slogan for economic justice was, "From each according to his abilities, and to each according to his needs." One problem with this theory was that centrally planned economies are not as efficient as decentralized, free-market economies. This has to be so under ideal conditions, because perfect competition maximizes efficiency. In Table 11.2, the free-market distribution in the top row maximizes total resources, but is highly unequal with Tom doing much better than Ron and Sal. The centrally planed economy in the middle row results in equality of welfare, but everyone is doing less well because the centrally planned economy is inefficient. Modern liberal egalitarians claim the best form of egalitarianism will use the free market to maximize the production of primary goods, but then redistribute primary goods to the benefit of the least advantaged.

#	Theory	Ron	Sal	Tom	Total
1	Free-market with no redistribution	$1,100	$1,100	$3,000	$5,200
2	Centrally planned equality of welfare	$1,000	$1,000	$1,000	$3,000
3	Free-market with redistribution	$1,600	$1,700	$1,800	$5,100

Table 11.2: Three illustrative distributions of financial resources.

As we have seen, Rawls's **difference principle** says that a distribution of rights and responsibilities is just if, and only if, everyone receives the same resources unless an unequal distribution results in the least well-off receiving more than in the strictly equal distribution. This preserves the incentives and efficiencies of the free-market by allowing some inequalities, and results in the least advantaged being as well off as they can be. We can see this in the third row of Table 11.2, where the least well off do better than in either of the other distributions, but with some reduction in the overall aggregate financial resources available. Liberal egalitarianism also provides an ethical justification for a free-market economic system, provided we add to it a system of proportional income tax and a redistributive welfare system.

GLOBAL JUSTICE

The same tension between the efficiency and the fairness of the market system occurs at the global level. A comprehensive view of moral standing requires that we consider the interests of everyone in the global community when we reflect on these issues.

Once upon a time, the world was divided into many local economies, each roughly self-sufficient in the necessities of life. People specialized, divided the labour, and cooperated with one another to produce goods efficiently. As transportation technology improved, people in one market economy specialized in what they did best, and traded with people in another market economy who specialized in something else. In the contemporary world, very few national economies are self-sufficient in life's necessities, let alone in its luxuries. The global economy has become highly interdependent, with most countries depending on imports for food, technology, and consumer goods.

Are we ethically obliged to consider the interests of everyone in the global economy, or do our ethical obligations extend only to participants in our local economy? Do distant people in other parts of the globe have moral standing? Should we strive for global justice as well as national justice?

One argument for the moral standing of distant people goes like this. Distant people have all the same natural features as nearby people. Whatever natural feature is sufficient for moral standing in ethical theories distant people have it also. Therefore, distant people must also have moral standing. Just as the ethical egoist cannot point to some morally relevant personal feature that implies that only he has moral standing, we cannot point to any morally relevant feature of ourselves that implies that only we local people have moral standing.

Certainly, distance does not seem to prevent distant people from having moral standing in our ethical decision-making. Suppose Nora lives near her mother in New York City. Nora has certain moral obligations to her mother. One day, Nora's mother moves to Melbourne, Australia. Do Nora's moral obligations to her mother disappear when her mother moves 10,360 miles away? If not, then physical distance does not affect moral standing.

Virtue ethics, with its emphasis on the character traits that make community cooperation work well, seems to suggest that we have moral obligations to other members of our local community that we do not have to outsiders. Nevertheless, a virtuous local community should itself develop community character traits that enable it to cooperate at a wider level. It is difficult to see how a local community can fulfil its obligation to be just and fair at a global level without also developing a sense of global justice in its individual members.

Furthermore, consequentialist and principle-based ethical reasoning both consider the interests of everyone in the global community. If free enterprise will maximize human welfare in the domestic marketplace, then free trade will likely maximize human welfare in the global marketplace too. If unrestricted, untaxed free enterprise leads to problems of distributive justice at the domestic level, then free trade will likely lead to problems of distributive justice at the global level too.

INTERNATIONAL FREE TRADE

Many of the utilitarian and distributive justice arguments we have just considered with respect to domestic free trade apply in similar ways at the international level. Once upon a time, international relations consisted of one city-state conquering another and demanding tribute. The conquest-tribute game is a zero-sum game with huge transaction costs; what one city-state gained in tribute, the other more than lost. The trade-trade game, however, is potentially a positive-sum game; because of specialization and the division of labour, both parties will gain from trade. This realization has led to improved international relations.

In his 1848 economics textbook, John Stuart Mill pointed out a character-based reason for encouraging free trade. "It is commerce which is rapidly rendering war obsolete, by strengthening and multiplying the personal interests which are in natural opposition to it. And it may be said without exaggeration that the great extent and rapid increase of international trade ... is the great permanent security for the uninterrupted progress of the ideas, the institutions, and the character of the human race." (Mill, 1909, III.17.14) Free trade, and the contact with different people that it facilitates, has the potential to make people everywhere more peaceful and tolerant, and to help create a cosmopolitan and multi-cultural global community.

By generalizing the libertarian view of Lock and Nozick, we can also see an argument based in negative rights in favour of free trade and against protectionism (tariffs and quotas). The argument begins with the usual libertarian premises that people have a natural right to own property, and that people have a natural liberty to exchange their property as they see fit. It first concludes that all government restrictions on free trade in domestic markets are illegitimate. Then the argument observes that natural rights are human rights, rights that any human being may claim. Natural rights are not political rights, such as the right to vote, that only citizens of a country can claim. Globally, every human being has these natural rights because every human being has moral standing. Natural rights do not stop at national borders. Therefore, all restrictions on free trade in international markets are illegitimate. In addition, all quotas, tariffs, and, border closures are illegitimate. Rectifying income inequalities that result from free trade is illegitimate as well.

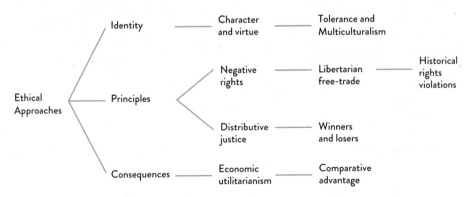

Figure 11.5: Conceptual map of ethical considerations regarding global free trade.

The main weakness of libertarian argument is that it is a historical entitlement view. The distribution of property rights in the world is just only if it started from fair initial acquisition. Evidence does not support the view that the history of the current global distribution of property violated no rights. The current global distribution has its origin in earlier zero-sum games of conquest and tribute. Earth has a history of violent conquest, colonization, and expropriation. For example, the Spanish conquest of Mexico in the sixteenth century brought great wealth to Europe, but killed millions of native Mexicans through warfare and disease and involved the theft of huge amounts of gold and silver.

Figure 11.5 gives a conceptual map of some ethical considerations for and against unrestricted free trade. We have discussed virtue ethics and negative rights considerations. Now we will look at the economic utilitarian argument and the concerns of distributive justice that it raises.

THE ECONOMIC UTILITARIAN ARGUMENT FOR FREE TRADE

Let us start from the premise that specialization and the division of labour is a positive-sum game that will produce an increase in aggregate material goods. Then let us add the premise that trade under conditions of perfect competition maximizes these aggregate material goods. Suppose that we have two countries producing two goods, but that each country can produce one of the goods more cheaply than the other country. We should conclude that if the two countries each specialized in the good that they produced most efficiently and both freely traded the results, then total production and consumption of the goods would go up. For example, if Hither has land that is better suited to the production of corn and Yon has better land for beans, then it makes sense for Hither to specialize in corn, Yon to specialize in beans, and for Hither and Yon to have free trade in corn and beans.

In this example, each country has an absolute advantage over the other in the production of some commodity. One country has an **absolute advantage** over a second country in the production of a commodity if, and only if, the first country can produce that commodity more cheaply than the second country can. Suppose, however, that one country can produce both goods more cheaply than the other country can. At first glance, it seems that there will be no benefit to this efficient country to engage in trade. This first glance would be misleading.

It turns out that both Hither and Yon can profit from free trade even if Hither is more efficient at producing both corn and beans than Yon is. The nineteenth-century English economist, David Ricardo formulated the **law of comparative advantage**, which says that there exist terms of trade under which two countries will both gain from trade if they specialize in producing goods in which they have a comparative, not an absolute, advantage. Both the efficient and the inefficient countries will gain from free trade. For example, even if the USA can produce both corn and automobiles more cheaply than can Mexico, Ricardo says that both the USA and Mexico can still gain from trade.

One country has a **comparative advantage** over a second country in the production of a commodity if, and only if, the first country can produce that commodity more cheaply in terms of another commodity than the second country can. Table 11.3 illustrates Yon's

	Hither	Yon
Corn (tons per acre)	6	1
Beans (tons per acre)	3	2
Absolute advantage in corn	√	
Absolute advantage in beans	√	
Comparative advantage in corn	√	
Comparative advantage in beans		√

Table 11.3: Hither has an absolute advantage in both corn and beans, but Yon has a comparative advantage in beans.

comparative advantage in the production of beans. Hither has an absolute advantage in bean production because it can produce 3 tons per acre to Yon's 2 tons per acre. Yon has a comparative advantage, however, in bean production. Yon can produce 2 tons of beans at the cost of giving up the production of 1 ton of corn. (Students of economics will recognize this as the opportunity cost of corn in terms of beans.) For Hither to produce 2 tons of beans, Hither would have to give up two-thirds of an acre of corn production, which would have produced 4 tons of corn. Yon can produce beans more cheaply than can Hither when costs are measured in terms of forgone corn production.

We can construct a little model that shows how specialization and free trade can lead to greater overall production of corn and beans. Suppose that yields per acre are as in Table 11.4, that people need equal amounts of corn and beans for a balanced diet, and that both countries have 10,000 acres of land.

	Hither		Yon	
	Corn	Beans	Corn	Beans
Productive capacity per year on 10,000 acres	60,000	30,000	10,000	20,000
Self-sufficient corn + bean production	20,000 + 20,000		6,666 + 6,666	
Total self-sufficient production (beans + corn)	26,666 + 26,666			
Yon 100% beans, Hither 5/9 corn, 4/9 beans	33,333	13,333	0	20,000
Total production with free-trade (beans + corn)	33,333 + 33,333			

Table 11.4: Gains from trade with comparative advantage.

Working through the numbers, we can see that if each country has a comparative advantage in one commodity, and if Yon specializes totally in the production of beans, then total production after free trade of each commodity will increase from 26,666 tons to 33,333 tons.

We can see the reason why each country is better off to trade if we imagine their situations when the terms of trade are one ton of corn for one ton of beans. To produce beans, Hither can either use an acre of land to produce 3 tons of beans or use that same acre of land to produce 6 tons of corn, which it can trade with Yon to get 6 tons of beans. Hither is better off to trade.

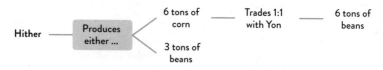

Figure 11.6: Hither's potential production per acre with terms of trade = 1:1.

To produce corn, Yon can either use one acre of land to produce 1 ton of corn, or use that land to produce 2 tons of beans, which it can trade with Hither to obtain 2 tons of corn.

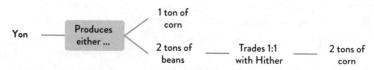

Figure 11.7: Yon's potential production per acre with terms of trade = 1:1.

Both countries will be better off if they produce the commodity in which they have a comparative advantage and engage in trade. The introduction of trade is like the introduction of a new technology for agricultural production.

The economic utilitarian argument for free international trade is that both countries will gain overall from free trade in terms of material goods. This will lead to higher overall supply and lower prices. The argument applies under conditions of both absolute and comparative advantage. However, the argument says nothing about the fair distribution of the gains from trade. Nor does the argument say anything about how comparative advantage is achieved. For example, countries can achieve a comparative advantage through banning unions, having low labour standards, permitting tax loopholes for businesses, or having lax environmental standards. International businesses often take advantage of these loopholes in taxation and accountability by shifting parts of their operations to different regions. Again, the economic utilitarian argument for unrestricted free trade says nothing about these issues of global justice.

WINNERS AND LOSERS IN INTERNATIONAL TRADE

In addition to Ricardo's law of comparative advantage, there is another, lesser-known economic law regarding international trade, the factor-proportions law. The factor-proportions law does say something about the distribution of the gains from free trade: "The owners of a country's relatively abundant factors will gain from free trade, while the owners of a country's relatively scarce factors will lose." (Krugman and Obstfeld, 2006, p. 64)

A country's abundant factor of production is a resource of which the country has a relatively larger supply than does its trading partner. A country's scarce factor of production is a resource of which the country has a relatively smaller supply than does its trading partner. In the following example, even though Home is a bigger country and has both more capital and more labour in absolute terms, it has a relatively larger supply of capital as compared to Away, and a relatively smaller supply of workers.

	Home	Away
Capital	100 billion dollars	25 billion dollars
Labour	2 million workers	1 million workers
Ratio of capital to labour	$50,000 per worker	$25,000 per worker
Ratio of labour to capital	1 worker per $50,000	2 workers per $50,000
Relatively abundant factor	Capital	Labour
Relatively scarce factor	Labour	Capital

Table 11.5: Relatively abundant and relatively scarce factors of production.

Here is a sketch of an explanation for the factor-proportions law based on the argument of Stolper and Samuelson. (1941, pp. 65–66) Suppose that Home and Away start to trade in clothing and automobiles. Manufacturing automobiles uses a higher proportion of capital than does manufacturing clothing. Home's relatively abundant factor is capital, its relative advantage is in automobiles. Clothing production is labour intensive and uses 1 unit of capital for each 2 units of labour. The figure below represents Home using 4 units of capital and 8 units of labour to produce clothing. ($ represents 1 unit of capital and ☻ represents 1 unit of employed labour.)

[$$$$ ☻☻☻☻☻☻☻☻]

Automobile production is capital intensive, and uses 1 unit of capital to 1 unit of labour. The figure below shows Home using 4 units of capital and 4 units of labour to produce automobiles.

[$$$$ ☻☻☻☻]

We will assume that a country has an advantage in producing goods that are intensive in the country's relatively abundant factor. Since Home's relatively abundant factor is capital, Home will export automobiles and import clothing.

Therefore, Home will increase automobile production and decrease clothing production. Decreased clothing production will release labour and capital:

[$$$$ ☺☺☺☺☺☺☺] → $$$$ & ☹☹☹☹☹☹☹☹

Decreased clothing production will release more labour (2:1) and less capital than is required to increase automobiles (1:1). The figure below shows Home using all its 8 units of capital to produce automobiles. Now it only needs 8 units of labour, leaving 4 units of labour unemployed.

[$$$$$$$$ ☺☺☺☺☺☺☺] & ☹☹☹☹

This will create a surplus of labour and a shortage of capital in Home's domestic factor markets. Therefore, in Home, wage rates to labour, its relatively scarce factor, will fall and returns to capital, its relatively abundant factor, will rise.

Similarly, in Away, returns to its relatively abundant factor, labour, will rise and returns to its relatively scarce factor, capital, will fall. Generalizing, free trade will cause owners of relatively abundant factors to be winners in the post-trade income distribution, and owners of relatively scarce factors to be losers. This is the factor-proportions law.

Because of the factor-proportions law, free trade is not Pareto efficient. For free trade to be Pareto efficient, someone must gain, and no one must lose, yet according to the factor-proportions law, the owners of relatively scarce factors will lose. Stolper and Samuelson, however, defend international free trade by appealing to another type of economic efficiency.

> ... our argument provides no political ammunition for the protectionist. For if effects on the terms of trade can be disregarded, it has been shown that the harm which free trade inflicts upon one factor of production is necessarily less than the gain to the other. Hence, it is always possible to bribe the suffering factor by subsidy or other redistributive devices so as to leave all factors better off as a result of trade. (1941, p. 73)

According to Ricardo, free trade will increase the amount of material goods available in each country, while creating winners and losers inside the country. This larger amount of material goods available should enable the winners to compensate the losers and still to have some goods left over for themselves. Free trade passes the compensation test for economic efficiency. However, there is nothing in economic theory that implies this potential compensation will actually take place, and this raises questions of distributive justice.

DISTRIBUTIVE JUSTICE IN INTERNATIONAL TRADE

Egalitarian theories of justice generally hold that policy decisions should increase the benefits to the poor and least advantaged. For example, Rawls's difference principle says that a distribution of rights and responsibilities is just if, and only if, everyone receives the same resources unless an unequal distribution results in the least well-off receiving more than in the strictly equal distribution. However, we do not have to accept Rawls's full theory to share the intuition that any policy decision is unfair that makes the least well-off group in absolute terms even more badly off.

	India		USA	
Factor	unskilled labour	capital	unskilled labour	capital
Relative abundance	abundant	scarce	scarce	abundant
Winner/loser	winner	loser	loser	winner
Advantage	absolutely least	relatively most	relatively least	absolutely most

Table 11.6: Free trade in manufactured goods between India and USA.

We can illustrate this with two cases. Table 11.6 shows what happens when India and the USA begin to trade freely in manufactured goods. India's unskilled labourers are more badly off than all other groups, so they are the least well-off group in absolute terms. In this case, unskilled labour is India's relatively abundant factor, and unskilled Indian labourers will be winners in this deal. The least advantaged group in absolute terms will benefit from a free-trade deal. Because of Ricardo's law, the USA will benefit overall, and its winners could compensate its losers. If the wealthy winners in the USA fail to compensate the unskilled labourers who lose out, then this will become a major political issue.

Table 11.7 shows the case of China and Canada beginning to trade freely in food. The least advantaged group, in absolute terms are Chinese peasants, who we will assume are worse off than unskilled labourers in Canada, who are in turn worse off than are Canada's farmers. Since unskilled labour is relatively abundant in China, Chinese peasants will be losers.

	China		Canada	
Factor	unskilled labour	land	unskilled labour	land
Relative abundance	abundant	scarce	scarce	abundant
Winner/loser	winner	loser	loser	winner
Advantage	relatively most	absolutely least	relatively least	absolutely most

Table 11.7: Free trade in food between China and Canada.

In this example, the poorest and least advantaged are losers from free trade in both countries. Global egalitarian justice would say no to free trade unless the winners actually will pay compensation to the losers in both countries.

Free trade will generate winners and losers. Often the losers will be the least advantaged. Free trade also generates a larger economic "pie" to divide among everyone. The gains from trade make it possible for the winners to compensate the losers when the losers are the least advantaged. Distributive justice requires that this happen.

Free trade in goods also creates problems of distributive justice because of the differential mobility of capital and labour. Capital is free to move across national borders. Labour is not mobile because of immigration laws. When returns to capital fall in Away, owners of capital can go to other countries for better returns. When wages fall in Home, workers cannot take their skills to other countries to earn better wages.

SUMMARY

1. A contractarian ethic justifies a market economy by showing that enforcing its legal rules will enable self-interested participants to avoid the dilemmas of cooperation.

2. A rights-based, libertarian justification of a market economy argues that if the economy has arisen historically from fair initial appropriation and a fair sequence of exchanges, then even an unequal distribution of income and wealth is justified.

3. An indirect, economic utilitarian justification of a market economy argues that, under conditions of perfect competition, the self-interested actions of market participations will lead to equilibrium in the prices and quantities of goods. This equilibrium will maximize overall net benefits as measured in financial terms.

4. The assumptions of this utilitarian justification for a market economy include no monopolies, no returns to scale, no positive or negative externalities, no public or open-access goods, no lack of information, no transaction costs, and no problems with willingness to pay as a measure of the strength of preferences. In practice, market failures arise from the violation of these assumptions.

5. A liberal egalitarian justification of a market economy points out that we can use market mechanisms to efficiently produce goods and services, and then use redistributive taxation to better the condition of the least advantaged members of the market society.

6. Moral standing does not vary with distance, so there is no morally relevant distinction between local and faraway people. Therefore, justifications for free trade in domestic markets should also be arguments in favour of free trade, and against protectionism, in the international market.

7.   Ricardo's law of comparative advantage suggests that when two countries trade freely, the total amount of goods in both economies will go up, even if one country can produce all goods more efficiently, in absolute terms, than the other can. This provides an economic utilitarian justification for free trade.

8.   Aggregative utilitarian reasoning often creates distributive justice problems. The factor-proportions law shows that the abolition of trade restrictions between two countries will create winners and losers within each country. Both countries are better off overall because of free trade, so the winners in each country could potentially compensate the losers.

9.   Global distributive justice requires winners from free trade to compensate losers whenever the losers are the least advantaged.

ONLINE LEARNING RESOURCES

You will find a collection of learning resources associated with this chapter on the book's website: http://sites.broadviewpress.com/businessethics/. Working through this material will help you understand and remember important concepts that we have discussed, and will help you apply them to issues in business ethics.

STUDY QUESTIONS

Answering the following questions will help you to understand the ethical theory in this chapter and will help you to create a set of review notes on the textbook.

1.   Summarize in a few sentences the contractarian justification for the enforcement of free market rules.

2.   Why does a libertarian justification for the free enterprise system permit unrestricted capitalism and ownership of the means of production by a wealthy few?

3.   Condense the indirect economic utilitarian argument justification for the free-enterprise system into a few sentences.

4.   Explain why air pollution is a negative externality and why unregulated markets create inefficient amounts of pollution.

5.   Explain why the enforcement of the legal rules of the market is a public good, and why the market requires a coercive enforced system of taxation.

6.   Why is liberal egalitarian distributive justice an improvement over centrally planned egalitarianism?

7.   Why should utilitarian and rights-based ethical reasoning apply globally?

8. Why can a rich country that is more efficient than a poor country in the production of all goods, still gain from trade with the poor country?

9. Summarize why the start of free trade between two countries will create winners and losers.

10. What type of clauses would egalitarian global justice require in all international free-trade agreements?

DECISION QUESTIONS

The whole point of learning ethical theory is to understand and ask questions like the following when you are analyzing an ethically problematic situation or case.

- Can a decision be justified because it is in accord with the rules of the economic market?
- Will the decision contribute to the efficiency of the economic market?
- Will the decision create external costs for nearby, distant, or future people?
- Would a decision that maximizes aggregate financial resources actually maximize well-being?
- Will the decision make the distribution of income and wealth less fair?
- Will a decision to engage in international trade make a developing country better off?
- Will a decision to engage in international trade lower anyone's welfare in the developing country?
- Can winners in a trade deal compensate losers for their lost economic welfare?

CASE STUDY

Analyze this case study using the ethical theory that you have learned so far. You will find a collection of learning materials applying to the case on the book's website: http://sites.broadviewpress.com/businessethics/. These materials will help you in your analysis.

Should Kate Recommend a Sweatshop?

Kate Bond is the CEO of Seinfeld Textiles, which manufactures clothing in a single factory in Canada. Canada has recently signed a free trade deal with Ismiristan that removes all barriers to trade on clothing between the two countries. The ST board of directors is unhappy with the prospective future profitability of the ST clothing factory in Canada.

Most of the financial value in ST is in its brand, in its reputation for quality clothing, and in its contracts with retailers. If ST were to sell its brand and its goodwill to another clothing company, then its owners would receive a good price. Its owners could then easily find new, more profitable investment opportunities in Canada. Kate thinks that if ST continues production in Canada, then competitors offering cheaper imported clothing will probably take away some of ST's customers.

ST provides well-paid, unionised jobs, and is the biggest employer in its community. Kate has lived all of her life in that community. Some of her family and many of her friends work for ST, and her best friend runs the local department store. ST closing its factory would be a disaster for all of them.

Kate has asked her VP of production to recommend how to cut costs, and his committee has recommended that ST close the local factory, and contract with a broker to arrange for the same lines of clothing to be manufactured in garment factories in Ismiristan, where wages are much lower than in Canada.

Out-sourcing clothing production to garment factories in Ismiristan could be a financial blessing for the people there. Most of the garment workers in Ismiristan are young, rural women who come to the cities, stay in dormitories, work long days in the factories, and send money home to their families. Their wages are very low in absolute terms, but higher than the wages they would receive in the countryside, if they could find any work. They are usually very poor and would otherwise have no employment prospects or sources of income.

Though they do relatively well financially, the garment workers face other problems. They pay high rents to the companies for their dormitory accommodation, and they must buy their food at the company store. Managers often order them to work overtime at straight wages. Supervisors treat them disrespectfully, and sometimes ask for sexual favours. No laws permit them to form unions. Their culture is patriarchal, so fathers, brothers, or husbands control the money that they send to their families. Many of them are young mothers who must go long periods without seeing their children.

If ST were to outsource its clothing production, its employees in Canada would receive small severance packages, as well as six months of employment insurance from the government, though at about half of their regular salaries. They would have other employment opportunities in Canada, though most such opportunities would require relocating to a different, oil-rich, province, or require a long commute every few weeks to see their families. Selling their homes would be difficult if ST closed its factory, and their houses would lose much of their value.

What should Kate recommend to the board?

SUSTAINABILITY AND THE ENVIRONMENT

What are our obligations to future generations and to the environment?

Can an economic approach to the environment be ethical?

How should we think about sustainable development?

In this chapter, we will look at ethical concerns regarding the effect of our market economy on our planet. To apply ethical reasoning to the market economy, we need to understand how environmental problems arise from failures of the market system. Pollution problems are often external cost problems. Resource depletion problems often arise from the existence of open access resources. Solutions to environmental problems are often difficult because the solutions involve public goods for which it is hard to get market participants to pay. Economic thinking can help us develop cost-effective answers to environmental problems using cost-benefit analysis and market-based approaches to pollution control. Nevertheless, these economic techniques themselves raise ethical questions of rights, justice, virtue, moral standing, and the quantification of sustainable development using financial indicators such as the GDP.

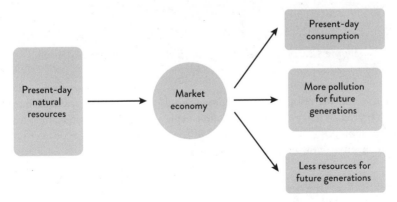

Figure 12.1: The market economy as a potentially destructive machine.

Economic activity often creates environmental pollution. These external costs fall, not only on market participants, but also on both the wider global community and future generations. A less-than-virtuous business disposes of a noxious effluent into a river, saving itself a little money, but causing problems for anyone who lives downstream. The river flows across an international boundary, and now the effluent becomes a problem for the global community. The river remains polluted even after the business goes bankrupt, leaving an environmental mess for future generations. Greenhouse gasses, toxic wastes from nuclear reactors, the depletion of non-renewable resources such as oil, and the exhaustion of underground aquifers, all create global environmental problems for posterity to solve. If we are not careful, the market economy will become like a giant machine creating welfare for present people, and problems for future generations: depleted resources and increased pollution.

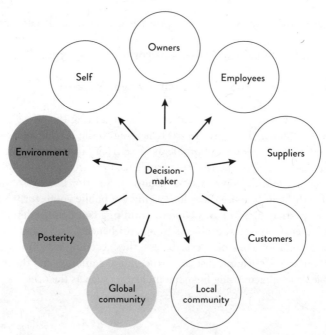

Figure 12.2: Comprehensive moral standing in business ethics.

These considerations suggest that we should employ a comprehensive theory of moral standing. When polluting or resource depleting market activities impose external costs, we should not forget the interests of the global community, posterity, and the non-human environment.

EXTERNAL COSTS

We saw in the last chapter that, according to economic utilitarian thinking, ideal market economies maximize total human welfare, on the questionable assumption that total human welfare is equivalent to an efficient market equilibrium. Ideal markets maximize the total net benefits of producing and consuming goods and services. This reasoning provided an indirect justification for self-interested maximizing behaviour within the market. Unfortunately, real market economies are not ideal. For example, because present markets do not account for the external costs of greenhouse gas production, the resulting climate change will be a giant market failure.

As well as monopolies, asymmetries of information, and so on, the sources of market imperfection include transaction costs, open-access resources, public goods, and external costs. An **internal cost** is a cost arising from the economic activity of a producer that is incorporated into the producer's asking price for the product. For example, the producer's cost of labour and the producer's cost of raw materials are internal costs for the producer. An **external cost** or negative externality is a cost arising from the economic activity of an agent that is born by others because the producer's asking price for the product does not incorporate this cost. For example, if the producer can dump his effluent into a river without cost rather than paying the cost of its proper disposal, then the producer can externalize the cost of pollution control.

If producers of a good are able to externalize some of their costs of production, then economic theory predicts that the market will produce too large a quantity of

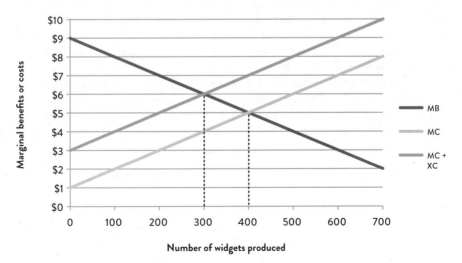

The effect of external costs

*Figure 12.3: Failure to incorporate external costs leads
to inefficient overproduction of widgets.*

this good at too low a price for true efficiency. In the example in Figure 12.3, widget producers are able to externalize $2 per widget of their production costs, perhaps by externalizing the actual costs of their waste products by dumping the waste in a river. The full marginal social cost of producing widgets is the marginal internal cost to the producer (MC) plus the marginal external cost born by downstream neighbours (XC). The full social cost supply curve (MC + XC) will be above the revealed supply curve for widgets (MC) because if producers were to include the external costs, then they would ask higher prices. If MB is the demand curve for widgets, then the market equilibrium between MB and the revealed supply curve, MC, will result in 400 widgets at a price of $5. If the supply curve incorporated the full social costs, MC + XC, then the result would be 300 widgets at a price of $6. The latter is the equilibrium that truly maximizes net benefits.

Failure to take into account the full social costs of the pollution created by widget production will, from an economic utilitarian point of view, result in the production of too many widgets (400 instead of 300), and the production of widgets at too low a price ($5 instead of $6). The net social benefits of a polluting activity should include the following:

+ Internal benefit to consumer of the polluting activity
− Internal cost to the agent of polluting activity
− External cost to everyone else of polluting activity
= Net social benefit for everyone of the activity

In the previous chapter, we examined the economic utilitarian argument that intends to show how, under ideal conditions, a free market reaches a maximally efficient economic solution. However, we can see now that this argument succeeds only if businesses include all social costs, internal and external, when producing and selling goods. Therefore, if we are to justify the market economy on economic utilitarian grounds, we must require that businesses be responsible for all of the costs of the unintended by-products of their economic activity.

It is important to remember that polluting activities not only impose external costs on participants in the local market economy, but also impose external costs on faraway members of the global community and on generations of people not yet born. Perhaps the majority of the external costs created by pollution will fall on future generations and on distant people.

ECONOMIC APPROACHES TO PROTECTING THE ENVIRONMENT

We can identify three different approaches to protecting the environment within economic thinking. **Market fundamentalism** is the view that, whatever the environmental effect of an economic market based on existing individual property rights, those effects are ethically permissible. Market fundamentalism is typically grounded in the moral theory of either libertarianism or contractarianism. Within the libertarian approach, individuals are free to use their property in any way that does not infringe the rights of others. Within the contractarian approach, individuals submit only to such laws as will prevent dilemmas of cooperation, and do not consider the interests of anyone outside their social contract. Market fundamentalism sees a minimal role for government in the protection of the environment. Individuals can sue one another for pollution damages to their own property, but this is the only protection that the environment receives. The government is there just to enforce property and tort law, and has no role in fixing environmental problems.

Free-market environmentalism is the view that the bad environmental effects of market behaviour are not ethically permissible, but that the best solution to environmental problems is to privatize the environment properly. The role of the government is to create those property rights that will generate efficient solutions. The reasoning behind free-market environmentalism is economic utilitarian. As we will see below, one justification argues that free-market environmentalism offers a solution to the problems created by open-access resources, and another justification uses the Coase Theorem to show that, with fully defined private property rights, the free market will solve pollution problems by efficiently internalizing external costs.

Environmental economics is an approach that recognizes market failures regarding the environment and studies how we can take collective action to fix environmental problems in a cost effective manner. It envisions a much larger role for government than the other two approaches. Typically, this approach uses the tools of cost-benefit analysis to find solutions to environmental problems that maximize overall net financial benefits, which is an obviously economic utilitarian strategy.

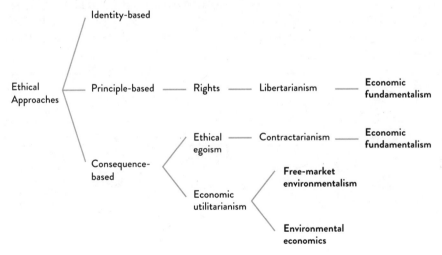

Figure 12.4: Conceptual map showing economic approaches to environmental problems.

We will do an ethical examination of these the latter two economic approaches in the remainder of the chapter. It is important to consider the fairness issues that each raises, and to examine how comprehensive is the view of moral standing that each presupposes.

THE TRAGEDY OF THE COMMONS

Garrett Hardin's "tragedy of the commons" is a particular type of external cost situation, which spreads the external costs of any individual participant's actions over all the participants in the situation. This gives each participant both a positive net internal benefit and an incentive for doing the action. Yet the result of similar actions by all participants is to create such large external costs that all participants are worse off. The tragedy of the commons is a multi-party cooperation dilemma.

Here is an example. Ten farmers each graze 10 cows on a "commons"—an unowned pasture. The carrying capacity of the pasture is 100 cows. If the number of cows on the pasture is 100 or below, the farmers will have revenue of $40 per cow, or $400 for 10 cows grazed. If the number of cows on the pasture exceeds the carrying capacity of 100, then, for each extra cow grazed by someone, the revenue will fall by $1 for every cow on the pasture. In other words, if one farmer grazes one more cow, then she will create a loss of revenue on all 101 cows of $101. Her loss will be $11 on her 11 cows, but she will externalize a loss of $90 onto the other farmers.

We can analyze this situation like we analyze a prisoner's dilemma. For simplicity, we will look at it from the perspective of one arbitrary farmer, Farmer X, and then generalize to the behaviour of all farmers. If the other farmers graze 10 cows each and Farmer X grazes 10 cows, then she will receive total revenue of $400. This is the payoff in the upper left cell of Figure 12.5. If the other farmers all continue to graze 10 cows each and Farmer X grazes 11 cows at $39 each, her revenue will increase to $429. This is the payoff in the upper right cell.

		Farmer X	
		10 cows	11 cows
Other Farmers	10 cows	10 x $40 = $400 --	11 x $39 = $429 √ --
	11 cows	10 x $31 = $310 --	11 x $30 = $330 √ --

Figure 12.5: The tragedy of the commons as a cooperation dilemma.

If the other nine farmers also graze 11 cows each, then this will create a loss of revenue of $9 per cow. If she grazes only 10 cows, then her payoff will be $310, as shown in the lower left cell. However, if the other farmers graze 11 cows, and she grazes 11 cows, then despite the lost revenue of $10 per cow, her total payoff will be $330, as shown in the lower right cell. Therefore, if the other farmers graze 10 cows, she will be better off to graze 11 cows as well. No matter what the other farmers do, Farmer X will graze 11 cows. She has a dominant strategy, which is always to graze one more cow.

Because Farmer X is an arbitrarily chosen farmer, what is true of her is true of all farmers. Each farmer has a dominant strategy, which is to graze an 11th cow. Therefore, all farmers will graze an 11th cow. Similarly, all farmers will graze a 12th cow, and so on, until finally their individual decisions ruin the common pasture and lead to a complete loss of revenues for all the farmers involved.

Tragedy-of-the-commons situations are common sources of environmental problems. People overfished the cod in the Grand Banks because every fishing boat had an internal incentive to keep fishing. People emit too much carbon dioxide because each polluter has an internal incentive to use the atmosphere as a sink for their emissions. The external costs of these greenhouse gasses will be born by future generations, not them.

Avoiding tragedy-of-the-commons situations is one justification for free-market environmentalism. The problem is that the pasture is an open-access resource. The pasture (or fish stock, or atmosphere) is common property. One solution is to privatize the common pasture by creating private property rights for the farmers. If each farmer owns a portion of the pasture for her exclusive use, and which she can sell to others, then she will have an incentive to preserve the value of her property. She will have no incentive to overgraze her private pasture. Free-market environmentalism claims that if people have marketable private property rights in what are currently open-access resources, then resource depletion would stop.

However, free-market environmentalism raises new ethical questions. How should we distribute private shares in what was previously common property? Should every farmer receive an equal share? Should we distribute shares according to historical usage? Should we distribute shares on a first-come/first-serve basis? Should other, non-farming people receive shares? Before the imposition of a private property regime, everyone was at liberty to graze cattle on the pasture. Imposing a private property regime will reduce people's liberty. Should we compensate them? If an alternative solution would be to create a legal authority to regulate grazing on the common pasture in a fair and equitable manner, then would this be better from an ethical point of view?

THE COASE THEOREM

Free-market environmentalism has another argument for using marketable private property rights to deal with the external costs of environmental pollution and resource depletion. Economists think of externalities as examples of market failure. However, the Coase Theorem suggests that, under certain circumstances, the market will actually be able to handle externalities. The **Coase Theorem** states that if agents can negotiate the selling of rights to do activities that cause external costs, and do so with perfect information and no transaction costs, then they can always find solutions to the problems caused by external costs that maximize total net social benefits. (Coase, 1960)

The Coase Theorem can provide an indirect economic utilitarian argument for a system of private property rights regarding the emission of pollution.

We can see the reasoning behind the Coase Theorem by constructing three simple scenarios. In the first scenario, there are no transferable or marketable property rights regarding pollution. The ABC Co. builds a chemical factory upriver of Carol's fishing spot, and emits noxious effluent that lowers her catch. Table 12.1 summarizes the payoffs to Carol and to ABC for the two scenarios where ABC chooses either to install pollution control or not to install it.

	Scenario 1 No pollution control	Scenario 2 Pollution control
ABC's net benefit	$130	$100
Carol's net benefit	$50	$100
Total social benefit	$180	$200

Table 12.1: Net benefits to ABC and Carol when ABC either installs or does not install a pollution control system.

In the first scenario, ABC's pollution lowers Carol's net benefits from her fishing spot from $100 to $50. Because ABC's internal costs are lower when it does not control its pollution, ABC's net benefits will be higher, at $130 rather than $100. ABC will use no pollution control and the total social benefits will be $180. However, if ABC installs pollution controls, the total net benefit to both parties will be higher at $200. The first scenario is inefficient.

In the second scenario, Carol has the right to stop anyone from creating pollution at her fishing spot. Carol can use her right to force ABC to install pollution control equipment. As shown in Table 12.1, ABC will suffer $30 loss over the first scenario, while Carol will have a $50 gain. This scenario maximizes the total social benefit at $200 instead of $180. Giving Carol this property right will create the socially optimal level of pollution for the two parties.

In the third scenario, ABC owns the right to emit pollution. The surprising result is that, provided a free market in pollution rights exists, the self-interest of ABC and Carol will lead them to maximize total social benefits. Table 12.2 shows this scenario in the third column. Because the right to pollute is marketable, Carol can offer ABC a side payment of $40 to install and use pollution control. Carol would offer this deal because her net benefit will rise from $50 without pollution control to $60 with pollution control ($100 minus the $40 side payment), which is a net benefit to her. ABC would accept this deal because its net benefit will now be $100 for running with pollution control plus the $40 side payment, which is higher than $130 for running with no pollution control. Both ABC and Carol are better off, though Carol is not as well off as when she owned the right that no one pollutes her fishing spot. The third

	Scenario 1 No pollution control	Scenario 2 Pollution control	Scenario 3 Pollution control with side payment
ABC's net benefit	$130	$100	$100 + $40 = $140
Carol's net benefit	$50	$100	$100 - $40 = $60
Total social benefit	$180	$200	$200

Table 12.2: net benefits with side payments when pollution rights are marketable.

scenario shows that, as long as pollution rights are marketable and there are no transaction costs, then two rational economic agents will maximizes their net social benefits at $200.

From the economic utilitarian point of view, that of maximizing the total net economic benefits of the polluting activity, it does not matter whether society assigns the property rights to ABC or to Carol. If Carol has the right not to receive pollution, then the net social benefits will be at a maximum of $200. If ABC has the right to pollute and this right is marketable, then the net social benefits will also be at a maximum of $200. Ronald Coase got the Nobel Prize in economics for seeing this.

From the justice-based point of view, however, it seems unfair that Carol would have to pay to reduce ABC's pollution of her fishing spot. If we were to suppose that ABC's factory was there first, and then Carol came along and started fishing, then it might seem fair that ABC has the right to pollute, and that Carol should pay to have ABC reduce its emissions. Yet we have a strong intuition that polluters should pay. This principle derives from the Harm Principle, the principle that people's rights do not allow them to harm others, as ABC's emissions do to Carol's fish catch. People who engage in potentially harmful activities, such as emitting noxious pollution, cannot use the defence that they were doing the activity before their victim came along. For example, someone who is shooting arrows at a target cannot use the I-was-here-first defence if they hit someone else who wanders between them and their target. The Coase Theorem maximizes efficiency with no regard for pre-existing rights, informed consent to infringement, compensation, or fairness.

The defence of free-market environmentalism using the Coase Theorem assumes that parties like Carol can quantify, in financial terms, the value to her of having her fishing spot ruined. Is value to her just the market value of the reduction in her fish catch? Is her offer of a side payment to ABC a true measure of the value of the pristine fishing spot to her? Or is it influenced by her ability to find the cash to pay ABC?

The defence also assumes that parties can negotiate side payments with little or no costs. The Coase Theorem only works if there are no transaction costs. This assumption is satisfied only in very simple cases, when there are few parties affected and when they can communicate easily. However, negotiations become expensive when there are many recipients of pollution, many polluters, non-point-source pollution, or accumulative pollutants. When the cause of pollution is difficult to prove, or when there are legal fees involved, then the Coase Theorem approach does not work. Applying the approach requires that we identify a direct connection between the rights of one party and the rights of another. Many cases of environmental pollution involve non-point-source or accumulative pollution. A rights-based or harm-principle-based approach does not work correctly in the presence of non-point-source or accumulative harms.

ENVIRONMENTAL ECONOMICS

Market fundamentalism and free-market economics have the idealistic goal of solving all environmental problems through the exchange of well-defined property rights in a market free of government regulation. The approach of environmental economics, however, is to admit the need for government regulation in solving environmental problems, but to use the techniques of economics to design cost-effective solutions to these problems.

The principal conceptual tool of environmental economics is the notion of the socially optimum level of pollution. The **socially optimal level of pollution** (SOL) is the point at which people consider the financial cost of reducing pollution by one increment to outweigh the cost that this increment of pollution will impose on them. This is an economic utilitarian notion because its point is to maximize net economic benefits. Environmental economists find the socially optimal level of pollution using analogues of supply and demand curves to find the socially optimal level of production and consumption.

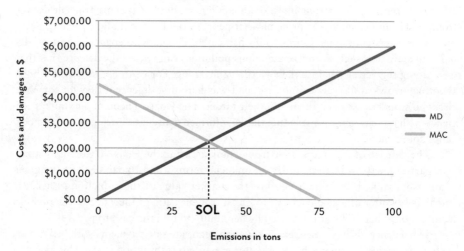

Figure 12.6: Graph of MAC and MD showing the
Socially Optimal Level of pollution (SOL).

Environmental economists use the notion of a Marginal Damages curve (MD) to represent the benefits forgone by failing to clean up pollution, and the notion of a Marginal Abatement Cost curve (MAC) to represent the incremental costs of preventing pollution or of cleaning it up. The **Marginal Damage** (MD) is a measure of the social costs that each additional increment of pollution imposes on everyone. The **Marginal Abatement Cost** (MAC) is a measure of the cost of decreasing pollution by one increment. Figure 12.6 illustrates the MD and MAC curves. The horizontal axis of the graph shows level of emissions on an increasing scale. The marginal abatement cost (MAC) is zero when there is no pollution control. Therefore, the MAC line intersects the horizontal axis at the level of emissions (75 tons) where no one makes any effort to control pollution. Marginal abatement costs rise as we reduce emissions from this point of no control, so the MAC curve slopes upward to the left from there. Marginal damage increases with emissions, so the MD line slopes upward to the right.

When there is no emission control, at emission levels of 75 tons and above in Figure 12.6, then there are zero marginal abatement costs, but there are high marginal damages. As we reduce emissions, marginal damages decrease, but marginal abatement costs rise. As we reduce emissions and move left on the graph, we can ask, whether the MD of each incremental reduction in pollution is greater than the MAC of preventing it. If the MD of decreasing emissions is greater than the increase in MAC, then the net benefits of the decrease will be positive. The maximal utility net benefits will occur at the point where MD = MAC. Any greater lowering of emissions will have negative net benefits because the increased costs of preventing the pollution (MAC) will exceed the increased costs caused by the pollution (MD). The point where MD = MAC is the socially optimal (SOL) level of pollution.

The ethical justification behind the normative use of environmental economics to make policy recommendations is economic utilitarianism. Consequently, the idea of the socially optimal level (SOL) of pollution approach has all the usual ethical weaknesses of utilitarian ethical reasoning.

As with reliance on the Coase Theorem, the moral justification of the Socially Optimal Level of pollution approach relies on the questionable assumption that the total benefits and costs of pollution can be measured and assigned a monetary value. And because this approach is grounded in economic utilitarianism, it also fails to address some of the concerns raised by competing ethical theories. For example, it is not clear that this approach respects the rights of all those affected by polluting activities, or that it leads to a just distribution of the burdens and harms caused by pollution. Other non-utilitarian ethical perspectives would likely lead to very different analyses of the merits of the SOL approach.

COST-BENEFIT ANALYSIS

Environmental problems often originate in external costs, and their solutions often involve providing public goods. Unfortunately, prices in a market economy cannot measure the external costs of environmental pollution because producers and consumers do not consider them in their pricing decisions. Prices in a market economy cannot measure the value of public goods because society cannot exclude people from public goods. If people cannot be excluded from a public good such as a solution to an air pollution problem, then the benefits of the solution are essentially free to all. Markets depend on producers being able to exclude consumers from a good unless the consumers pay for it. A **cost-benefit analysis** is a technique of environmental economics where economists measure the costs and benefits of different environmental policies according to people's willingness to pay for them. The total net benefits of each policy are calculated and used either as a factual input to a policy decision, or as an ethical reason for a policy decision.

Environmental economists use several methods of measuring costs and benefits. Sometimes they can measure revealed WTP by observing existing market values. For example, if water pollution causes a decline in the fish catch, then they can calculate the cost of this from known market prices for fish. When they cannot compute the value of the consequences of a policy from WTP revealed in existing prices, they can use the contingent valuation method, which involves a carefully designed survey to measure expressed WTP. Economists ask people to say how much they would be willing to pay for some benefit, or how much compensation they would expect for bearing a cost. For example, if pollution causes increased health risks, then economists could ask people how much they would pay for insurance against these risks. As well, economists can measure imputed WTP by looking at similar goods that are different only in respect of their non-market cost, and using statistical methods to value the non-market cost. For example, the difference in price of two houses, one in a polluted area and the other not, will indicate how much homeowners are willing to pay to avoid pollution.

Next, economists add up the costs and benefits for each policy under consideration, as in the simple example in Table 12.3. If the economists stick to positive economics, then they will offer the results as inputs to a wider policy making process. If the economists accept economic utilitarian ethical assumptions and do normative economics, then they will recommend Plan B over business as usual (BAU), because Plan B has the higher net benefit.

	BAU	Plan B
Mike	$100	$50
Nancy	$200	$400
Peter	$300	$300
Aggregate:	$600	$750

Table 12.3: Example of a simple cost-benefit analysis.

Economic utilitarian reasoning, like all utilitarian reasoning, has difficulties with fairness. For example, in Table 12.3, an economic utilitarian policy maker should choose Plan B. Yet under Plan B, Nancy benefits by +$200, while the burdens fall on

Mike (-$50). Nancy is a winner under Plan B and Mike is a loser. From the point of view of distributive justice, this is unfair.

Under Plan B, the total net benefits are larger than under BAU. Therefore, the potential exists for the winner to compensate the loser, while still gaining from Plan B. By giving $50 to Mike, Nancy can restore him to his net benefit under business as usual, and still have an increased net benefit for herself.

	BAU	Plan B	After compensation
Mike's net benefits	$100	$50	$50 + $50 = $100
Nancy's net benefits	$200	$400	$400 - $50 = $350
Peter's net benefits	$300	$300	$300
Total net benefits	$600	$750	$750

Table 12.4: Nancy compensates Mike for his loss under Plan B.

Unfortunately, just because the winners can potentially compensate the losers in a cost-benefit analysis, it does not follow that they actually will compensate them. The situation is analogous to the creation of winners and losers by free trade, which we examined in the previous chapter.

DISCOUNTING THE FUTURE

The market-based methods and cost-benefit analyses of environmental economics should not forget the interests of future generations. Environmental economics does consider the interests of posterity, but it does so by discounting future external costs to present values. Environmental economics uses a **discount rate** to compare present and future benefits and costs. The idea is that $100 now is worth more than $100 in one year. For example, someone could invest $100 now in the stock market with 7% return and have $107 in one year's time. This suggests a normative, economic utilitarian decision rule: Determine the present value (PV) of the future value (FV) of all external costs, and choose the policy with the lowest PV of total costs.

We all prefer receiving benefits now and paying costs in the future. The reason is partly psychological; we tend to be impulsive about benefits and procrastinators about costs. Yet, preferring benefits now and costs in the future is also rational. There is some risk that we will not be alive to receive future benefits or to pay future costs. If a person believed that he would be dead in six months, what discount rate could make him postpone receiving a benefit for a full year, especially one that he could not bequeath to anyone else? Discount rates are only helpful when we must make a choice within our individual lives.

Another reason we discount the future is that we expect, through economic growth, that we will be richer in the future. For example, a student may borrow money to buy a copy of Microsoft Excel because the cost will fall on his future self, who will have a job by year-end and, being richer, will miss the money less. Income, like every other good thing, has a declining marginal utility. In the future, we will be better able to afford the high clean-up costs of our polluting activities. Therefore, we should use a high discount rate for future external costs. One problem with this argument is that, with potential environmental catastrophes like climate change, it may be false that growth will continue and that the future will indeed be a lot richer than the present.

As well, a decision rule that works within one person's life may not be fair when we apply it to more than one person. As Keynes said, in the long run, we are all dead. In the case of greenhouse gas pollution, we will not be alive when the most damage occurs, and we will not be the ones who pay the clean-up and adaptation costs. Discounting the future for groups of people over a period in which some of them will die and new people will be born, is not the same as discounting the future within our own individual lives.

The choice of a rate at which to discount the interests of posterity is an ethical choice. Environmental economics prefers to use market discount rates because they seem to embody no value judgments and are easily determinable by empirical observation. Nevertheless, one problem with using market interest rates to set future discount rates is that different markets have different discount rates. Savings accounts, government bonds, corporate bonds, loans at prime, mortgage loans, and returns on the stock market all suggest different market interest rates. Insofar as market interest rates do embody value judgments, at least they are the democratic values of consumer preferences. However, decisions by individual consumers are all choices within one life. Further ethical issues arise when we must make decisions involving choices between different lives, which happen when we make decisions involving a future society whose members will not be the same as the members of contemporary society.

To see the effect of a choice of discount rate on policy decisions, we will look at a simplified version of the disagreement between two economists, Nicolas Stern and William Nordhaus, regarding whether to take action now to prevent climate change. (Broome, 2008) Both economists assume that climate change will cause one trillion dollars worth of damage to the planet in 100 years. They agree that the cost, now, to prevent this damage is 50 billion dollars. The two economists, however, disagree about the appropriate discount rate: Stern, after an economic and ethical analysis, says 1.4% while Nordhaus, using market interest rates, says 6%.

The economic utilitarian decision rule says to choose a policy by comparing PV of future damage with present cost of preventing the damage. The choice of a discount rate makes a big difference to the policy recommendations of the analysis when we make decisions affecting the interests of future generations. While they agree on the future external costs, Stern says to act now, whereas Nordhaus says to delay. From the ethical point of view, is the Nordhaus conclusion fair? The present generation benefits from burning fossil fuels while the future generation, which is not composed of the same people as the present generation, pays the costs. The choice of a small discount rate for future costs considers the interests of future generations more strongly than

	Stern	Nordhaus
FV of damages	$1 trillion	$1 trillion
Years in the future	100	100
Discount rate	1.4%	6%
PV calculation	=PV(1.4%,100,0,1000000000000,0)	=PV(6%,100,0,1000000000000,0)
PV of future costs	$249 billion (approx.)	$3 billion (approx.)
PV of prevention	$50 billion	$50 billion
Policy	Act now!	Delay!

Table 12.5: Cost-effectiveness analysis of acting or delaying action on climate change using the Microsoft Excel formula for PV.

does a large discount rate. Choosing a discount rate in a cost-benefit analysis requires considering issues of intergenerational justice.

SUSTAINABLE DEVELOPMENT AND GDP GROWTH

Considerations regarding intergenerational justice also enter into the definition and measurement of sustainable development. The Brundtland Report to the United Nations of 1987 defined **sustainable development** as development that meets "the needs of the present without compromising the ability of future generations to meet their own needs." (World Commission, 1987) The implications of this definition are ambiguous. Does our generation maintain stocks of particular resources to meet the needs of future generations? Alternatively, does our generation have a duty to ensure that the income flow from whatever stocks of resources are left is sufficient to meet the needs of future generations?

The economist, Robert Solow, suggested that sustainability should refer to flows, not to stocks. He claimed that "the duty imposed by sustainability is to bequeath to posterity not any particular thing—with the sort of rare exception I have mentioned [he mentions Yosemite National Park and the Lincoln Memorial]—but rather to endow them with whatever it takes to achieve a standard of living at least as good as our own and to look after their next generation similarly." (1993, p. 168) It follows, for example, that we do not have a duty to maintain stocks of fossil fuels at present levels, provided we bequeath to future generations the expertise to produce at least as much usable power by other methods. Technological innovation and upward pressure on prices will make it economically more attractive to use substitutes for scarce natural resources.

The usual way that economists measure development is by using the Gross Domestic Product (GDP). The GDP of an economy is the market value of all final goods and services produced in a country during a year. GDP is a measure of total market activity. From the normative perspective of economic utilitarianism, we have a duty to grow the GDP in order to grow, and thus maximize, the total amount of preference satisfaction. Economic utilitarianism entails that we should seek GDP growth.

GDP growth has weaknesses both as a measure of increased human welfare and as an indicator of sustainable development. GDP is an abstract measure of market activity, not of human welfare. All economic activity adds to GDP, even if it is destructive, regrettable, or unsustainable. GDP ignores non-market transactions, such as housework, which add to welfare. GDP ignores income inequalities and the diminishing marginal utility of income. A highly unequal society will have a lower overall level of satisfaction than will a more egalitarian society with the same GDP. As well, it will be less fair. In addition, GDP ignores both human rights abuses and the benefits of living in a free country.

Nor is GDP growth a very good indicator of sustainable development. Cleaning up present day pollution will raise GDP while taking resources away from activities that could contribute to sustainable development. For example, the US GDP actually went up with the multi-billion dollar costs of the clean up of the Exxon Valdez oil spill in 1989. GDP ignores the future external costs of present day pollution. For example, pollution-caused health care costs incurred by future people do not reduce GDP. GDP ignores future resource depletion because it contains no depletion allowance.

A better indicator of sustainable development, such as the Genuine Progress Indicator, would begin with estimates of personal consumption expenditures. It would adjust these consumption expenditures for inequalities, and add value of socially productive non-market activities, such as unpaid childcare. It would then deduct the present and future costs of undesirable effects such as pollution, crime, etc. It would then deduct the present and future costs of the degradation and depletion of natural resources.

GDP growth may appear to be an empirical, value-free indicator of development. We measure GDP by an internationally agreed procedure, using raw economic data compiled by economists. Nevertheless, a GDP measurement makes value judgments despite its appearance of objectivity. It makes value judgments in its choice of what to include and what to leave out. For example, it chooses to include the present internal costs of pollution clean up and to exclude the future external costs of pollution mitigation. Future external costs are hard to estimate and including them requires an explicit value judgment regarding what discount rate to use. Even so, excluding costs such as the future external costs of climate change from GDP makes GDP an unfair indicator of sustainable development.

INTER-GENERATIONAL JUSTICE AND GREEN VIRTUES

The moral equality of persons is the basis for social justice and global justice. It is also the basis for inter-generational justice. Treating people as equals requires that morally arbitrary features of people do not determine how we treat them. Time of birth is a morally arbitrary feature of people. Therefore, inter-generational justice is concerned with the distribution of benefits and costs between present and future people. It treats all people, present and future, as equals in the assignment of costs. Of course, in treating future people as moral equals we will not always treat them in exactly the same way. For example, in considering the costs of pollution to future generations, we may still discount future costs to account for people being richer in the future. Nevertheless, generally an analysis that is sensitive to concerns of intergenerational justice, such as that of Nicholas Stern, will use lower discount rates for future costs than will a policy, such as that of William Nordhaus, that is not.

Inter-generational justice may well require that individual people develop green virtues. **Green virtues** are character traits that enable people and corporations to cooperate and flourish in environmentally sustainable societies of people and corporations with similar dispositions. A flourishing society is a sustainable society, and some character traits help create an environmentally sustainable society. For example, environmental sustainability will require that present and future people develop dispositions to reduce resource consumption and environmental pollution, dispositions to reuse resources, and dispositions to recycle resources.

Solutions to environmental problems are often public goods. A car-pooling policy that lowers carbon dioxide emissions will benefit everyone, yet it is impossible to prevent anyone from enjoying the benefits of slower climate change. Since we cannot exclude people from the benefits, people will tend to become free riders, accepting the benefits without contributing to the costs. Free riders will avoid car-pooling whenever it is inconvenient. In a society where people develop green virtues, the costs of preventing free-riders and policing the policy will be lower.

Business corporations, too, can have character traits. Corporations can develop green virtues through the design and implementation of codes of ethics, incentive structures, and ethical climates. For example, corporate incentive structures that rewarded managers for reducing greenhouse gas emissions would contribute to the green character of corporations. Businesses with corporate characters that were disposed to reduce greenhouse gas emissions would help create a sustainable economy that would not be subject to the business risks posed by global climate change. Businesses with such green virtues would not be prone to free-ride on a collective social policy that benefits all businesses. By developing green virtues, businesses can flourish in an environmentally sustainable society.

SUMMARY

1. Environmental problems often arise from market failures such as negative externalities, open-access resources, and the failure to provide public goods.
2. External costs will fall on local people participating in the market, on distant people outside the market, on future people not yet able to participate in the market, and on the non-human environment.

223

3. A comprehensive view of moral standing in business ethics reminds us to consider the interests of the global community, posterity, and the environment in making ethical decisions.

4. The existence of negative externalities such as pollution will result in the inefficient production of too many goods at too low a price.

5. Libertarian and contractarian reasoning both suggest market fundamentalism as an approach to environmental problems, whereas economic utilitarian reasoning suggests either free-market environmentalism or an environmental economics approach.

6. Open-access resources lead to tragedy-of-the-commons situations. Free-market environmentalism suggests that privatizing all environmental resources will prevent their over-use. Privatizing the environment, however, raises questions of fairness and liberty.

7. The Coase Theorem shows that, in the absence of transaction costs, free-market environmentalism will deal efficiently with external costs. However, transaction costs are very high in environmental problems such as non-point-source pollution, and, as usual, this utilitarian approach raises questions of fairness.

8. Environmental economics aims to produce the socially optimal level of pollution. This level is not zero. Instead, it balances the benefits of producing pollution against the costs of preventing it.

9. Environmental economics uses cost-benefit analyses to find ways of fixing environmental problems with the highest net benefits for all concerned. Such analyses can generate winners and losers, and thus problems of distributive and compensatory justice.

10. Cost-benefit analysis consider the interests of future people, but uses a discount rate for future environmental costs. We have reasons to discount future costs within our own individual lives, but we also have ethical reasons not to discount costs for unborn generations. The choice of a discount rate is an ethical decision; using a high discount rate for future costs may unfairly privilege the interests of the present generation.

11. GDP growth has weaknesses both as an indicator of increasing human welfare, and as an indicator of sustainable development.

12. If both business people and business corporations develop character traits that dispose them to protecting the environment, then this will help sustain development for future generations.

ONLINE LEARNING RESOURCES

You will find a collection of learning resources associated with this chapter on the book's website: http://sites.broadviewpress.com/businessethics/. Working through this material will help you understand and remember important concepts that we have discussed, and will help you apply them to issues in business ethics.

STUDY QUESTIONS

Answering the following questions will help you to understand the ethical theory in this chapter and will help you to create a set of review notes on the textbook.

1. What reasoning justifies a comprehensive view of moral standing?
2. Summarize why market forces will result in people producing an inefficient quantity of commodities whose production creates external costs.
3. Why would libertarians tend to justify a market-fundamentalist approach to the external costs of environmental pollution?
4. Explain how we can analyze greenhouse gas emissions as a tragedy-of-the-commons situation.
5. Why is the Coase Theorem unlikely to apply to situations involving non-point-source pollution?
6. Describe a rights-based criticism of using the socially optimal level of pollution in environmental policy decisions.
7. Explain how the use of a cost-benefit analysis to make a policy decision might create winners and losers, and thereby generate a problem of compensatory justice.
8. Discounting future costs within our own lives seems reasonable. What is the problem with generalizing this procedure to future generations?
9. What are two problems with using GDP as an indicator for the sustainable development of the environment?
10. How might the development of green virtues by business corporations help solve the public goods problem often involved in solutions to environmental problems?

DECISION QUESTIONS

The whole point of learning ethical theory is to understand and ask questions like the following when you are analyzing an ethically problematic situation or case.

- Does the decision properly consider the interests of future generations?
- Does the decision properly consider the non-human environment?
- Does the decision assume market fundamentalism, free-market environmentalism, or environmental economics?
- Why do real-world markets fail to maximize economic well-being?

- Will the decision create external costs for nearby, distant, or future people?
- Can the decision maker negotiate fair compensation for external costs?
- Does the decision take unfair advantage of open-access resources?
- Does the decision free-ride on an environmental public good?
- Will the decision result in a socially optimal level of pollution?
- Is a cost-benefit analysis appropriate?
- Does the cost-benefit analysis properly consider issues of fair compensation and distribution?
- Does the cost-benefit analysis use an ethically appropriate discount rate?
- Will the decision benignly increase GDP?
- Will the decision contribute to truly sustainable development?

CASE STUDY

Analyze this case study using the ethical theory that you have learned so far. You will find a collection of learning materials applying to the case on the book's website: http://sites.broadviewpress.com/businessethics/. These materials will help you in your analysis.

Should Lars Pollute at Home or Away?

Lars Olsen is the CEO of Electronic Manufacturing Inc. EMI is a large manufacturer of hi-tech wireless mobile devices. Recently the government of Homeland, where EMI's principal factory and all of EMI's consumers are located, has brought in new environmental legislation that regulates the disposal of the toxic materials that go into the manufacture of electronic devices. This regulation makes manufacturers responsible for the recycling of any electronic devices that contain toxic materials, even after consumers have purchased the devices. This new policy will be costly for EMI. EMI will have to charge distributors, and thus consumers, a large, refundable deposit in order to get the devices back. As well, EMI will now be responsible for the costs of recycling the devices. Sales will fall, and costs will rise.

EMI has no choice but to comply. Lars's job is to recommend to the board of directors of EMI how to lower the costs of recycling. The board will collectively make the final decision on what to do. Lars knows that, in his recommendation, he should consider not only the internal costs to EMI, but also the external costs to society of the considerable pollution caused by the recycling process. The emissions from the recycling process will cause health problems for the whole country. Because the emissions will not break down, but instead will accumulate in the national environment, their cleanup will become a big problem in the future.

Lars sees only two ways to proceed. Firstly, EMI could locate its recycling facility at its principal factory in Homeland to take advantage of the transport efficiency of employing back-hauls of recycled devices from distributors. Secondly, EMI could ship the returned devices to Awayland, a country on the west coast of Africa where labour is much cheaper, and contract with a local recycling company there to dispose of the devices.

Homeland has strong environmental laws and a legal system that makes polluters pay for the damages that they cause. Its citizens earn high incomes, and any days that they take off work because of environmental sickness lose them a lot of money. Healthcare in Homeland is very good, but also very expensive. Capital markets in Homeland are very efficient and interest rates there are low. The GDP growth rate in Homeland is also low because its economy is already large and highly developed. Returns on investment are stable and moderate.

Awayland has environmental laws that are very favourable to polluters. Emissions are legally permissible and protected unless specifically forbidden by regulation. Awayland currently has no regulations regarding electronic waste, and is unlikely to change this policy. Many people are unemployed in Awayland, and average incomes are very low. Healthcare is inexpensive, but rudimentary. Capital markets in Awayland have not yet developed, so interest rates are relatively high, as are returns on investment. Awayland is starting to industrialize, so its GDP is growing quickly.

Which option should Lars recommend to the board?

GLOSSARY

One country has an **absolute advantage** over a second country in the production of a commodity if, and only if, the first country can produce that commodity more cheaply than the second country can.

Absolute duties are over-riding obligations that people have no matter what happens.

Ethical reasons are **action-guiding** because they motivate us to act in ways that we think are morally right, or at least ethically permissible.

Act utilitarianism uses maximizing utility as a decision procedure for which actions people should perform.

Ethical reasons are **agreement-seeking** because we offer them as justifications to others for acting in a certain way. They are reasons about which there can be argument and debate, and they have justifications on whose truth or falsity and applicability we want others to agree.

Altruism requires agents to maximize positive mental states in others with little consideration for their own interests.

A **care ethics** is an ethical approach based in the special relationships, like that of mother and child, which people have to one another, and in the relationship skills and emotional traits that make such attachments possible.

A **categorical imperative**, is a moral principle of action that does not depend on anyone's wants or desires.

Someone is **causally responsible** for an outcome if, and only if, some action that he intended to perform and then did perform caused the outcome to happen.

A **character-based approach** to ethics focuses on what sort of person or organization the agent is becoming, on whether he, she, or it is virtuous.

Coercive power is the ability to dominate through force or the threat of force.

A **coercive threat** that interferes with autonomy is a perpetrator's morally unjustified declaration of the intent to cause harm to the victim under certain circumstances.

One country has a **comparative advantage** over a second country in the production of a commodity if, and only if, the first country can produce that commodity more cheaply in terms of another commodity than the second country can.

Compensatory justice ensures that people who infringe the rights of others without consent fairly recompense those who they harm.

The **comprehensive view of moral standing** holds that a decision-maker has an obligation to consider the interests of people in distant countries, of future generations, of animals, and of the environment, as well as the interests of the firm's owners, employees, suppliers, customers, and members of the community in which the firm is located.

A **conceptual framework** is a mutually supporting, seldom questioned, and resilient set of fundamental assumptions about the world, about human nature, and about ethical values, that affects how people think and act in the world.

Conditioned power is the ability to dominate through internalized beliefs and attitudes. Subordinates see their unquestioned submission as natural, and the dominant understand their dominance as ordinary and normal.

A **consequence-based approach** to ethics focuses on the results or outcomes of the action, and maximizes net benefits to all concerned.

A legal **contract** is composed of two legally enforceable promises: a conditional offer, and its acceptance.

A **contractarian ethical theory** is a theory claiming that ethics consists in an enforced contract among ethical egoists designed to prevent dilemmas of cooperation, such as the Prisoner's Dilemma situation.

If one person has a right that a second person does some act, then the second person has a **correlative duty** to do this act that she owes to the first person.

Deception is a non-linguistic action or omission that the perpetrator intentionally uses to cause her victim to believe something false.

Derivative rights are moral rights that are justified as on the bases of an ethical theory that is not itself rights-based.

The **difference principle** says a distribution of rights and responsibilities is just if, and only if, everyone receives the same resources unless an unequal distribution results in the least well-off receiving more than in the strictly equal distribution.

Direct utilitarianism treats utilitarian reasoning as a decision procedure and judges each case according to a calculation of the utilities it causes.

Distributive justice ensures that society allocates benefits and burdens in a way that treats people as moral equals.

Divine command theories of ethics hold that the commands of God create people's duties.

A **dominant strategy** in game theory is a strategy that yields a higher payoff regardless of the strategy chosen by the other player.

Duties are overriding ethical obligations that agents have to act in certain ways.

In **duty-based theories** of ethics, the agent should follow the principle of doing his or her duty, regardless of the consequences.

Economic power is the ability to dominate through economic incentive or economic threat.

Economic utilitarianism is a form of preference-satisfaction utilitarianism where we measure the utility of a good or service to someone according to her willingness to pay for it.

Equal consideration of interests holds that a distribution is just if, and only if, it assigns the same weight to everyone's interests in the aggregation of interests for purposes of utilitarian maximization.

Equality of opportunity says that a distribution is just if, and only if, it assigns positions in society according to morally relevant criteria such as ability or merit and not according to morally arbitrary criteria such as race or gender.

Equality of welfare holds that a distribution of property rights in resources is just if, and only if, it results in everyone having the same level of welfare.

Ethical egoism is the ethical theory that agents ought always to maximize their own self-interest.

Ethical pluralism is the view that we should make ethical decisions by considering the (often-conflicting) ethical reasons that follow from all ethical theories, and then judging how to proceed.

Ethical relativism is the metaethical view that the truth or falsity of ethical judgments is relative to the traditional practices of a cultural group.

Ethical theories are ways of systematizing ethical reasons that philosophers have developed over the many centuries during which philosophers have been thinking about ethical problems.

Experience-based utilitarianism aims to maximize the positive mental experiences that an ethical decision brings about.

An **external benefit** or positive externality is a benefit arising from the economic activity of an agent for which the market price of the product does not compensate the agent.

An **external cost** or negative externality is a cost arising from the economic activity of an agent that is born by others because the market price of the product does not incorporate this cost.

Fair equality of opportunity requires both that there be formal equality of opportunity and that society provide a uniform quality of education for all to give everyone a fair chance to acquire the skills needed to compete for social positions.

Formal equality of opportunity requires that there be no legal impediment to a person with certain talents competing for a position that requires those talents.

Fraud is obtaining a benefit from a victim by lying or deception.

A **general right** is a right whose correlative duty falls on everyone.

Green virtues are character traits that enable people and corporations to cooperate and flourish in environmentally sustainable societies of people and corporations with similar dispositions.

The **harm principle** says that people (or the government) may interfere with someone's freedom, liberty, or exercise of their rights only in order to prevent harm to others.

A **hypothetical imperative** is a strategic principle that will help someone get what he wants.

An **identity-based approach** to ethical reasoning focuses on what sort of person (organization) the agent (organization) is becoming, on whether she (it) is virtuous and has a good character.

An **indirect utilitarian theory of justice** claims that equal consideration of interests will lead to equality of resources because of the diminishing marginal utility of income.

Indirect utilitarianism treats utilitarian reasoning as a justification procedure, and advocates obedience to rules, respect for rights, inculcation of virtues, and the creation of whatever policies are necessary to produce maximum aggregate utility.

Informational privacy is the condition of being able to control access by others to information about oneself.

The **informed preference theory of value** holds that a state of the world is valuable if it would satisfy the preference that someone would have if she had full information and were reasoning rationally.

Initial equality of resources says that a distribution of rights and responsibilities is just if, and only if, it is the result of people's free choices after everyone starts life with strictly equal distribution of resources.

The **interest theory** of natural rights holds that the inherently valuable natural features that justify possession of moral rights are the crucial interests of the right-holder.

The **"is/ought" gap** means that we cannot derive an ethical conclusion from an argument consisting of purely scientific or factual premises.

In **justice-based theories**, the moral principles that agents should follow in their decisions involve treating others as moral equals.

Ricardo's **law of comparative advantage** states that there exist terms of trade under which two countries will both gain from trade if they specialize in producing goods in which they have a comparative, not an absolute, advantage.

The **law of diminishing marginal utility** states that as the consumption of a given economic good increases, the marginal utility produced by the consumption of one additional unit of the good tends to decrease.

The **law of increasing marginal cost** states that, in the short-run, the marginal cost of producing each additional item will tend to increase.

Legal rights are legally enforceable rights.

Libertarianism holds that a distribution of rights and responsibilities is just if, and only if, it respects people's natural rights to self-ownership.

A **lie** is a linguistic communication which the perpetrator believes to be untrue and with which the perpetrator intends to deceive his victim.

A **logic of domination** is a structure of argumentation that justifies relationships of domination and subordination within an oppressive conceptual framework.

Conditions where the assumptions of perfect condition do not hold and markets are not efficient are **market failures**.

The **marginal utility** of an economic good or service is the additional utility gained through the consumption of one additional unit of that good or service.

An entity has **moral agency** if it is capable of understanding moral principles, is capable of responding to moral reasons, and is able to accept praise or blame.

A **moral agent** is an entity to which we are prepared to assign praise or blame, which can respond to moral reasons, and which we are prepared to hold morally accountable. To possess moral agency, an entity must have capacities for moral sensitivity, responsiveness to ethical reasons, and decision-making abilities.

Moral autonomy is the capacity to govern oneself according one's own ethical reasoning.

Moral rights are rights that are justified by moral theories.

A person, organization, or nonhuman entity has **moral standing** if we must consider his, her, or its interests in making an ethical decision.

An agent is **morally accountable** for an action and its consequences if, and only if, we should be prepared to praise or blame her for her freely made decision and for its results.

A person, organization, or nonhuman entity is **morally considerable** if we must consider his, her, or its interests in making an ethical decision.

According to the doctrine of **natural rights**, rights-bearers have rights because they have certain natural features. These natural features are inherently valuable and thus require protection by moral rights.

One condition is a **necessary condition** for a second if the first state of affairs is required for the production of the second one.

Someone's **negative autonomy right** is the right that others not interfere with his decision-making.

A **negative right** imposes a duty on everyone else not to interfere with the right holder.

Someone's **negative liberty** is the right that others not interfere with her actions.

A **NESS condition** is a Necessary Element in a Set of Sufficient conditions.

A **normative cost-benefit analysis** is a decision-making technique that measures the financial costs and benefits of different policy options according to people's willingness to pay for them, calculates the total net benefits of each policy, and uses the results to justify a policy decision ethically.

Normative economics uses economic science to make policy decisions. It tells decision-makers what policies they ought to implement based on an economic analysis of the policy alternatives.

Objective consequentialism requires agents to make those decisions which lead to the best consequences from a point of view that is independent of the psychological states of individual people.

An **open-access resource** (a commons good or a non-excludable resource) is a resource from which it is difficult to exclude other individuals.

Oppression is the unjust or cruel exercise of power by means of the structure of a group, a community, or a society as a whole.

An **oppressive conceptual framework** is a conceptual framework that makes relationships of domination and subordination seem normal, natural, and unquestionable.

The metaethical principle that **"ought" implies "can"** means that a person cannot be morally obligated to perform an action or bring about a consequence if he is unable to do so.

Ownership of a tangible or intangible thing consists in a bundle of rights and liabilities regarding that thing.

The **paradox of egoism** says that there exist states of affairs in the self-interest of ethical egoists that these same ethical egoists cannot achieve because they ought always to act selfishly.

An outcome is **Pareto-efficient** if no other outcome is possible that makes at least one person better off and no person worse off.

A **payoff matrix** for a game is a table that shows each player's payoff for every possible combination of strategies.

Personal autonomy is the capacity to make authentic decisions about one's own life. It is the ability to choose freely one's conception of the good life, to pursue this conception, and to either endorse or change one's choices.

Physical privacy is a person's condition when she is free from intrusion by other people.

Someone's **positive autonomy right** is the right that others assist her with her decision-making.

A **positive cost-benefit analysis** is an economic technique that measures the financial costs and benefits of different policy options according to people's willingness to pay for them, calculates the total net benefits of each policy, and uses the results as a factual input to a policy decision.

Positive economics is a science that creates models describing the behaviour of economic markets and participants in those markets.

A **positive right** imposes a duty on others to assist the right bearer is some way.

Preference-based utilitarianism aims at maximizing the production of states of affairs that people want.

Prima facie duties are ethical obligations that people have, but which may yield to stronger obligations.

A **principle-based approach** to ethical reasoning looks at the decision-maker's motivations. It assesses the decision as right or wrong according to what ethical principles the agent follows, or does not follow, when she makes her decision.

A game is a **prisoner's dilemma game** when both players have dominant strategies that, when played, result in an outcome with payoffs smaller than if each had played another strategy.

Psychological egoism is the *empirical* theory that people always *do* act to maximize to their self-interest.

Public goods are goods whose use by one person does not diminish their availability to others, and from the use of which it is difficult to exclude other individuals.

A **reservation price** is the maximum amount of money that a consumer would be willing to exchange for one more unit of a commodity in the absence of a defined market price for that commodity.

Retributive justice ensures that society holds people accountable for harming others or violating their rights.

A **right** is a justified claim by one person that other persons owe duties to her.

In **rights-based theories**, the moral principles that agents should follow in their decisions involve respecting the moral rights of others.

Rule utilitarianism uses maximizing utility as a standard of rightness for which rules people should follow.

The **shareholder view of moral standing** in business ethics holds that a decision-maker has an obligation to consider only the interests of the owners of the firm.

A **specific right** is one whose correlative duty only falls on a determinate person or group.

The **stakeholder view of moral standing**, which is associated with the doctrine of corporate social responsibility, holds that a decision-maker has an obligation to consider the interests of the firm's owners, employees, suppliers, customers, and members of the community in which the firm is located.

Strict equality of resources holds that a distribution of property rights in resources is just if, and only if, it results in everyone having the same amount of resources.

Structural equality of opportunity requires that organizations design positions in such a way that persons doing the necessary work of society, such as those responsible for the care of young children, can still fill those positions.

A **sufficient condition** is a condition that is enough to bring about a second condition even if it is not required to bring about the effect. Whenever the sufficient condition is present, the second condition is also present.

The **total utility** of a group of economic goods or services is the sum of all the utility produced by the consumption of those goods or services.

Transaction costs are the costs of reaching and enforcing an agreement between negotiating parties. They include the costs of researching information about the situation, negotiating the agreement, and legally enforcing the agreement.

Utilitarianism requires agents to make those decisions which lead to the best consequences judged in terms of the sorts of mental states that they bring about in others.

Utility is an abstract measure of the welfare that people get from consuming something as a product or service.

A **vice** is a stable character trait with negative moral significance. Examples are avarice, cowardice, dishonesty, and sleaziness.

A **virtue** is a stable character trait with positive moral significance. Examples are courage, generosity, benevolence, and fairness.

A **virtue ethics** holds that persons and organizations ought to cultivate a virtuous or morally excellent character.

The **will theory** of natural rights points to how the holder of a right has the power either to insist that others follow their correlative duties, or not to insist that they do, according to the right-holder's will on the matter.

Willingness to pay is the maximum amount of money that someone would be willing to exchange for an economic good or service.

BIBLIOGRAPHY

AFL-CIO. "CEO-to-Worker Pay Gaps." http://www.aflcio.org/Corporate-Watch/
CEO-Pay-and-You/CEO-to-Worker-Pay-Gap-in-the-United-States/Pay-Gaps-
in-the-World (accessed June 12, 2013).

Audi, Robert. 2009. *Business Ethics and Ethical Business*. New York: Oxford UP.

Bowie, Norman E. 1999. *Business Ethics: A Kantian Perspective*. Oxford: Blackwell.

Broome, John. 2008. "The Ethics of Climate Change." *Scientific American*
298: 96–102.

Coase, Ronald. 1960. "The Problem of Social Cost." *The Journal of Law and
Economics* 3: 1–44.

Crane, F.A.A., and Dirk Matten. 2004. *Business Ethics, a European Perspective:
Managing Corporate Citizenship and Sustainability in the Age of
Globalization*. Oxford and New York: Oxford UP.

Freeman, R.E., and William M. Evan. 1990. "Corporate Governance:
A Stakeholder Interpretation." *Journal of Behavioral Economics* 19(4): 337.

Friedman, Milton. 1970. "The Social Responsibility of Business Is to Increase
Its Profits." *New York Times Magazine*, 13 September.

Frye, Marilyn. 1983. *The Politics of Reality: Essays in Feminist Theory*.
Freedom, CA: Crossing P.

Galbraith, J.K. 1983. *The Anatomy of Power*. Boston: Houghton Mifflin.

Gilligan, Carol. 1982. *In a Different Voice: Psychological Theory and Women's
Development*. Cambridge MA: Harvard UP.

Goodpaster, Kenneth G. 2010. "Corporate Responsibility and Its Constituents."
In *The Oxford Handbook of Business Ethics*, George G. Brenkert and
Tom L. Beauchamp, eds. 126. Oxford: Oxford UP.

Hardin, Garrett. 1968. "The Tragedy of the Commons." *Science* 162: 1243–48.

Hobbes, Thomas. 1651. *De Cive*. London. http://ebooks.gutenberg.us/
WorldeBookLibrary.com/decive.htm (accessed October 16, 2013).

Honoré, A.M. 1961. "Ownership." In *Oxford Essays in Jurisprudence*,
A.G. Guest, ed. 107–47. Oxford: Oxford UP.

Institute for Policy Studies. "Executive Excess 2012: The CEO Hands in Uncle
Sam's Pocket." http://www.ips-dc.org/reports/executive_excess_2012
(accessed June 13, 2013).

Kant, Immanuel. 1959. *Foundations of the Metaphysics of Morals*.
Lewis White Beck, tr. Indianapolis: Bobbs-Merrill.

Kernohan, Andrew. 2012. *Environmental Ethics: An Interactive Introduction*.
Peterborough: Broadview P.

Krugman, Paul, and Maurice Obstsfeld. 2006. *International Economics:
Theory and Policy*: 7th Edition. Boston: Addison-Wesley.

MacIntyre, Alasdair. 1981. *After Virtue*. Notre Dame: U of Notre Dame P.

Mill, John Stuart. 1909. (1848) *Principles of Political Economy,* III.17.14.
    7th Edition, London; Longmans, Green. http://www.econlib.org/library/
    Mill/mlP.html (accessed February 4, 2014).
———. 1859. *On Liberty.* http://www.gutenberg.org/
    files/34901/34901-h/34901-h.htm (accessed May 27, 2013).
Nozick, Robert. 1974. *Anarchy, State, and Utopia.* New York: Basic Books.
Rachels, James. 1975. "Why Privacy Is Important." *Philosophy and Public Affairs*
    4: 323–33.
Ross, W.D. 2002. *The Right and the Good.* Philip Stratton-Lake, ed. Oxford:
    Clarendon P.
Sandel, Michael. 2009. *Justice: What's the Right Thing to Do?* New York:
    Farrar, Straus and Giroux.
Solow, Robert. 1993. "An Almost Practical Step Toward Sustainability."
    Resources Policy September: 162–72.
Stolper, Wolfgang F., and Paul A. Samuelson. 1941. "Protection and Real Wages."
    The Review of Economic Studies 9(1): 58–73.
Warren, Karen. 1990. "The Power and Promise of Ecological Feminism."
    Environmental Ethics 12: 125–46.
World Commission on Environment and Development. 1987. "Report of the
    World Commission on Environment and Development." 96th plenary
    meeting, December 11, 1987. http://www.un.org/documents/ga/res/42/
    ares42-187.htm (accessed April 12, 2011).

INDEX

Golden Rule, 74
good life, 119
government regulation, 24, 82, 186, 216
government regulation and redistribution, 186
government role in protection of the
environment, 211, 216
governments
informational privacy and, 164
greed. *See* avarice
green virtues, 223
guilt, 48

Hardin, Garrett, 212
Harm Principle, 74, 79–80, 85, 123, 176, 215
hedonism, 113
Hobbes, Thomas, 47–48
holism, 157, 165
honest disclosure, 28
honesty, 109, 117–18, 124
Honoré, A.M., 83
honour killing, 25
human flourishing, 111
within a corporation, 121
need for good character, 124
social circumstances relevant to, 114–15
as understood in virtue ethics, 113
human rights, 6, 10, 12–13, 68, 149, 195
human rights abuses, 7, 12, 222
human rights violations, 65–66
human welfare, problems of measuring, 54
Hume, David, 22–23
Hume's Guillotine, 22, 25
hypothetical imperative, 76

identity-based approach to ethical reasoning,
6–8, 155
identity-based feminism, 138
In a Different Voice (Gilligan), 137
incentive structures, 121, 223
indignation, 48
indirect economic utilitarian argument
for private property rights regarding
pollution, 214
indirect economic utilitarianism justification for
a market economy, 186–89, 202
indirect utilitarian argument for equal
distributive shares, 99
indirect utilitarian theory of distributive justice, 100
indirect utilitarian theory of justice, 97
indirect utilitarianism, 54, 66–67, 97–98, 111
keeping promises, 81
utilitarian reasoning as justification
procedure, 67–69
individual members of a corporation
moral accountability, 154, 157–59, 166, 178
individual rights, 54, 65. *See also* rights
informational privacy, 164, 175, 177–78
connections to personal autonomy, 176
informed consent to infringement, 215

informed preference theory of value, 59–60
injustice, paradigm examples of, 91
insider trading, 177
interest theory of rights, 175
intergenerational justice, 221, 223. *See also*
future generations
internal costs, 209
international businesses, 198
international free trade, 194–96, 198
Internet
informational privacy and, 164, 176
reduced transaction costs in the market, 191
interpersonal comparison of preferences, 104
intolerant cultures
ethical relativism and, 25–26
*An Introduction to the Principles of Morals and
Legislation* (Bentham), 56
invisible hand, 48, 67, 183, 189
"is/ought" gap, 22–23, 25, 40, 148

joint-stock company, 156
decision-making process, 166
as example of complexity and divisibility of
ownership, 84
just society, 110
justice, 74, 90–91, 104, 110, 117–18, 125,
141, 207
egalitarian theories of, 200
transplant surgeon example, 65
justice-based point of view
on protection of the environment, 215
justice-based theories of ethics, 8, 111
justice considerations, 11, 13, 15

Kant, Immanuel, 85, 123
Categorical Imperative, 76–78
on duty, 74, 81
on motivation of moral agent, 75
Kantian duties, 76–78
weakness of, 77–78
Kantian rights theory, 118
Kantian theory of natural rights, 174
Kantian tradition
personal autonomy in, 174

law of comparative advantage, 196, 199, 201, 203
law of declining marginal benefits, 188
law of diminishing marginal returns, 94
law of diminishing marginal utility, 97, 187, 192
law of increasing marginal cost, 187–88
legal concept of "deep pockets," 154, 159
legal contracts, 73, 80, 157
social cooperation through, 117
legal reasoning, 156
legal responsibility, 153–54, 159, 166
legal rights, 79, 91
levelling down objection, 101–02, 104–05
liberal egalitarian justification of a market
economy, 192–93, 202

From the Publisher

A name never says it all, but the word "Broadview" expresses a good deal of the philosophy behind our company. We are open to a broad range of academic approaches and political viewpoints. We pay attention to the broad impact book publishing and book printing has in the wider world; we began using recycled stock more than a decade ago, and for some years now we have used 100% recycled paper for most titles. Our publishing program is internationally oriented and broad-ranging. Our individual titles often appeal to a broad readership too; many are of interest as much to general readers as to academics and students.

Founded in 1985, Broadview remains a fully independent company owned by its shareholders—not an imprint or subsidiary of a larger multinational.

For the most accurate information on our books (including information on pricing, editions, and formats) please visit our website at **www.broadviewpress.com**. Our print books and ebooks are also available for sale on our site.

On the Broadview website we also offer several goods that are not books—among them the Broadview coffee mug, the Broadview beer stein (inscribed with a line from Geoffrey Chaucer's *Canterbury Tales*), the Broadview fridge magnets (your choice of philosophical or literary), and a range of T-shirts (made from combinations of hemp, bamboo, and/or high-quality pima cotton, with no child labor, sweatshop labor, or environmental degradation involved in their manufacture).

All these goods are available through the "merchandise" section of the Broadview website. When you buy Broadview goods you can support other goods too.

broadview press
www.broadviewpress.com

All of the years that passed by
You're all I think my aunt lear
I think all of the these we could do
When I am breaking down (2X)
I want to meet you soon
Oh Thank God he gave me you
You're the reason I breath cry *keep me fighting*

When I am breaking down (2X)